In Strength and Faith: A Cobber Memoir

In Strength and Faith: A Cobber Memoir

PAUL J. DOVRE

CONCORDIA COLLEGE
MOORHEAD MINNESOTA

DEDICATION

To Mardeth Louise Bervig Dovre, without whom....

Contents

About the Contributors

About the Author

Dr. Paul J. Dovre served as president of Concordia College in Moorhead, Minnesota, from 1975 until his retirement in 1999. Previously, he served the college as a faculty member and vice president for Academic Affairs. Dr. Dovre came to Concordia from Northwestern University in 1963, where he earned his M.A. and Ph.D. degrees and served as a faculty member. After his retirement, Dovre served interim assignments as dean of students at Luther Seminary and interim president of Concordia College and Capital University. He also co-directed the Lutheran College Leadership Development Program for twelve years.

Dovre's community activities include service on the boards of the Moorhead Chamber of Commerce, FM United Way, FM Symphony, Oak Grove Lutheran School, member and chair of the Heritage Hjemkomst board, United Way campaign chair, member of the Moorhead Rotary Club, and hospice volunteer. He received the prestigious 2024 Legacy Leader Award from the 2024 Fargo Moorhead West Fargo Chamber of Commerce to recognize his leadership and contributions in the metropolitan region. Statewide service includes member and chair of the Regent Candidate Advisory Committee and member of the Judicial Selection Committee and the Minnesota Humanities Commission. Dovre also has been active in the ELCA, serving as vice-chair of the Lutheran Council of the USA, delegate to the Lutheran World Federation in 1990, and co-chair of the ELCA Task Force on Education in 2003-2007.

The government of Norway designated Dovre Knight, First Class of the Royal Norwegian Order of St. Olaf in 1979. Dovre received the American Norway Heritage Fund Award in 1993 and the Norwegian Ambassador's Award in 1999. In 1980, Dovre was recognized among the one hundred college presidents identified by their peers as the most effective chief executive officers in higher education. Dovre holds honorary degrees from Wartburg, Luther, St. Olaf, and Concordia College as well as Capital University. He served as a visiting scholar at Harvard University in 1992, 1999, and 2005.

Dr. Dovre's publications include *The Future of Religious Colleges*, editor, Eerdmans, 2002; *The Cross and the Academy*, Lutheran UP, 2011; *A Holy Restlessness*, Augsburg, 2009; *In Strength and Faith: A Cobber Memoir*, Concordia College, (pending).

Paul Dovre grew up on a farm near Porter, Minnesota. He graduated from Canby High School and earned his B.A. degree from Concordia College in 1958 following service in the United States Army. He is married to the former Mardeth Bervig. They have two children: Erik, a physician in Eau Claire, Wisconsin, and Louise, a member of the Minnesota State Court of Appeals. The Dovres are members of Trinity Lutheran Church in Moorhead, Minnesota.

About the Editor

Dr. Joan Kopperud is Professor Emerita of English and former director of integrative learning at Concordia College. A strong proponent of experiential learning, Kopperud co-authored *The Service-Learning Companion* (Duncan and Kopperud, Houghton Mifflin, 2008). In 2010, Concordia recognized her service with the Ole and Lucy Flaat Distinguished Teaching Award and in 2018 with the Alma and Reuel Wije Distinguished Professor Award. In 2020, Minnesota Campus Compact awarded Kopperud the Civic Engagement Leadership Award for the successful initiative she led to reduce food waste at Concordia. Kopperud co-chaired "Food for Good," the fall 2020 Faith, Reason, and World Affairs symposium at Concordia. Kopperud currently serves on the Cass Clay Food Commission, which advises policy makers in the Fargo-Moorhead metropolitan area to ensure that residents have access to safe, nutritious, and affordable foods. Joan (Whitchurch) Kopperud and her husband Kevin are Cobber alumni from the class of 1975. They have two sons, Judd and Adam, and five grandchildren.

Preface

I began working on this memoir about a decade after my retirement in 1999 from the presidency of Concordia College. Mardy and I have continued to live in the Fargo-Moorhead community since my retirement, and we have retained close connections with the college in a variety of ways. Some connections have been more active, including serving as interim president at Concordia on two occasions, and some connections less so, such as assisting with alumni and constituent relationships. Regardless of the capacity, we value our continuing ties with Concordia College.

This memoir is not a formal history, rather, the reminiscences of one of the participants in that history. This is a subjective account; that is, it is an informal account of how I experienced and perceived events. I acknowledge and respect the reality that other participants in the life of the college may have experienced in different ways over these years.

This memoir does not include footnotes or numerous references; however, that does not mean the absence of research. Through the good graces of then archivist Lisa Sjoberg, I had excellent assistance in accessing relevant files. In addition, I made extensive use of my personal files. Colleagues James Hausmann, Dr. Carroll Engelhardt, Tracey Moorhead, and Catherine McMullen provided helpful responses to the manuscript. I also extend special thanks to Dr. Joan Kopperud, Professor Emerita of English, for improving the flow of the text with countless helpful edits.

I hope *In Strength and Faith: A Cobber Memoir* will be a useful resource to future generations of scholars, faculty, staff, students, family, and friends.

Paul J. Dovre

1. Before Concordia

My early years were spent on a farm in west central Minnesota near Minneota until age eight and near Porter, Minnesota, thereafter. I was the fifth in a family of five children born to Inga Borson Dovre and Nels Edwin Dovre, both second generation Norwegian-Americans. My parents had difficulty speaking English when they began school, so for that reason, they did not encourage their children to learn Norwegian. Nonetheless, we were made aware of our Norwegian heritage and took pride in it. We feasted on Norwegian foods, observed Norwegian customs, sang Norwegian hymns, and heard stories about the old country, which, sadly, we never recorded and soon forgot.

The grandparent I knew best was Ben Borson, my mother's father, who came to America by himself as a teenager just after completing confirmation, an important event in Norway that marked the transition from childhood to adulthood. Once in America, he worked off his fare on an uncle's farm near Story City, Iowa, a job he left as soon as the debt was paid. From then forward, my grandfather was at various times a farmer, realtor, farm advocate, co-founder of a farmers' co-op and insurance company, insurance agent, and tax preparation agent. He was, in a real sense, a public man. In the 1920s, he became president of the local Farm Bureau and wrote a regular series of editorials for the local newspapers in which he advocated for, among other things, Robert Lafollette, a candidate for President of the United States on the Progressive Party platform. Ben Borson was self-taught and well-read. I remember frequent conversations between my parents and grandfather about contemporary affairs. Upon reflection, I see how these conversations were formative in my own interest in public affairs.

During World War II, my grandfather was especially concerned for family members in Norway. I recall my mother sending Red Cross packages of clothes and personal care items to them. He also loved playing games and telling stories at family gatherings. But for some personal demons, I expect that his material success would have been substantial, or he would have pursued a career in politics. I barely knew his wife Anna, my grandmother, who died when I was five years old. Anna was the second eldest in a family of fourteen. She had immigrated to America as a young girl. I recall hearing that my grandparents' home was the gathering place for Norwegian immigrants, called "Newcomers," so my mother grew up in a house filled with people, food, music, and good fun, which were largely present in my upbringing as well.

My other grandfather, Ole Dovre, died before my birth, but stories of his life were also woven into my family heritage. He was one of a family of nine, most of whom had emigrated from Valdres, Norway, to America. Like my other grandfather, Ole first worked for an uncle in Kansas before setting out on his own. He, too, was largely self-educated and had a love for public discourse with the local attorney and newspaper publisher. He spent several years working in Northfield, Minnesota, for an uncle, Harold Thorson, who was one of the founders of St. Olaf College. When my grandfather retired, he and his family moved to Northfield, where he liked to gather for morning coffee with a group of men that included St. Olaf faculty members Ole Rolvaag and F. Melius Christiansen. Between his early and later years in Northfield, Ole Dovre was a successful farmer near Minneota. The signs of his success were a new home, a new barn, and herds of purebred cattle and hogs. In the 1920s, my father and uncle bought the farm, so that is when my grandparents moved to Northfield for their retirement, a retirement that was interrupted by the agricultural commodity depression in the twenties. This forced them to sell their home in Northfield and return to the Minneota farm. From what I have heard from his family, he never really recovered from this event and died a few years later.

My grandmother, Inger Dovre, had also grown up in the Valdres valley of Norway. Whether or not my grandparents knew each other in Norway is unknown to me. They attended different churches and lived in different valleys, so it is uncertain. My grandmother was an outgoing and hospitable person, who specialized in needlework, cooking, and baking. She was mother to eight children and loved to dote on her grandchildren. The return to the farm in the 1920s following the agricultural crisis was difficult for her, as was the death of Ole. For the next twenty-odd years, she would live with family members for short periods of time until settling in with her daughter Ruth in Wyoming for the last decade of her life. Despite the challenges in my grandmother's later life, she and my father remained especially close, so stories of Inger Dovre were woven into the fabric of my family heritage as well.

Although none of my grandparents had extensive opportunities for formal education, from stories and experiences I came to understand that Norwegian heritage, hard work, family, education, and public discourse were valued. I see how these values were also carried out in the next generation in Inga Borson Dovre and Nels Edwin Dovre, my parents. Both of my parents attended high school, a fairly new opportunity at that time. My father attended the local high school at Minneota, followed by mechanics school in Kansas City, while my mother attended Madison Lutheran Normal School, a boarding school that prepared parochial and public-school teachers in the norms of curriculum and pedagogy, in Madison, Minnesota. My mother spent some years teaching before marrying my father, who had been farming with his brother. My parents married in their mid-twenties and began their life together on a rented farm south of Minneota. Their next move was to a rented farm west of Minneota, where the landlord, a local livestock buyer, would build them a new home, sufficient to accommodate what would become our family of seven. By 1940, the economy was improving, so my parents bought the first of what would be four major land acquisitions near Porter, Minnesota. The move to our Porter farm was a major turning point for our family. The house was, by standards of the day, large and luxurious with electricity and running water. No more running to the outhouse for physical relief or the windmill for a pail of water to wash the clothes or dishes as had been the case on the Minneota farm.

My father was a progressive farmer, always attentive to the latest scientific developments. He enjoyed the challenge of new ideas, new machines, new varieties, and new farm practices. Nels Dovre set an example of hard work and high standards, which shaped our family culture and the life habits of my siblings and me. While my father largely managed the farm business responsibilities, my mother was the keeper of the family hearth as homemaker at a time when there were few conveniences and many mouths to feed, including the hired help. Mother was a listener and an encourager, always available to hear about our victories and challenges. She played the piano for our family of singers. She also brought with her from the Borson clan a love for games, kidding, and stories. As I grew up in a household of hard work balanced with love and encouragement, over time I came to better understand my parents' relationship. Like other couples in the day, my parents were not given to displays of affection; in later years, however, we discovered a trove of letters filled with eloquent expressions of love that my father had written to my mother in their courting days. My father regularly brought flowers to my mother with affectionate expressions boldly stated. The way they looked at each other and conformed to one another's preferences left a lasting impression on me, one that shaped my own relationships with others and a commitment to hard work and the priority of family.

My siblings were a wonderful influence in my life as well. Our parents affirmed that each of us was endowed with unique and significant gifts. Wanda, ten years my elder, was our leader. She was a bright, positive, buoyant, and inspiring person, who had a great career in education. Ardis, next in line, was perhaps the brightest. She became a registered nurse and dealt with health issues her whole life, which led to a quiet determination to counter her physical vulnerability. In counterpoint to the challenges she faced, whenever she came home from nurse's training school, she brought candy, which, due to war time shortages, was not available in our hometown. She often brought friends home, and one of her favorite summer activities was sunbathing, which earned her a good deal of teasing from her brothers. Ardis got married and had a fulfilling career, but she had a difficult and taxing marriage that ended in divorce. She died in her mid-seventies.

Florence, also a teacher, was the most sensitive sibling, able to discern the needs of others with loving care. Her second marriage to John Spann brought many gifts of discovery and joy to her life. The next sibling, Ralph, five years my elder, is in many ways the rock of our family—strong, steady, dependable. He has always been my "best man." He was a highly successful farmer and the source of steady leadership in the community and church. He and his wife Norma, now deceased, were parents to six gifted and loyal children. As I reflect on my relationships with my siblings, I see how the business of farming touched all of us, teaching us habits of economy, discipline, faith, and hard work. We were Depression-era kids who have never taken the good life for granted. We were very loyal to each other and enjoyed frequent reunions that always featured family stories and at least one card game.

Growing up, my siblings and I experienced our social life in a variety of ways, beginning with family. We had several aunts, uncles, and cousins in the community, and we gathered frequently for special celebrations like birthdays and other celebrations as well as for routine Sundays for dinner and visiting. I enjoyed my cousins, with whom I played and explored our universe. Brother Ralph and I frequently went hunting together, sometimes with neighborhood friends. Luther League and 4H provided additional venues for social interchange with peers. There were basket socials, softball games, and hayrides, among other activities. I formed good friendships at Canby High School, where social life centered on concerts, athletic events, and school parties and dances. My peers and I attended movies and community dances as well. It was a dating culture and we often double dated.

Faith and religious practice were taken for granted in our family. As a boy, I was not much impressed by our pastors, who seemed pious and uninteresting. Then, just after World War II, a new pastor came to our congregation. J. David Larson had been an Army chaplain, who soon became a significant role model for me as an articulate, handsome, and action-oriented leader. To me, his God and his faith seemed virile, engaged, and real world. In our confirmation class, we spoke of sex, death, and human failings—he didn't pull any punches. During his years as our pastor, we also had a strong Luther League program. Our meetings were well attended, and our programs featured a combination of good fun and serious reflection on matters of faith. As I consider my personal journey of faith, I feel fortunate to have been grounded in a family that held deep faith traditions, but equally fortunate to have later experienced what it means to live an active, questioning, vibrant faith.

As the youngest in the family, I spent some years as the only child at home, so, understandably, I was very close to my parents. At fifteen, we began a tradition of evening devotions that became a meaningful part of my upbringing. I also saw that my mother was active in her faith, taking her turn as Bible study teacher and president of the ladies aid, a common church group for women at the time. As a teenager, I often challenged my father, despite his patience and my mother's intervention. Some of my siblings said he and I were so much alike that the stress between us was inevitable. In retrospect, I recognize that our relationship ran deep all along and has been a significant factor in my life's journey. As I grew older, my father, like Mark Twain's, grew wiser and our relationship grew into a mutually affirming one.

My parents had always valued education, so my formal schooling played an important part in my upbringing. I enjoyed school from first grade in Minneota through twelfth grade at Canby High School. In between, I spent five years attending a one-room country school near our farm. In particular, I enjoyed history, biology, math, and geography. Although I was not a top-of-the-class kind of student, I was a steady learner. I sometimes tried to rationalize my slightly-above-average academic performance by pointing to my taxing schedule of 5:30 a.m. wake-up chores and 5:00-7:00 p.m. evening chores, but several of my peers had similar schedules. I missed the senior honor roll by one position but earned recognition for leadership and speech activities. I sang in the choir and boys' quartet and competed on the debate team. I also tried football, but never got beyond the third team "hamburger" squad. (I suppose it may have built character?)

My principal extracurricular activity in my high school years was in 4H, an organization of young farm people that encouraged good health, engaged citizenship, and best practices agriculture. While I engaged in a variety of projects, including conservation and even gardening, my main focus was raising and showing beef cattle. I started with one calf, and by my junior year, I was training and showing three calves. This was an opportunity to compete with farm kids from across the state since I often qualified for competition at the state level. I developed a good eye for the finishing potential of cattle and learned how to provide the right diet and training regimen. My success at working with cattle earned me enough money to pay for much of my first years of college and to buy a straw and hay baling machine, which enabled me to earn additional money doing custom baling work for neighbors. Once in college, I used the proceeds of selling the hay baler to buy my first car. I hasten to add that the purchase was not an investment but an expenditure.

My foundational years growing up in west central Minnesota grounded me with the endowments of a nurturing family, vibrant faith community, and excellent educational opportunities. I knew this to be a salt of the earth environment in which I felt the encouragement and support of both my immediate and extended families. My siblings and I were expected to amount to something, to contribute to the common good, and to act with integrity and humility. There was both law and gospel in our lives, accented by grace and expectation.

2. The College Years: 1952-1958

I was motivated to go to college in several ways. First, many of my high school teachers provided encouragement. My scores and grades also indicated that I was qualified academically. Several of my high school friends were headed to college, and three of my four siblings had already pursued further study, two in education and one in nursing, so going to college seemed like a logical next step for me as well. Most of my father's siblings had attended college or professional school, and my mother, as previously noted, had attended Madison Lutheran Normal School in preparation for her teaching career. While the door was open to join my father and brother in farming and I was undecided about a career preference, college still seemed like the right choice for me.

Why Concordia? There was not any one reason why I eventually chose to attend Concordia, but several reasons. Don Hanson, a good friend from my Luther League group in Minneota, had gone to Concordia a year earlier and gave his college experience at Concordia rave reviews. His girlfriend, my cousin Bonnie Borson, decided to follow him there, as did another fellow Luther Leaguer, Darlene Swanson, so peers also played a role aiming me in Concordia's direction. In addition, there were significant adults who were contributing factors as well. My former pastor, J. David Larson, was a strong Concordia advocate as was Helen Dale, the wife of our pastor at the time. My high school involvement in music also influenced the eventual decision to attend Concordia. I was very involved in the choral program at Canby High School, and our conductor had a high regard for the Concordia choir, and his wife, who had been my voice teacher, had sung in the Concordia choir. During my junior year, Paul J. Christiansen, conductor of the Concordia choir, directed our district music festival choir and that experience made a great impression on me. In the spring of that same junior year, our high school choir was invited to the spring choir festival at Concordia, which was my first visit to the campus. I was impressed by the campus, especially by Brown and Fjelstad Halls, and the Concordia choir was awesome! I had visited the campuses of Augustana and Gustavus Adolphus, and St. Olaf might have seemed a logical choice because of some family history on my father's side connected to the institution, but Concordia turned out to be my strong preference.

On an early September Sunday in 1952, my cousin Bonnie Hanson and I set out for our Concordia adventure. Bonnie's mother and grandparents also made the 165-mile trip to Moorhead. In addition to the five of us in the 1950 two-door Ford, the car contained all the clothes and other necessaries we thought we would need for our college experience, including the portable typewriter my parents gave me as a graduation present.

New students were organized into clubs for various orientation activities. Orientation stretched into the semester for about two months, with Saturday morning activities designed mostly, I believe, to keep us from going home. My orientation club counselor was Alan Turmo. He had written to me before my arrival and was present to provide support and counsel as needed. Early on, I met my faculty advisor, Dr. Allwin Monson, professor of speech. I still recall the initial meeting of several of his other advisees out on the lawn in front of what is now Grose Hall. Among Monson's other advisees was Carlton Paulson, who, like me, would one day join the faculty, but as first-year students adjusting to college life away from home, that thought never occurred to us, I'm sure. Among the orientation traditions was the annual "shakathon" when all students, new and returning, gathered in the old gymnasium in a series of interlocking circles; there we would shake hands with hundreds of students, beginning the assimilation process. The "shakathon" tradition continued for several years.

The fall enrollment in 1952 at Concordia was 1,020, up from 890 the year before. Over 800 of us were Lutheran, 453 of us were from Minnesota, and 416 of us were farm kids. Our homogeneity was further indicated by the straw vote for U.S. President when Eisenhower won 233 votes to Stevenson's sixty-nine votes. New students were joined by four new faculty and staff members who would serve long and distinguished careers at Concordia: Walther G. Prausnitz, Hiram Drache, William A. Smaby, and Howard Osborn.

In retrospect, Concordia was a pretty homogeneous place, but so were almost all of the regional colleges, public and private. At Concordia, our commonalities centered around our Lutheran identity, small town and rural connections, generally conservative attitudes, and cultural and intellectual naiveté. Concordia was a wonderful place of transition for most of us to stretch those commonalities into broader ways of thinking and experiencing life. The faculty was patient with our naiveté, and the religious environment was familiar and nurturing; the academic and cultural milieu provided wonderful opportunities, and the social environment was informal and hospitable. In short, Concordia was a great place for farm kids like me to grow into a wider world. Indeed, I think for many decades, Concordia's sweet spot was in serving students from farms, small towns, and regional centers (e.g. Great Falls and Havre, Montana; Devil's Lake, Minot, and Grand Forks, North Dakota; and Fergus Falls, Alexandria, Detroit Lakes, Minnesota, and beyond.)

Four major clusters of activity shaped campus life in those days. To understand the first cluster of activity, a bit about the religious makeup of the campus at the time may be helpful. The Lutheran constituency of Concordia was defined by a variety of religious streams dating to the settlement period in the late 1800s. There were the liturgically formal and confessionally-oriented Lutherans, who traced their history to the Norwegian Synod. There were also the more evangelical and pietistic patrons who traced their origins to the Hauge Synod and the Lutheran Free Church. The largest group of constituents were members of the United Synod in the early century. They were meliorists, or centrists, and although they included people with pietistic leanings, they were focused on the matters that unified them: mission and evangelism. All three groups were represented in the founding of Concordia, although United Synod members were clearly in the majority. These three groups came together to form the Norwegian Lutheran Church in 1918, and although there were subsequent name changes and mergers, these remained the key constituents of the college. The three groups agreed that Concordia should be strong in its faith commitment, focus on the preparation of lay people for vocation, maintain a Christian environment, focus on the liberal arts and preparation for careers, and that there should be an emphasis on Christian inspiration through daily worship and a range of organized religious activities. Those commitments held the college and these diverse constituencies together.

In view of this cultural framework, it is understandable that students brought to the campus some diversity in habit, conviction, and practice. For example, some students came from homes where card-playing, dancing, and smoking were acceptable practices, whereas others came from homes where such practices were strictly forbidden. Some students came from congregations with a strong tradition of evangelism, gospel music, and personal affirmations of faith. Others came from homes where faith was a personal matter, not usually expressed in public forums. Some came from communities of faith that were quite informal and lay centered, while others came from faith traditions that were more formal and clergy centered. All this variety and more was to be found on Concordia's campus. During my first year, I compared experiences with my roommates, two of whom came from homes with the strictures noted above—this in comparison to my home setting where card playing and dancing were acceptable. These differences were in no way dividing on campus, but with respect to student activities, students tended to gravitate to the practices with which they were comfortable, and the community accommodated that diversity.

Religious life at Concordia was both dynamic and diverse. Initially, chapel was a daily event required of all students for their first five months on campus. Services were held in the Old Main Auditorium during the first semester and then in the new Memorial Auditorium following Christmas. It was shortly after the change in venue that the college dropped the chapel attendance requirement. Incidentally, I believe Concordia might have been the first of the Midwestern Lutheran colleges to make this move. At that time, chapel was organized by the Religion Department, and most of the speakers were from the faculty and Lutheran congregations in the area. President Joseph L. Knutson, Concordia College president at the time, spoke frequently and was a campus favorite. Students were responsible for chapel services on Fridays, which featured a senior speaker (usually someone planning to attend seminary) and a soloist or music ensemble.

Concordia organized campus-wide themed events during the academic year. For example, each year there was a major Religious Emphasis Week on campus. Throughout the week, two or three prominent and articulate evangelists, pastors, and teachers from the Evangelical Lutheran Church were featured. These speakers spoke in chapel, various religion courses, evening services, and a variety of informal settings. Among the speakers whom I remember was Alvin Rogness, subsequently, president of Luther Seminary. Also, each spring the campus hosted a world mission festival organized on similar lines.

In addition to chapel and campus-wide themes, there was LSA, Lutheran Students in America, a national organization with chapters on campuses across the country. As I recall, LSA met once a month on Sunday evenings for the purpose of education, inspiration, and outreach activity. Members were organized into what we called "deputation teams" of about 8-10 members that visited area churches, which usually provided Sunday evening programs. I was a member of such a team and led one team during my sophomore year. In addition to LSA, there were the Mission Crusaders group, Friday Prayer Fellowship, and the Tract Club, each reflecting a unique area of ministry.

A second major cluster of activity was purely social and centered on the literary (not so much) societies. When I arrived, there were six brother/sister societies. The number would grow as the student population expanded in the 1960s. Most students joined a society in the second semester of their freshman year. The societies met weekly on Saturday mornings and sponsored a range of social events. In the spring, there were teas for the women's societies and smokers for men's societies, followed by pledging, initiation, and a spring banquet. I joined Sigma Tau Pi, the newest men's society. I enjoyed great fellowship in this group, particularly in my second and third years. Initiation activities often skirted the boundaries of propriety, which led to disciplinary action and periodic calls for reform, but societies continued to flourish for decades at Concordia.

A third major cluster of campus activity consisted of cultural events—lectures, theater productions, recitals, and concerts. The campus hosted world class artists and scholars. In addition, there were three or four major theater productions each year and periodic concerts by the choir and band. These events drew strong student attendance. I rarely missed any of the campus cultural events, which broadened my cultural literacy.

The fourth cluster of campus activity revolved around athletic events, specifically, football and basketball, both men's events in those days. In my first year at Concordia, our football team was the conference champion, led by co-captains Paul Simonson and David Rostad and Coach Jake Christenson. And the basketball team? They hustled.

All these college activities were significantly enhanced with the advent of Memorial Auditorium in 1952. At the time, Memorial was the best sports venue in the Fargo-Moorhead community and in the entire athletic conference. In addition to athletic events and chapel, Memorial hosted concerts, lectures, recitals, theater productions, and "square games" as well as some Fargo-Moorhead community events. Although the campus at this time lacked a dedicated, centrally located student gathering place—and this was a frequent complaint—the fact is, as students we gathered frequently and in large numbers at these various campus events, and there was something for almost every interest.

As I noted earlier, I came to campus with a strong interest in music. I wasn't interested in studying music, but I hoped to participate in the extracurricular music program. Since I had done well in high school music, I supposed that I would be a strong candidate for one of the two Concordia choirs. As a freshman, I went through the tryout process, but was not called back for either of the two choirs. It turns out that I was a "tweener," that is, I had the tone of a tenor but the range of a baritone. I just didn't fit. That was a great disappointment. (Years later, as a junior, I got to know choir director Paul J. Christiansen, and on one occasion, he asked me why I had not tried out for his choir.)

In my early years at Concordia, besides attending campuswide events, I found other ways to stay engaged on campus. As a freshman, I learned of a job opportunity working at athletic events as a sort of security monitor. My job was to prevent people from getting into events without paying admission or from venturing into restricted areas. This was a good, low-stress job that paid well. I also did yard work for Rudy Bergland, who lived across the street from Brown Hall. In addition to being involved in LSA (Lutheran Students in America), I served on the properties committee for a fall theater production. I did so with the encouragement of my speech teacher, who was directing the play. Incidentally, the chair of the properties committee was Esther Grundhovd Allen, who later would serve as assistant to the president.

Academically, my grades at Concordia were average. I aced first semester biology with Professor Ed Fuglestad, and he invited me to move to the advanced section for the second semester. While I again got A's in the lecture and text dimensions of the course, I simply was unable to solve the intricacies of life as seen through a microscope.

While the campus did not have a student union, and we complained about that, I had no problem making social connections. I dated a bit, often attending campus events or going to movies downtown. I developed close friendships with Roger Swenson and LeRoy Ness that would last a lifetime. I lived in unit one of Brown Hall with three classmates, and while closet and dresser space were limited, only one of us had much to store. Two of my roommates, Merle Olson and Richard Mathison, were sons of pastors and gave me insight into that life. The third roommate, Loren Johnson, was the son of an attorney and would follow in his father's footsteps after graduation. Dorm life agreed with me and was a good venue for expanding my social circle.

Campus rules were strict in those days, not just at Concordia but across the collegiate landscape. Colleges at that time were expected to be *in loco parentis*, that is, to act in place of parents. For example, at Concordia, women had hours in the dorm, meaning they had to be in their dorms with lights out by 10:00 or 11:00 p.m. In addition, social dancing was not permitted on campus at that time. The hours and lights out policies for women drew some editorial attention in *The Concordian*, the campus newspaper. By my second year, I was dating someone with local connections that included house parties and dancing. Also in my second year, we had a new dean of women, Dorothy Olsen, and the first major decision she made was to liberalize women's hours and end the lights out policy in women's dorms. She was a very popular dean.

Expanding my extracurricular interests, in my second year at Concordia I decided to participate in forensics. I was a member of the debate team, and this provided an opportunity to hone my skills in analysis and communication and to meet some interesting, bright people from other colleges. In terms of competitive success, I was about average as a debater—and that may be stretching it. This was also about the time when I decided on majoring in economics and speech. I thought that economics would be a good background if I decided to enter the farming operation with my dad and brother Ralph. And speech—well, I was good at it and enjoyed it.

By my second year, Walther Prausnitz (English) had taken over responsibility for the college's artist and lecture events. This was a banner year that included presentations and performances by the great actor Charles Laughton, the educator Robert Maynard Hutchins, theologian Marcus Barth, economist Gabriel Hauge, the Minneapolis Symphony Orchestra, and more. I still recall those events because they opened new worlds to many of us, even though we surely did not understand or appreciate all of what we were hearing. Upon reflection, I am sure the caliber of guest lecturers and performers was good for the college's growing reputation for academic seriousness.

Besides enjoying the outstanding artist and lecture series on campus, I was beginning to explore other opportunities as well. For example, television came to Fargo-Moorhead in 1953, and along with it, the student-produced "Cobber Campus" aired by WDAY-TV. In addition, students produced a religious program, "Thy Kingdom Come," on KFGO radio. I participated in one of the broadcasts. I was also the secretary of my society, Sigma Tau Pi, and put my toe in campus politics by running unsuccessfully (very) for student body treasurer. I was increasingly finding out that

Concordia was the right choice for me, as I enjoyed my classes, extracurricular activities, and expanding interests.

The college continued to grow in enrollment and was expanding in other ways as well. In the fall of 1953, the enrollment was 1,107, and planning for a new library was authorized as well as the renovation of the old gymnasium into the Art Barn. There was some disagreement about the esthetic shape of the campus going forward. Ed Sovik, an architect from Northfield, Minnesota, was hired to design the library. At about that time, former Concordia President J. N. Brown wrote a guest editorial in *The Concordian* (11/13/53) urging retention of the Gothic style of Fjelstad and Brown Halls. Sovik enjoyed the confidence and support of esteemed art professor Cy Running as well as President Knutson and business manager William Smaby. Balancing the retention of Gothic design in some places on campus, Ed Sovik's esthetic in other parts of the campus would shape the look and feel of the Concordia campus for the next four decades.

While I had enjoyed my first two years at Concordia, in the summer of 1954 following my sophomore year, I needed to do some soul searching because I was still undecided about my career direction. Part of me was inclined toward farming, but another part leaned toward business or a profession. I also had some angst that would take me years to resolve, whether to prepare for the ministry. While my academic record was okay, it was not stellar. Clearly, I lacked focus. By way of further context, in those days, military service was a near certainty for young men. While young men could be deferred to attend college, they were only delaying the national obligation. My lack of vocational clarity and the reality of my military obligation led me to the decision to volunteer for a two-year period of service in the U.S. Army. I was not alone in weighing completion of my military service because several of my classmates also enlisted.

During my military service, I was stationed at Fort Leonard Wood, Missouri, and Camp Rucker, Arkansas, for my training, followed by Fort Bliss, Texas, for my permanent duty. I was trained as a radio operator in a service company that was part of a guided missile battalion. In the early 1950s, guided missiles were an innovation in the Cold War and received a lot of attention. I was rarely called upon to operate a radio, however, and spent most of my time in training and various service duties. The biggest take-away from my military experience was my exposure to ethnic, religious, and racial diversity, which was a positive, eye-opening experience that would serve me well for the rest of my life. For example, one of my friends was a

Jew who attended synagogue every Friday evening. One of my roommates was an Inuit with incredible technical skills. Another friend was an African American from St. Louis, another a Polish Catholic from Chicago, and the list goes on. The result was that I became comfortable with and enriched by the diversity I experienced in those years. I found that I could work effectively with people from many different places in the cultural landscape.

During the interim of my military service from 1954-56, I kept close track of Concordia College through my college friends and various publications. It was clear to me that the college was on the move. In the fall of 1954, enrollment had grown to 1,255, the acclaimed novelist John Dos Passos lectured on campus, and the noted soprano Eileen Farrell presented a recital. *The Concordian* reported that 3,000 people attended a production of *The Caine Mutiny Court Martial*, starring the famous actor, Wendell Cory. Beyond the cultural life at Concordia, the physical campus was changing, too, with priorities on building and change. Ground was broken for the new library, which eventually would be named in memory of Carl B. Ylvisaker, longtime and beloved professor of religion, who inspired Cobbers in the dark days of the Depression by referring to Concordia as a "College of Destiny." In March of 1955, the post office and bookstore were moved to new quarters. Students felt that it was time for a student union, and, once again, expressed those views at various campus forums and in *The Concordian*, but a dedicated student union of any sort would be a while.

President Knutson was ably leading the charge in this most momentous time of building in the history of the college. Here is how he made the case in the December 1954 issue of *The Quarterly Review*:

> Most of our church people are not rich. Perhaps this is more cause for repentance than gratitude. Our Lutherans have been slow scholars in the matter of stewardship. Most of the buildings at Concordia are not only old, they are barracks. Concordia has to make up for the deficiency of buildings and equipment in the superiority of her faculty, student body, spiritual emphasis and the quality of scholarship provided. Concordia needs $5,000,000 during the next decade for capital improvements. Can the church do it? Yes, when the members of the church realize that Concordia belongs to the church.

A few months later in the June 1955 issue of *The Quarterly Review*, he continued to press the case:

> Frankly, it is difficult to be patient and to exercise faith when one faces up to Concordia's opportunity and future. So much to do but so little time with which to do it. I sometimes wonder how long Paul J. Christiansen and his staff will have to wait for a music hall? How long our fine science departments will have to carry on in a government barracks?

In addition to President Knutson's persistent and eloquent urging, lay leaders were stepping up. The college was in desperate need of a new library but lacked a funding plan. Two local businessmen, J. Luther Jacobson and Gene Paulson, produced the most important development strategy of the decades to follow, the C400 Club. The idea was to enroll four hundred people with each committed to a gift of $1,000 over a four-year period. This was a dramatic change in the normal stewardship pattern of Concordia patrons, and it worked! Through a series of meetings and mini-campaigns, the project gained momentum. Once the library project was funded, the C400 Club adopted other capital projects. The C400 idea gained national prominence. In fact, C400 was the primary fundraising strategy of the college into the 1980s. Equally significant would be the availability of federal grants for the construction of residential facilities and, eventually, classrooms and libraries.

The forward momentum of Concordia in the 1950s was apparent, not only regarding the physical campus vision but also with student life in general. For example, the imagination for the future of the college was illustrated by a sketch of what the campus might look like when fully developed, which appeared in the June 1955 issue of *The Quarterly Review*. It is an interesting sketch to revisit. A campanile had been envisioned at about the location where the structure now stands. The site of the Ivers building was to have been a chapel. Plans for new dorms to accommodate a growing number of students were not far off. It was clear that Concordia's strong, bright future that President Knutson and many early leaders of the fifties envisioned was well underway. In addition to the physical changes on campus, the flow of student life continued on its course as well. In athletics, Concordia had yet to find its stride. In the early fifties, Gustavus dominated the conference in football and Hamline in basketball, leading *The Concordian* editor to write:

"It would certainly be nice to have a basketball season without Hamline and a football season without Gustavus—being virtually certain to capture the conference championship." In not too much time, however, the dominance of those two institutions in the conference would change.

In the academic arena, a decision was made to alter class attendance policy by no longer requiring students to present a formal excuse from the dean of students after an absence. This was seen as a very progressive move and was applauded by students. Moving into leadership among the faculty was Carl Bailey, professor of physics. He was an eloquent spokesman for the liberal arts as illustrated in this essay from the May 1954 issue of *The Alumni Magazine*:

> We try to give the student some understanding of his relationship to God; some understanding of the nature of the world and of his own nature. We want to develop his powers of thought; to make him a critical person, in the best sense, capable of discriminating analysis and independent reason. We want to uncover for him the incredible riches of pleasure and enlightenment which lie hidden in art and music and literature. We want to make him know that his specialty is not the world but only a small part of the world. We want him to be curious; to be questioning; to be **thinking**: in a word, to be alive.

Concordia's faculty, enrollment, and cultural events in the 1950s were marks of the institution's increasing strength. The college continued to build a distinguished faculty with the addition of Olin Storvick (Classics), Otto Bratlie (Religion), David Green (Modern Languages), and Sonny Gulsvig (Physical Education)—all joined the faculty in 1955 and all of whom would serve the college long and well. Enrollment in the fall of 1955 totaled 1,354, which represented an increase of 105% since 1951. The cultural events program continued to feature distinguished artists and speakers, including the Robert Shaw Chorale, the Juilliard String Quartet, and historian Gerald Priestly. Also worth noting, 1956 was an election year and Estes Kefauver and Adlai Stevenson, aspirants for the Democratic presidential nomination, both visited the campus among the many distinguished notables who found their way to address the growing Concordia community.

The theater arts scene was also changing at Concordia in the mid-fifties. Donald Spencer joined the faculty in 1954 and quickly built a strong theater program that featured four productions during the school year, plus an additional four to six productions in the summer. All performances were held in the Old Main Auditorium, a limited facility for theatrical productions. Spencer gathered around him talented and highly motivated students, and the theater events became go-to events on campus for the Fargo-Moorhead community.

Another sign of Concordia's momentum was the creation of a five-year cooperative program in economics and the completion of the library. Dr. Otto Nieuwejaar, department chair, built a program in which students alternated a semester of internship in a business setting with a semester of study on campus during their fourth and fifth years. There were few programs like this in the region, and it was one of the key building blocks in the growth and development of the college's economics/business program. Another encouraging development was the completion of the Carl B. Ylvisaker Library. To accomplish the monumental task of moving an entire library to the new site, there was a procession of students and staff carrying books from the old library in the basement of Fjelstad Hall to the new facility located mid-campus. The Carl B. Ylvisaker Library, later known as "the Carl B.," would serve Concordia's growing faculty and student enrollment for years to come.

Financial support for a growing and changing Concordia continued. In 1956, the college was awarded a $239,800 grant from the Ford Foundation to be invested, and the earnings used to enhance faculty salaries. This was the largest grant in the college's history and provided the foundation for the college's endowment fund. Concordia's leadership team sensed growing opportunities for the college. President Knutson expressed it this way: "Concordia has the largest natural supporting constituency of any college in the upper North Central area. Her size and program should be doubled and multiply her influence." His vision would become reality.

In campus life, changes were afoot as well; examples abound. One highlight was on the gridiron, where the Concordia football team defeated Gustavus, a rare occurrence, since Gustavus often dominated the conference. Students also took an active interest in the future of Concordia. For example, they suggested adding a jazz musical event to the cultural offerings, but that idea didn't take root. Nationally at this time, the Civil Rights Movement was in its infancy, and one student columnist for *The Concordian* expressed doubt about whether legislative action could really change the human heart. Worth mentioning for me on a personal level, there was a note in *The Concordian* announcing that Mardeth Bervig was the secretary of the Spanish Club. More on Mardeth Bervig later.

By the spring of 1956, I was contemplating the end of my military service obligation. Since the military was over-staffed then, soldiers could apply for an early discharge to return to college. I applied for both an early discharge and re-admission to Concordia, both of which were granted. Although I had left Concordia for military service with uncertainty about my major(s) and future, I would return to campus with a sense of clarity and direction. I would complete my majors in economics and speech, pursue graduate work in speech, and seek a teaching career at the college level.

During my summer leave, I visited the campus and, after exploring housing options, decided to live on campus in Grose Hall, which had been converted to a men's dorm following the completion of Park Region Hall, a women's dorm. My roommate would be John Elster, who, like me, had gone into the Army after his sophomore year. When I returned to campus, my friendship circle centered on other returning veterans, including both Jerry Bjelde and Curt Lundeen, friends from my earlier stint at Concordia. Jay Spoonheim, Rick Paulson, Richard Hvidsten, and Wayne Cease were other veterans who became new friends. All of us were members of the college Veterans Club, a group that functioned much like the literary societies on campus, absent from the pledging and initiation activities; we thought of ourselves as too old and experienced for that.

The fall of 1956 featured another record enrollment of 1,463 students, up eight percent from the previous year. In addition to the still new library, Park Region Hall opened in the fall semester. The lower level included space for a snack bar to be open during the afternoons and evenings—not quite a student union that we all hoped for, but an improvement over the past. I was a member of the committee designated to choose a name for the new space. After soliciting ideas, we settled on The Corn Crib, a name that has lived on in several campus venues (and with adulterated spellings).

As I pursued my majors and plans for the future, my academic schedule featured upper-level courses in economics and speech and extracurricular work in debate. In addition, I was the speech and debate coach at Oak Grove Lutheran High School in Fargo, a job I inherited from my friend LeRoy Ness, who had graduated the previous spring. My debate partners were Bruce Weber and, for most of the year, John Serkland. John was very sharp, and we had some success on the debate circuit. On the academic side, it took me a while to find the groove. I had been away from academic study for two years and found many of my texts dense and dull. I had to learn to read and take notes all over again. By the second semester, however, I found my stride and began building a solid academic record.

Amidst an ambitious fall semester of classes, I attended athletic, cultural, and religious events during my junior year. The most significant of my cultural experiences was the opportunity to hear the Dave Brubeck Quartet on the North Dakota Agricultural College campus, now North Dakota State University. I became a life-long fan. The fall spiritual emphasis week included two speakers with whom I subsequently would become well acquainted: Paul Hanson, a pastor from Willmar, who would become our pastor at Trinity Lutheran in Moorhead, and David Preus, a pastor from Brookings, South Dakota, who would go on to serve as bishop of the American Lutheran Church. The political context was 1956, an election year, so many of my friends and I went to NDSU to hear Republican Vice President Richard Nixon. Democratic vice-presidential candidate Estes Kefauver spoke on the Concordia campus. In the campus straw poll, Eisenhower received 73.8% of the vote, including my own.

Then, as now, homecoming was a big event at Concordia. The homecoming queen was Judy Gryte, and her roommate, Mardeth Bervig, was one of the attendants. While I had known who Mardeth was since her first year when she worked in the cafeteria, I had not met her. I had dated during the fall semester, but there were no serious relationships. One fall day while on the Oak Grove campus for a meeting, I stopped for lunch in the school cafeteria. At the same time, Mardeth Bervig, now a student teacher at Oak Grove, arrived for her lunch break. We exchanged greetings. Later in the semester, as Christmas approached, my debate students planned a Christmas party, and they suggested I bring a guest. So, out of the blue, I called Mardeth Bervig to ask if she would join me. I had wanted to meet her, and now I had the perfect excuse since she knew a number of my speech students from her student teaching stint at the school. Mardeth accepted my invitation and the rest is history. One more special memory from that Christmas party: The students had planned a program that included various games. One of the games involved impromptu speaking on a topic drawn from a hat. In what was obviously a setup by the students, Mardy drew the topic "Three Things I Like about Paul Dovre." Mardy and I had really only met, so the topic put her in an impossible position, but I'm happy to report that she managed her way out of the situation with great dexterity.

Upon my return to Concordia for my junior year, I made many new friends on campus besides my friendships with the other returning veteran friends. I socially kept busy most days and many evenings. On mornings when I did not attend chapel, many of us would go out for coffee to a neighborhood restaurant on 7th Avenue between Concordia and the campus of Moorhead State Teachers College, now Minnesota State University Moorhead. Dorm life included an evening time for devotions Monday through Thursday at 10:00 p.m. The devotions were led by students and usually included a hymn, a Bible passage, brief reflection, and a closing prayer. These gatherings were attended by upwards of half of the dorm residents. Then in the evening, often after the dorm devotions concluded, six or eight of us would gather at The Barn, a restaurant in the FM Hotel on Center Avenue, where we would have coffee, pie, and discuss both the affairs of the world or some new idea we had picked up in class. On other occasions, I would join some of my veteran friends at a local watering hole for prohibited beverages.

In the second semester, I was involved in several campus activities. The societies produced a variety show called Cobber Capers, and I co-chaired the event. The student body was considering adoption of an honor system that would dispense with conventional academic monitoring and place responsibility on students. I was an advocate for the honor system and participated in some campus forums, including an all-campus event in which I supported the proposal, while faculty member Hiram Drache of the History Department opposed it. Although the campus vote fell short to enact the change, the seeds were planted and within two years an honor system was in place.

As spring elections for student body president approached, several of my friends urged me to run for president. Agreeing to run, I survived the primary election, but lost in the finals by twenty-nine votes to my STP society friend and classmate Gary Glomstad. Although I won the votes among upper-class students, I lost the freshmen vote. It was surprising that I had done that well in the election, having been on campus a relatively brief time, but I acknowledge the principal reason was the ambitious effort of members of the Vets' Club.

Springtime on any college campus is a wonderful time, and Concordia was no exception. Campus activities ended with various celebrations, and students were honored for their achievements. The warming weather invited picnics and other outdoor activities, and societies conducted the annual rites of initiation. A memory I still recall is that my STP society went a bit over the top at spring initiation, and some new members and their upper-class sponsors ended up at a Fargo watering hole. Word got back to dean of men, Victor Boe. Through a rather imaginative process, I came to represent my errant brothers in their dealings with Dean Boe. I negotiated a deal whereby the students admitted the infraction and agreed to donate a pint of their blood to the local blood bank. I vividly recall the parade of a dozen or so men as they went to meet with Dean Boe on a spring afternoon to accept the consequences of their actions.

By spring 1957, Mardeth Bervig and I were more than an item, and in the summer, we were engaged. We visited one another's families, and I joined in the celebration as she graduated that spring. Mardeth had been a four-year member of the Concordia choir and a featured soloist in her senior year. She had also worked in the Music Department. Mardy majored in business education and was bound for Elbow Lake, Minnesota, to begin her teaching career. For all the reasons cited above, my junior year was the most significant of my college years. I spent the following summer working on my dad's farm, but with frequent visits to Halstad, Minnesota, where Mardy lived.

By this time, I was anticipating my post-graduate plan by gathering information about various graduate schools. My advisor, Professor Allwin Monson, a highly respected member of the faculty, was of great help to me. He supervised my senior reading program through which I became acquainted with the great classical theorists of rhetoric—Aristotle, Plato, Cicero, and Quintilian. Monson had grown up on a Montana farm and really connected with us farm kids. He had a special gift for discovering the talents of his students and encouraging them to do their best. He saw in me possibilities that I did not recognize in myself, and his encouragement was a mainstay in my professional growth. As our relationship grew, Monson invited me into his home, where he and his wife Dorothy extended their warm hospitality.

After a summer on the farm back in west central Minnesota, I was eager to return for my senior year. I continued to find myself fully engaged on campus, like many of my fellow students at Concordia. From a student point of view, we were proud when our newspaper received all-American honors and our football team won the conference championship. My roommate, Craig Johnson, was one of the stars of the basketball team, and I rarely missed a home game. I continued to work as the speech and debate coach at Oak Grove Lutheran School but dropped my participation in debate at Concordia. In addition to my work at Oak Grove, I became a "Top 40" weekend disk jockey at KFGO, the local radio station. Early in the second semester, Professor Monson developed a throat condition that required total rest for his vocal cords, so I was invited to teach a section of the beginning speech class. This was a helpful experience for me in anticipation of my work as a graduate assistant the following year. In addition, I was the Inter-Society Commissioner, which meant that I coordinated work among the societies and presided over pledging and initiation. Elbow Lake, Minnesota, where Mardeth was teaching, was a seventy-mile trip one way. Regardless of the distance, we were together most weekends in either Elbow Lake or Moorhead.

On the academic front, Concordia continued to move ahead with several significant developments, including the creation and publication of *Discourse*, a review of the liberal arts, under the leadership of Walther G. Prausnitz. The cultural events and lecture series that year at Concordia included Rita Streich, a German soprano; the New Art Wind Quartet; the Minneapolis Symphony Orchestra; and lecturers Richard Dyer Bennet, artist Albert Christ-Janer, and theologian Joseph Sittler. Also on the academic front, the faculty was contemplating a change in the Core Curriculum. Lloyd Svendsbye (Religion), Rodney Grubb (Political Science), and Al Bartz (Psychology) were new to the faculty that year. I developed a friendship with Svendsbye, and he provided helpful counsel as I contemplated my future.

I decided to spread my wings academically during my senior year by taking elective courses in political science, philosophy, art history, and English literature. One consequence was that I fell one course short of completing a major in economics, but I thought the tradeoff was positive. Among other benefits was the opportunity to take classes from Harding Noblitt (Political Science) and Cy Running (Art), two of the giants on the faculty. As I reflect on my education at Concordia, I recognize that I am certainly a product of the liberal arts, which has forever shaped my critical thinking about and engagement with the world.

The college expansion continued apace. Enrollment now stood at a record 1,504. The C400 club claimed many members toward a goal of four-hundred, and gifts totaled a record $658,610.70. President Knutson's leadership achievements were celebrated by the students when we gave him a fishing boat, and by the faculty and staff, who held an appreciation event in honor of the president, Dean Carl Bailey, and business manager William Smaby. The college was buoyant and optimistic for its future.

Springtime and commencement season in late May and early June in 1958 were glorious. With the arrival of spring, the campus was once again verdant. As usual, there were many spring parties, banquets, concerts, and late-night picnics. Ah, yes, youth springs eternal. That same spring, I applied for admission to five graduate programs. I was accepted by all of them, but I chose to attend Northwestern University. While the monetary value of my assistantship at Northwestern was less than other offers, the institution was one of the top graduate programs in my discipline. While I had excelled academically in my last two years at Concordia, my first two years had been about average, so I was delighted by the opportunity to attend Northwestern, where I could study with the best and brightest in my field.

Mardeth and I were married in her home church in Halstad the day after commencement in 1958, a friends and family event on a beautiful Tuesday afternoon. The wedding party included two of my best college friends, Wayne Cease and Richard Hvidsten. Most of my other college friends were also in attendance. Now you may ask, why did we get married on a Tuesday? The answer lies in the fact that some in our wedding party were members of the Concordia choir, and the choir was leaving the next day for a concert tour in Norway, so we scheduled our wedding around the choir rehearsal schedule. For Mardeth and me, that Tuesday was the best day of our lives.

3. Framing a Career: 1958-1965

In June of 1958, Mardy and I packed our earthly belongings in the back of our 1956 Chevrolet station wagon and headed for Evanston, Illinois, to attend graduate school at Northwestern University. I planned to enroll in summer school to get my academic bearings. We found a place to live, I registered for classes, and Mardy found a job in the Evanston school system, all within the first week of our arrival. We also visited Trinity Lutheran Church, which would become our worship home for the next several years, also where Mardy and I would become members of the church choir.

I took two graduate courses that summer, one in classical rhetoric and one in speech psychology. The rhetoric course was taught in seminar-fashion, a new experience for me. I earned A's in both courses and felt that I would be a successful graduate student. We got to know the Evanston community, attended summer theater on campus, and made occasional forays into downtown Chicago. Following summer school, I found a job at a local bookstore.

Just as summer was ending, we had another experience in vocational discernment. My father was contemplating purchasing a cattle ranch in South Dakota, about twenty-five miles from the home farm. As noted earlier, during my high school years I was an active 4H Club member and my specialty was livestock. My dad asked me if I would be interested in coming home to operate the ranch. While pleased by my dad's confidence in me, Mardy and I considered the offer and decided not to change our course. Looking back, this was a major crossroad decision, but one we never regretted.

At the beginning of the fall term, I met the graduate school faculty and my student colleagues, and I began work as a teaching assistant. I taught a class in beginning speech to adult learners on the downtown Chicago campus of Northwestern University, which was a good learning experience for me. We graduate assistants had regular meetings with the department chairman, Dr. Ernest Wrage, where we would talk about our experience teaching undergraduates as well as other matters—academic, political, and otherwise. Those were good meetings. Dr. Wrage would become my dissertation adviser two years later. The graduate assistant group was very congenial. Among them was Frank Nelson, a St. Olaf graduate whom I had met when we were both college debaters, and we became good friends.

My graduate work went well. Dr. Wrage was known as the most rigorous teacher in the department, and I was pleased to earn A's in all his courses. I entered graduate school with the goal of earning a master's degree, but soon Dr. Wrage and other faculty members were encouraging me to pursue a doctorate. While I was flattered by their encouragement, I was thinking again about the possibility of pursuing a career in the ministry. While this was not a new question for me, my interest had been piqued by new experiences. Most of my professors and student colleagues at Northwestern were critics of religion. The scientific ethos of the academy was strong, even in the humanities. This stirred me to think more deeply about my faith and to acknowledge doubt. I shared my vocational uncertainty with Dr. Wrage, and he suggested that I apply for a Rockefeller Theological Fellowship, a program designed for people who were not sure about their calling, but who were willing to spend a trial year in a seminary. Upon reflection, I am deeply grateful for the opportunity suggested by Dr. Wrage. I had long admired his intellect and experience in the academy, so I welcomed his mentorship. Subsequently, I applied for and obtained the fellowship, so the next step in my vocational discernment was to make plans to spend the coming year at Luther Seminary in St. Paul.

I was awarded my master's degree from Northwestern University at spring commencement in 1960 and spent the following summer working in a furniture store in Evanston, which had been home now for the past eighteen months. In August, Mardy and I packed up for our move to St. Paul. We were expecting our first child in November, so there was anticipation on many fronts. We found an apartment that was, to say the least, unusual. The owners of a two-story residence had simply split the upstairs down the middle, which made for an odd assortment of spaces; nevertheless, this would be our home as we awaited our growing family. We stayed close to home following the birth of Louise, a red-head with a wonderful disposition from the beginning. Mardy was a natural parent because, as the oldest of four daughters, she had a good deal of experience taking care of children. On the other hand, I was the youngest in a family of five with absolutely no experience with children, to say nothing of infants. Most evenings I returned to the seminary library to study. On other evenings, I studied at home. With our limited means, a new baby, and unique apartment space, our entertainment consisted of listening to good music, reading books, and playing card games. We attended several concerts by the Minneapolis Symphony and attended University Lutheran Church of Hope, a church our daughter would return to as an adult. Coincidentally, this is the church where President Knutson had served as pastor before coming to Concordia as college president. Mardy's family and mine were not far distant, so we often saw them on weekends. In addition, we made some good friends at the seminary, and Mardy served as an officer of the seminary spouses' group.

My year at Luther Seminary was pivotal in my vocational journey. First, I had many excellent teachers and was able to grow in my intellectual understanding of the faith, for as St. Anselm wrote, "Faith seeks understanding." In that year, I developed a rudimentary understanding of biblical criticism and systematic theology, gifts that would be of consequence to me years later. Second, I was able to clarify my calling. I had been looking for some breakthrough in this matter: Was I called to be a minister or not? Through my study, I came to understand my calling in broader terms than my career; that is, I was called by God to serve my neighbor and that was a calling that could be fulfilled faithfully in a variety of ways. There was not just one way or one career, and this was a key revelation for me. I came to understand that one should consider one's gifts, the counsel of others, and one's own inclinations in addressing the matter. This breakthrough insight took a load off my mind. I had gifts for teaching, had been encouraged by others, and was inclined in that direction rather than the more traditional path of ministry. I determined that I would return to graduate school, complete my Ph.D., and, hopefully, pursue my calling in a church-related setting. While I initially thought that the setting might be teaching homiletics at a Lutheran seminary, it did not quite work out that way.

At seminary, I was reunited with friends from my Concordia years, including Roger Swenson and LeRoy Ness. They were in their fourth and final years at Luther Seminary, while I was a first-year student. As I consider my year-long experience at the seminary, I was influenced the most by three professors: Dr. Roy Harrisville in New Testament, Dr. Eugene Fevold in history, and Dr. Warren Quanbeck in theology. Also, while at the seminary, I assisted homiletics professor Arndt Halvorson in working with some students who needed extra work on their communication skills. That experience convinced me that the seminary needed to do a better job in that area, which is why I considered pursuing a career in homiletics.

In the summer of 1960, we packed up and moved back to Evanston and Northwestern University. This time, we had an additional passenger in eight-month-old daughter Louise, who with her bright spirit was an endless source of joy to us. After getting settled, I resumed my study at Northwestern in summer school, and in the fall, I returned to my teaching duties as a graduate assistant. It was good to be back and renew acquaintances with faculty and student colleagues. In the early going, I explored a couple of new areas, behavioral studies and homiletics, but I soon zeroed in on my original focus in rhetorical theory and criticism.

Mardy secured a position teaching in the business department at a nearby high school. She made good friends and had a fulfilling two years in that position. At one point toward the end of her second year, the principal asked if she would consider becoming the department chair of a new high school that was in the planning stages. This was a real tribute to her good work, but did not quite fit with our plans, which included having another child and moving wherever my career might take us. Yes, this was back in the days when the husband's career set the course.

The summer of 1960 was also consequential on the academic side for a couple of reasons. First, I was invited to participate in a new doctoral track in which I could take whichever courses would best prepare me for the doctoral qualifying exams without having any grades assigned for the courses. In other words, students in this new track were on their own and could sit for their qualifying exams whenever they thought they were prepared to do so. I thrived in the program and elected to take my exams at the end of the 1960-61 academic year. The second matter of consequence had to do with completing the language requirement for the doctorate. I had studied Greek intensively at Luther Seminary and, while not ordinarily a qualifying language, students were routinely granted permission to fulfill the requirement in Greek. I spent the summer of 1960 studying Greek, and in the fall, I petitioned the graduate dean for permission to use the language. I was turned down. The dean was new to his position and decided to follow the book, so at the end of November, I began studying French with a tutor. I spent my Christmas break memorizing flash cards, preparing for the exam that was available in January. I signed up to take the exam, not expecting to pass it, but I wanted to see how close I could come. To my surprise, I passed the exam, so there was celebration in our home to have the language requirement fulfilled. During that same academic year, I was approached by Concordia College in Moorhead to accept an administrative position as director of communications, but my professional course was already firmly set, so I declined the offer in short order. This was another decision we did not regret, so continued on the track toward my Ph.D.

The selection and approval of a dissertation topic is a major crossroad for a doctoral student. I proposed doing a rhetorical analysis of the persuasive techniques of the Nonpartisan League, an agrarian political movement centered in North Dakota. I focused on the early years of the movement, from 1915 to 1922. My proposal was approved, and I commenced my research in the spring of 1961 after completing my qualifying exams. I never grew weary of my dissertation topic, as many graduate students do. I spent the summer of 1961 traveling to libraries in Minnesota and North Dakota and interviewing some veterans of the Nonpartisan League. It was an interesting summer. My research was well enough in hand by the fall, so I could begin writing. After reading the drafts of early chapters, my advisor, Dr. Wrage, suggested that I work with an editor. I engaged an editor who worked for *The Wall Street Journal*. He was demanding, but he taught me how to write tight, efficient prose, and I remain indebted to him.

In 1961-62, my graduate assistantship assignment shifted from speech classroom to debate lab where I worked with Frank Nelson, who by this time was a faculty member and the director of forensics. He was one of the best coaches in the country in one of the foremost programs in the country. In addition to the lab or practice work, I traveled to national tournaments at places like Purdue, Harvard, Dartmouth, Kentucky, and Kansas. Frank was an influential mentor, and by spring of 1962, he had decided to take a leave of absence to complete his dissertation. I was invited to become his replacement and a member of the faculty for the 1962-63 year. I accepted the position and spent the summer completing my dissertation and preparing for my fall assignment.

Just as the fall semester commenced, I successfully defended my dissertation. I had been in graduate school for four years, three years at Northwestern and one year at Luther Seminary. I was excited to begin my professional life as a teacher-scholar. I did not have specific aspirations regarding my career, but I was confident that things would play out in a salutary way.

The 1962-63 year was a busy one. In June of 1963, my parents came to Evanston for my graduation. It was a double celebration because our son Erik was born on June 5 of that year. Also, that spring I was contacted by various universities and was, in turn, applying to others for a permanent professional position. I was offered positions at Eastern Montana State College, Purdue, Wisconsin, and Concordia. My interviews at Concordia in the spring of 1963 included long conversations with Dean Bailey and Professor Monson. In addition, I visited with some of the younger faculty members, including David Green, Rodney Grubb, and Lloyd Svendsbye. They were encouraging and optimistic about the college. Mardy and I decided that I would accept the offer to become assistant professor of speech and director of forensics at Concordia. Although my decision disappointed my graduate school professors, who had encouraged a more scholarly/research focused career, Mardy and I knew Concordia was the right decision for us. The decision was the result of several factors, but the decision largely reflected my deep respect for President Knutson, Dean Bailey, and Professor Monson as well as my excitement about Concordia's future.

The rest of summer 1963 was equally busy. I spent June and July preparing for my first presentation at a professional conference of the Speech Association of America. I was also preparing for my teaching assignments at Concordia and for the upcoming forensic season. To add to this busy time of our lives in 1963, we began a summer vacation tradition of spending time at a Minnesota lake. Summer lake time eventually would lead us a decade later in the early seventies to purchase lake property on Bad Medicine Lake near Park Rapids, Minnesota. Our children loved the lake as much as we did because the lake was, and still is, a great place to relax, recreate, and build family ties. In addition, I enjoyed planting and trimming trees, improving lakeshore, and doing the myriad of other chores necessary while relishing lake time in Minnesota north country.

In August of 1963, we moved to Moorhead and found an almost new three-bedroom apartment on 19th Street South. The spaciousness of our new digs was in marked contrast to the cozy apartments we had lived in during our graduate school years. Among the occupants of the apartment building back in 1963 were Al and Anita Anderson. Al was in the Philosophy Department at Concordia and would become a valued friend and colleague. Mardy and Anita would become fast friends and, among other shared endeavors, they started a book club that included the wives of several faculty members, a group that was still active in 2018.

Eventually, in the summer of 1964, we found a small house on 4th Street South, about two blocks from the campus. The house was a good fit for us, in part, because of its ideal proximity to campus. As a veteran, I qualified for a GI loan, which did not require a down payment. Our monthly house payments were under a hundred dollars per month, which made the home affordable on my annual salary, somewhere in the $6,000 range. In the late sixties, we would expand the house to accommodate our growing space needs and would reside there until 1975.

Mardy and I were already feeling at home in Moorhead and at Concordia that summer of 1963, excited for the academic year 1963-64. Our college friends Jerry and Bev Bjelde were also new to the Concordia staff. Jerry was the director of Alumni Relations. We also reconnected with college friend Roger Swenson, a Development staff member, and wife LuJean, and Ed Ellenson, director of Admissions, and his wife Ann. In addition, we made friendships among the other new faculty and staff. Most of our friends had children about the ages of ours, so there were many shared interests and stories around childrearing. Our children, Erik and Louise, were cheerful and outgoing, easy to care for and a source of joy in our lives.

My instinct about accepting the position at the college had been correct—Concordia was indeed on the move and the future looked bright. Though I had been absent from the campus for four years, I had stayed in touch through my friend Roger Swenson in the Development Office and my mentor, Professor Monson. Before saying more about the beginning of my career at Concordia in the fall of 1963, first, a bit more about the college in the early sixties. I knew that Concordia was continuing to grow in enrollment and new buildings were being constructed, including the student commons, Livedalen Hall, and Hvidsten Music Hall. The construction of dormitories and the growth in enrollment were both aided by new federal programs that provided financial assistance to students and low interest loans for the construction of facilities. In 1962, A *Blueprint for Concordia College* was published, the result of a collaborative planning process directed by Dean Bailey.

Along with the positive sides of Concordia's growth, there were also growing pains, of course. For example, it was a challenge to find faculty qualified and sympathetic with the college's mission. In "The President's Report of 1960," President Knutson acknowledged that it was sometimes necessary to hire people who had never had a connection to a vital congregation or a Christian college. Knutson further clarified his point: "That does not necessarily mean that they are unchristian, but it is necessary for Concordia to be so positive and winsome in her Christian position and emphasis that they become convinced that her objectives are both good and right." Concordia had a growing academic reputation to uphold, so I now recognize that, in part, President Knutson's leadership and support for hiring faculty were key to moving the college forward at that time.

While the administration, faculty, and staff were busy with more serious matters, students—as students will do—found ways to pull a few harmless pranks on campus. There was one student prank that became legendary, in which a handful of students moved dishes from the cafeteria to the library via the heating tunnel and arranged place settings on each table in the reading room. It would be some time before the pranksters owned up to this deed. When the class of 1961 had its reunion years later, the dean of students, Victor Boe, absolved the pranksters of guilt in a fun-filled celebration. Placing the table settings in the library was such a good prank that the number of students claiming to have been part of the event grew from year to year. In another case, twenty-three members of the Young Republican Club attended the fall organizational meeting of the Young Democrats Club and elected two of their members to office. The next day, they appeared in chapel and resigned their positions. While Concordia students generally pursued their academics with necessary seriousness, they also found ways to inject the general atmosphere on campus with a bit of good humor as well.

Reflecting more serious concerns at the time, a group of students published a list of their concerns and proposals in what they called "The Blue Paper." This, apparently, caused President Knutson some distress, some issues more than others. One of the students' proposals was to hire a campus pastor, which was done with the president's hearty endorsement. Reverend Carl Lee was called to the position and served the college with distinction for many years. Emerging student concerns also related to the Civil Rights Movement, the escalating conflict in Vietnam, and the role of students in campus governance. These matters would mature in decisive ways in the following years.

My Concordia career began in late August of 1963 with the opening faculty workshop, and classes began a week or so later. The Speech and Theater Department consisted of four people: Al Monson, Clair Haugen, Carol Torgerson, and me. I was the only Ph.D. in the department, but at that time, few faculty on campus held terminal degrees. In the first semester, I taught two sections of beginning speech and an advanced course in persuasion. I still recall the advanced class, consisting of only five students.

But, as they say, they were the right five students because they were bright, talented, and hard-working. They enjoyed the class and spread the word, so the spring enrollment in the course was over twenty.

During the first week of classes, we held an evening meeting for students who might be interested in participating in the debate program. Remember that I was coming off two years of coaching with one of the top debate programs in the country at Northwestern, so I was used to experienced debaters who worked hard and knew the ropes. That first evening at Concordia attracted about fifteen students, including only 2-3 students with experience. Among them were two upper-class students, John Strandness and Paul Arneson, and three freshmen, Connie Farden, Loren Anderson, and Jim Nestingen. The three freshmen would quickly become the backbone of the program, but that first evening had not been auspicious. Mardy still recalls what I said when I came home from that meeting: "It looks like it could be a long year," and in many ways, it was.

My long-term goal was to bring the program along to a position of national stature. I was sure we had students at Concordia who could compete with the best in the country, but first we had to figure out who those students were, begin where they were, and then build a successful program. Our performance in the early tournaments and the early years was not impressive. I sent John Strandness and Connie Farden to tournaments at Harvard and Northwestern. They did not compete successfully, but they learned a lot. By the second semester, Loren Anderson was in the mix and then things started moving. In the second year, Mark Onstad, Lon Holden, Linda Jacobson, Chris Hindemith, Mark Engelstad, Betty Malen, and Linda Thorkelson joined the program, all of whom had some high school experience. Then we began to be competitive at regional tournaments and stronger at the national level. By the third year, we were being taken seriously at every level, and in the fourth and fifth years, Concordia debaters were winning tournaments at the national level.

In addition to the debaters, we had some outstanding orators, two of whom—Don Gaetz and Judith Simonson—would become national champions. Al Monson coached the orators and was also my assistant debate coach. He was patient and encouraging to students and a great companion to them on many road trips. It was striking that he, who had at one time been the director of forensics, including during my college years, would now be my assistant. His work and support were invaluable to me.

Meanwhile, back on the campus, I was serious about the work at hand. In my second year, I was promoted to associate professor and named department chair. Al Monson had proposed my move to department chair when I was hired, but I asked that we delay my assuming the role of department chair for a year. At the time, I felt the promotion was surely premature, but the decision also reflected my personal drive and early professional success with a couple of publications. When I assumed the role as department chair in the fall of 1964, I was eager to build the department. We made some additions to the curriculum, including a beginning section of speech for high ability students. We also added coursework in rhetorical theory and criticism. I initiated a move to require that students planning a career in teaching should be required to take beginning speech. To reach this goal, I first secured the support of the chairs of the Education and English Departments, and then I lobbied other faculty leaders. The proposal was adopted unanimously. Our department also decided to improve the department's Ph.D. ratio, so we financed a leave for Clair Haugen, director of theater, by each faculty member in the department taking on a course overload. Upon Clair's return and Carol Torgerson's departure, we hired a new faculty member in theater, Ken Bordner. The Speech and Theater Department was making positive changes, and I appreciated the opportunities to demonstrate my leadership, not only at the department level but also campuswide.

As I reflect on my leadership in the Speech and Theater Department and on campus in general at the time, I feel fortunate to have been positively influenced by several remarkable people—Allwin Monson, Ernest Wrage, Carl Bailey, and Joseph Knutson. In the contemporary era, we speak of the positive impact of mentors, and I believe these four individuals served as my mentors. It was not the case that I had some sort of formal agreement with any of them. Rather, they were mentors in the sense that they were as exemplars, sources of counsel and encouragement. Allwin Monson saw my potential and encouraged me, Ernest Wrage set high academic standards and expanded my professional horizons, Carl Bailey was the role model of a wise and effective leader, and Joseph Knutson inspired and counseled not only me, but a whole generation of Cobbers. I would be remiss not to include my father, Nels Dovre, as the first mentor-role model in my life. It was my father who, early in my life, set standards of work, ethics, and excellence that have forever shaped my life.

4. Crucible of Change: 1965-1975

In the early sixties, no one imagined what was coming in higher education in general or to Concordia College in particular. While there were some aspects of change that Concordia anticipated such as national growth in the number of college-age students, we did not foresee many of the other impact factors that were on our doorstep. For example, we did not anticipate the impact of the Civil Rights Movement or the Vietnam War. Individuals on campus who were keenly aware of the Vietnam conflict were few, and even they could not have imagined the chaos that would follow in American society and on college campuses across the nation. Also, at that time, we had not heard about or understood anything about student power. The revolution in moral standards also was not on our agenda, nor did we anticipate the religious awakening that would occur on the Concordia campus. Amidst this broader cultural context, there were also changes that accompany generational shifts in institutional leadership, which was the case at Concordia.

Chapter 4 is titled "Crucible of Change: 1965-75" because this period at Concordia was indeed a crucible, that is, a holding vessel in which elements combine, often the result of challenges and trials, to create a new reality. In short, Concordia College experienced more dramatic change from 1965 to 1975 than in any other decade in its history. As the result of the changing national context, the impact on Concordia was manyfold: The governance of the college was modified, the college made dramatic changes in its curriculum, and the campus hosted highly-visible speakers on many controversial subjects. In addition, Concordia initiated a highly successful international studies program, added new dimensions to the college's religious activities programing in response to the evangelical impulse of students, and established an ecumenical outreach center. Concordia also experienced transformational change in student freedoms, initiated efforts to achieve racial diversity, and expanded student opportunities to both experience and understand a wider world. The list could go on because the changes were rapidly occurring at all levels and within every facet of the campus community, it seemed. Living through these years and events was like living in a crucible, where Concordia was being refined by forces often beyond their control. The result, as with a crucible, was a refinement, whether constructive or otherwise, in the nature and character of the institution.

Before continuing, I must note that in this postmodern era, what you read here is clearly perspectival in describing the decade as I experienced it. I will tie this narrative to key events, activities, and decisions without claiming that the point of view shared is complete and fully objective. I will begin with a short assessment of the college's readiness for the change and transition that was coming. Then, in separate sections, I will explore the changes that were experienced at Concordia in the faculty and curriculum, student life, and religious life. I will explore some of the ways we experienced the Vietnam conflict and the Civil Rights Movement. What follows is a description of my personal journey through the crucible of change from 1965-1975.

INSTITUTIONAL TRANSITION

While the challenges and changes that characterized the decades of the sixties and seventies were unprecedented, the college was blessed by a thoughtful planning process, a highly capable and farsighted administrative team, and an abundance of loyal and capable faculty and administrative staff members. First, there was an effective planning process. On the eve of the sixties, it was apparent that there would be incredible opportunities for growth. J. L. Rendahl, vice president for Admissions, and later in the decade executive vice president, was perhaps the most farsighted. He also kept a close eye on the demographics and the regional competition. Rendahl was a master marketer as well, which kept Concordia far ahead of most private colleges in the region. He also was astute about emerging federal programs that would help build dining, housing, and academic facilities. Of equal importance were new programs of financial assistance, first to students in the high-demand areas of math, education, and science, but soon to include students who qualified for financial assistance. President Knutson often referred to Rendahl as our "Philadelphia lawyer," that is, a man who was well informed in matters not only like demographics and public policy, but also a master in navigating government relationships. The core leadership team of Rendahl, Smaby, Bailey, and Knutson shared an understanding that growth represented Concordia's most available opportunity to improve the academic quality and physical capabilities of the college. Their underlying assumption was that as a college, Concordia was called to serve the educational needs of the region to the extent possible.

It was clear to Carl Bailey that before Concordia could grow, the college and its leadership needed a comprehensive plan shaped by the institution's core commitments to mission and quality. To that end, a planning team was established that eventually developed a plan titled A *Blueprint for Concordia College*, which was a product of broad consultation among the faculty and staff. Essentially, A *Blueprint for Concordia College* was a document about fundamental matters such as the mission, the liberal arts, and the quality of experiences. This document turned out to be formative not only for the growth period of the sixties but also for the indefinite future. How was that so? I believe there were two primary reasons for the lasting success of the *Blueprint for Concordia College* document. First, because the mission statement of the college, composed by Bailey in 1961, set out language that would endure: "The purpose of Concordia College is to influence the affairs of the world by sending into society thoughtful and informed men and women dedicated to the Chrisian life." Those well-chosen words of the mission statement then, as now, reflected the values of Concordia and guided its vision.

A second reason for the enduring success of A *Blueprint* was that it established a clear planning process that has continued to the present. The document helped guide multiple facets of the college. For example, A *Blueprint* established some presuppositions about the role and characteristics of the faculty. The study document covered practical matters related to tenure, teaching loads, leaves of absence, research, teaching, and endowed chairs and professorships. In addition, key requisites of a sound academic program and student religious life were also identified. A *Blueprint* provided expectations and guidance related to academics and the campus itself. For example, since growth would mean expansion of the physical plant, an important element of the document was a section outlining the orderly expansion of the campus.

Many planning documents then, as now, are written with a certain amount of enthusiasm, but eventually are left to gather dust. What was different about the Concordia planning tradition is that the plans shaped the college's development almost daily. In the early going of the college, resources were scarce, so it was important to have clarity about plans and priorities, and the planning document did just that. In short, A *Blueprint for*

Concordia College not only contributed to the emerging strength of the institution in the 1960s, but also well beyond that decade because the document guided campus leaders to make effective decisions in clear support of the mission of Concordia College.

In addition to an effective, comprehensive planning document, another key to the strength of Concordia during the growth and change period of 1965-75 was the leadership team's ability and success in working together. They were loyal to each other, respectful of each other's capacities and authority, and united in support of the larger-than-life leader, Joseph Knutson. An example of Knutson's wisdom and strength as a leader was knowing what he didn't know and relying on the capabilities and capacities of those who did. To complement this ability, he was also the master of delegation. In addition, President Knutson kept his attention on the Lutheran constituency, Concordia's mission and Lutheran identity, and the big picture. Joe Knutson was also the voice and face of the college. Drawing on years of experience and habits prior to Concordia, Knutson had been seasoned by the political complexities of large congregations, church-wide leadership, and a prodigious habit of reading. I venture to say that he was one of the best-read people on campus, despite his busy schedule and various commitments. One can only speculate on what miracle of the Spirit brought these four individuals—Knutson, Bailey, Rendahl and Smaby—together for a nearly twenty-five-year leadership run. (As a side point worth noting, women are not mentioned in the Concordia leadership team of the early 1960s, but this isn't surprising for the time. In the sixties, higher education was generally dominated by men; similarly, it was men who often assumed leadership positions in the early history of Concordia.) Regarding campus leadership at the time, special note should be made of the contributions of the dean of women, Dorothy Olsen, and dean of men, Victor Boe, both of whom knew their jobs well and were highly effective in their relationships with students. As far as other campus leadership at the time, while the Advancement team did not play a significant role in the early sixties, that would change with the emergence of Roger Swenson as its leader in the late sixties.

Let me say a bit more about the members of the leadership team. I have already noted President Knutson's stature; he was a giant, literally and figuratively. Typically, he generally stayed out of faculty business, although he faithfully attended all faculty and Faculty Senate meetings, where he provided the opening devotions. He almost always spoke at the opening convocation, where he shared a world view shaped by Christian presuppositions. President Knutson, fondly known as Prexy Joe by many, had a good smile and a friendly demeanor, making conversation with everyone as he loped across the campus. In meetings of the leadership team, Knutson deferred to others in managing, usually Carl Bailey (and later me) and occasionally Bill Smaby on business matters or J. L. Rendahl on Admissions and campus development matters. When Roger Swenson joined the group, he would take the lead on matters related to fund-raising. Meetings of the President's Council took place in the president's office. Prexy Joe was not one for long meetings. In fact, he would often get up and leave the office for a few minutes to pick up his mail, which he would bring back to his desk and read as we continued our deliberations.

In addition to the leadership team's weekly meetings, we would gather for two-day planning sessions each June at Joe Knutson's cottage at Spider Lake near Park Rapids, Minnesota. Those retreat sessions were a highlight of the year. While on retreat, the leadership group expanded to include additional staff like Ed Ellenson from Admissions; Dave Benson and Morrie Lanning from Student Affairs; Don Dale, who served as registrar; Curt Danielson, director of the physical plant; Associate Dean Bob Homann, and usually some faculty members. The focus of these annual events was on broad planning issues, usually related in one way or another to the *Blueprint*. We visited about future capital projects, looked at enrollment trends, and addressed issues in student life and faculty development. Again, Joe deferred to others with expertise to lead the agenda and occasionally weighed in with his ideas. There also was a social dimension to the annual retreats, as we went to a local café in nearby Nevis for our meals and often played whist in the evenings. I will never forget playing cards with J. L. Rendahl and Vic Boe, only to discover how competitive they were. Bill Smaby usually brought along a box of cigars as an after-dinner treat for those of us who enjoyed an occasional smoke. While the weekly meetings and the two-day June retreats helped campus leaders carry on the essential decisions and work of the college, these times were also important for deepening not only our engagement with the tasks at hand but also our personal relationships. Our time together furthered the trust and respect we had for each other, which I believe benefited the college.

Because of their lasting impact on the college, let me return to brief descriptions of influential members of the council. Carl Bailey, a Cobber from the class of 1940 and a Ph.D. in physics, returned to Concordia as a physics professor and brought numerous strengths to the leadership team. Carl was quiet and a master of patient deliberation. He gave everyone time and room to breathe. Whenever he spoke, everyone listened because Carl was held in such high regard. He had a high opinion of the college and its possibilities, and because of that, Carl was a real confidence builder. He was a pipe smoker and made an art out of filling, tamping, and lighting his pipe, which often allowed others in the room a chance to think and contribute. Indeed, Carl's pipe etiquette was a sort of rhetorical tool of his leadership. In short, Carl Bailey was the Council's intellectual leader and the college's academic leader in establishing programs and policies.

On the other hand, Bill Smaby, business manager since 1952, was the leadership team's tactical leader. He knew how to plan and manage the budget in a way that inspired confidence. Equally important, he was masterful in his interpersonal skills. Bill's door was always open and his handshake firm, smile inviting, and voice warm. What great good fortune it was for the college to have Bill Smaby providing financial leadership for twenty-four of the most financially strategic years of Concordia's history. On a personal note, Bill always encouraged me and supported my work. When I became president of the college, he agreed to postpone his retirement for an additional year to aid us in the leadership transition. I am forever grateful for the extra year he gave to Concordia and to me.

J. L. Rendahl was probably the smartest man in the room—well read, creative, systematic, and thorough. He was on top of student demographics and federal aid programs. In addition, he had a well-honed marketing plan and surrounded himself with able staff. President Knutson greatly respected Rendahl and regularly leaned on his counsel. J. L. Rendahl frequently knocked on my door with valuable information he had gleaned from some report or publication. He was strategic and held his own opinions, but he also a good listener and carefully weighed the ideas of others. For example, I recall a time when he presented a well-reasoned argument in opposition to the idea of establishing the Tri-College University (TCU), a consortium that was designed to expand student opportunity through cooperation among NDSU, Moorhead State College, and Concordia. He thought this program would leave us at a disadvantage on enrollment. The consensus view of the Council was that the TCU would be an asset, as it proved to be. J. L. had stated his case, but his view did not prevail, and, of course, he was a gentleman about the decision to move forward with the TCU partnership.

As mentioned, Vic Boe, a former parish pastor, was our dean of students. He was our sage; that is, Vic rarely brought proposals to the table, but he consistently offered helpful insights. Vic's demeanor was mild and even-tempered, a rock of Gibraltar during those turbulent years of incredible pressure on student rights, civil rights, and life-style issues. While he had a good sense of humor and an easy-going manner, constant demands from dealing with the realities of student life in the sixties probably hastened his retirement. Vic made excellent staff appointments in David Benson and Morris Lanning, two men who emulated his model of patience and fortitude. Dorothy Olsen was Vic Boe's partner in Student Affairs as the dean of women. She was a respected voice and a real change agent in student life. Dorothy Olsen is regarded as one of the early influential women on campus. The college benefitted greatly from Olsen's work on behalf of and dedication to Concordia.

Another fine addition to campus leadership came with hiring Roger Swenson. Roger had joined the leadership cadre upon his appointment as director of Development. His gifts included his ability to think outside the box on issues like governance, administration, and fundraising. He was our house iconoclast and could break up a serious discussion with appropriate humor, especially when we may have been taking ourselves too seriously. Roger was the first member of our staff to attend the Institute for Educational Management at Harvard University. As a result, he brought back some excellent ideas about management and administration, including the creation of an executive structure with vice presidents. Morrie Lanning, then a graduate student, also contributed to this effort. I have intentionally focused this discussion on leadership team members who served for most of the decade from 1965-75. There were transitions during the decade that brought new members to the team, who will be referred to in later sections of this chapter.

In addition to an effective planning document in A *Blueprint for Concordia College* and an effective leadership team and council, the third factor that facilitated Concordia's successful run in the sixties and seventies was the presence of a gifted administrative staff. Consider the Admissions Office, where, as I noted above, J. L. Rendahl appointed both Ed Ellenson and Jim Hausmann to his staff. Ed would become vice president for Admissions and then vice president for Advancement, and Jim Hausmann would become vice president for Admissions and Financial Aid. Similar success in staff appointments occurred in Development as well, with appointees such as

Gerald Bjelde, Art Grimstad, Rosalie Lier, and John Pierce. Each brought their specific talents and energy to bear. Gerald Bjelde would become director of Alumni Relations and Communications, Art Grimstad would spark a dramatic growth in the C400 Club, Rosalie Lier put Concordia on the map in the foundation world, and John Pierce would become an incredibly successful major gift officer for decades to come. Other administrative staff worth noting were in the Office of the Dean of Students. Both Morris Lanning, known as Morrie to most, and David Benson were appointed to entry level positions shortly after graduating from Concordia. Morrie would become the vice president for Student Affairs, and Dave Benson would become, successively, director of College Relations and associate vice president of Development. In the academic dean's office, I would become dean and, eventually, president. Robert Homann would serve two terms as associate dean and two terms as vice president for Academic Affairs. There are others, of course, but this listing provides a clear sense of the core leadership team's success at spotting talent and then nurturing, guiding, and mentoring them in support of the mission of Concordia College.

During my first year as associate dean, the administrative leadership team, then called the Administrative Council, met weekly to discuss matters both routine and strategic. The council was made up of the entire administrative staff and would be replaced by the President's Council in the late sixties. I was eager to continue my leadership on campus, but I soon discovered I had much to learn in my new role. At my first or second meeting with the Administrative Council, the editor of *The Concordian* and a faculty member were called on the carpet for their coverage of some event. I was upset by this move and quickly defended the editor for his actions. Fools do indeed rush in where angels fear to tread. Following the meeting, I came to my senses about my indiscretion. Although I did not have any change of heart on the issue, I didn't have the experience yet to have had a more measured, thoughtful response. Before the end of the day, I appeared in the president's office and remarked that I realized that President Knutson had a difficult job, which was my back-handed apology, I guess. The president might have shouted me out of the office, but, instead, he responded modestly. In retrospect, and knowing Joe Knutson's *modus operandi*, I suspect that he had already relieved himself of his anger by expressing his thoughts about my actions to J. L. Rendahl, as was often the case in those days. I had a lot to learn, but, again, I was excited by the new challenges. I was also fortunate to be surrounded by strong mentor-leaders.

Those of us who were on the staff formed informal bonds, which I believed strengthened our capacity for leadership. I think of the hours spent with Homann, Lanning, Benson, Ellenson, and Swenson. We were emerging leaders, full of energy and our own ideas for change. We encouraged and challenged each other, and we also challenged the status quo of the college on a range of issues. Roger, in particular, led the effort to professionalize the management of Concordia's endowment funds. He also worked to expand the capacities of the Board of Regents through the selection process. Morrie and I worked together on several projects, including the establishment of the Committee on Student Affairs and the student rights document. David Benson had the pulse of students, and we collaborated on matters related to Intercultural Affairs and minority students. Morrie, David, and I were in frequent contact as we negotiated various student complaints and proposals. Ed Ellenson and I would kibitz about financial aid policies, enrollment goals, and the recruitment of minority students. While the sixties and seventies were certainly a crucible of change, I found my work to be challenging but rewarding, thanks in part to administrative colleagues who closely shared in the work.

A particular example comes to mind of this kind of administrative leadership and excellence from the Advancement leaders, their focus on deferred giving under Roger Swenson, and, subsequently, Ed Ellenson. While Concordia achieved national recognition for its C400 Club that provided funds for several building projects, the college had a difficult time raising money in the form of large gifts. The reality was that our constituency at the time was agrarian and, while a farmer might have considerable wealth in farm land, he/she needed that land to make a living. In short, they couldn't afford to give it away. In view of that reality, Roger and his colleagues decided that, in the long run, Concordia's opportunity lay in working with people (farmers and others) to structure their estate plans in such a way that the college might be an eventual major beneficiary. In other words, potential donors would have their property as a source of income as long as they lived, and when they no longer needed it, the college would benefit. In addition, the staff developed expertise in working with trust and annuity arrangements. The results were positive and largely explain the accelerated growth of the college's endowment in the eighties and nineties.

Leadership development in today's higher education is a formal academic discipline, and almost every contemporary leader in higher education can point to valuable learning experiences in one or more quality professional programs. Perhaps I would have been a better leader if I had had the benefit of such opportunities, but I am not complaining because I think I had the best mentors and colleagues anyone could have asked for. My own evolution as a college leader was largely serendipitous. When I came to Concordia as an assistant professor, I had no plan to become a college leader, much less the president of Concordia and spend my entire career at the college. In fact, in my second year at Concordia, I declined an opportunity to return to the faculty at Northwestern University. In the late sixties and early seventies, I was approached about several deanships, the chairmanship of a department in a significant university, and a couple of presidencies. What kept me at Concordia through those years were the college's deep commitment to the mission, Concordia's momentum with an eye for the future, its strong, capable institutional leaders, and opportunities for personal growth and career leadership.

FACULTY AND GOVERNANCE

In the early sixties, many new people joined the faculty, principally because of the growth in enrollment. To illustrate, in 1963 there were twenty additions to the faculty, seventeen in 1964, nineteen in 1965, and thirty in 1966. Many of us newcomers had terminal degrees at a time when most other members of the faculty did not. Increasing the percentage of doctorates was a high priority reflected in both the faculty leaves program and in the recruitment of new faculty. Most of us brought with us a loyalty to the college, whether or not we had graduated from Concordia. We also brought energy and ideas to make the college a better place. We found in Dean Carl Bailey a wonderful exemplar of the liberal arts tradition and a source of encouragement to us with respect to our energy and passion to move the college forward.

In my early years on the faculty, my closest colleagues were Lloyd Svendsbye (Religion), Al Anderson (Philosophy), Alan Graebner (History), Ted Heimarck and Roger Spilde (Economics), Jim and Eleanor Haney (Religion), Larry Falk (Sociology), Leonard Bird (English), and Bob Homann (Chemistry). Al Anderson convened about a dozen of us for occasional discussions.

Without question, he was our intellectual leader. We called ourselves "the brain pickers." The focus of our discussions was on the disciplinary work to which each of us was committed, but beyond the structured discussions, we were busy imagining the future of the college. To be sure, we carped about certain administrative actions, particularly the pursuit of enrollment growth, but we were fundamentally loyal to the college. We respected President Knutson, and we admired and followed our wise and sagacious dean, Carl Bailey.

In those days, from a demographic point of view, there were two faculties: one, the established, long-term members who occupied positions of leadership on the faculty and in the academic departments, and, two, the newcomers. The established faculty were people who had often sacrificed a great deal in the 1940s and 1950s, for that reason most of them lacked doctoral degrees. In the view of "the brain pickers," however, this group didn't want to move as quickly or dynamically as we thought necessary. As a result, some of us were elected to the Faculty Executive Committee, which, in effect, set the agenda for faculty discussion. The college had the good fortune of having some seasoned faculty members who mentored and joined hands with the newer faculty, thus avoiding any two-faculty divide. That group included Walt Prausnitz (English), Olin Storvick (Classics), Al Monson (Speech), and Harding Noblitt (Political Science). One of the first initiatives in the early sixties was the creation of a joint faculty administration planning group, with equal numbers of faculty and administrative staff. Dean Bailey led the group in identifying and then exploring institutional issues related to finance, facilities, curriculum, faculty, enrollment, the church, and public policy. This, in turn, led to faculty-wide discussions of these matters.

At about the same time and on a parallel track, the Faculty Executive Committee reviewed the faculty constitution. That review took a long time, but led to some fundamental changes in governance. The Faculty Senate became the principal decision-making body of the faculty, whereas in the past, many decisions had been reserved to the faculty as a whole. In the new constitution, the membership of the Faculty Senate more than doubled and included both administrators and students. The faculty, of course, predominated and included all department chairs and an equal number of faculty elected at-large. The effect of this change in governance was that it gave influence to several additional faculty members, which was a positive change. For example, it became much easier to get a hearing for a new idea, thus bringing more ideas and voices into decision-making conversations. Another change occurring in the late sixties was setting terms for department chairs at three years and involving senior faculty in the selection process for new chairs. This facilitated change at the departmental level and provided newer faculty with opportunities for leadership.

Dean Bailey's determination to avoid any two-faculty cleavage led to his support and leadership in both the long-range planning project and the review of the faculty constitution. In addition, and related to rapid growth in enrollment and faculty, President Knutson and Dean Bailey determined that there was need for an associate academic dean. Dean Bailey sought the counsel of selected faculty and, subsequently, invited me to assume the position, which I did in the fall of 1967 at the age of thirty-two. I had already served as a department chair in Speech and Theater for four years. In addition, I served as a member of the Faculty Executive Committee and as chair of the facility planning group for a new humanities and social science complex.

Carl Bailey gave me a great deal of responsibility and then left me alone to do the work. He gave me room to try new things, some of which he must have known were a bit farfetched. While on sabbatical leave, Carl handed his duties over to me when I had only one year of experience as his associate. Of course, I could and did screw things up from time to time, but all the while I was learning important lessons. When Carl left the Dean's Office in 1970 to return to the faculty, he recommended me as his successor, and the Faculty Selection Committee concurred. At that point, I came to work for President Knutson directly. He made it clear that I was the dean, and he wasn't going to look over my shoulder. He trusted me to do the work. I had a steep learning curve, but I also had the good counsel of Carl Bailey, Walt Prausnitz, and Bob Homann, my associate dean.

CURRICULUM INNOVATION AND REFORM

The sixties were a period of unprecedented innovation and change on the academic side, inspiring changes across many disciplines. There was a real sense of momentum and excitement. Following are just a few examples: In the early sixties, the Concordia Language Villages program was founded and began its expansion under the leadership of Gerhard Haukebo. A new program in healthcare administration, the first undergraduate program of its kind in the country, was established under the leadership of Ted Heimarck. The Modern Language Department moved to new pedagogy, featuring oral skills and language fluency under the leadership of David Green. The college received funding from the Research Corporation to support faculty research in the physical and natural sciences, and a similar grant was received from the National Science Foundation to support the research activities of the social scientists. A lay education program, subsequently to be named the FM Communiversity, was established in the Fargo-Moorhead community under the leadership of Jim Hofrenning. A student exchange program was initiated with Virginia Union University and Fort Lewis College under the leadership of Eleanor Haney, and the May Seminar study abroad program was initiated under the leadership of Odell Bjerkness. Courses in ethnic studies and human relations were added in the History and Education Departments, and independent study programs were extended to many more students. Clearly, Concordia was on the move, building a strong educational presence. I felt fortunate to be part of leading the exciting, positive momentum.

Another development in the academic program was related to the ecumenical movement that flourished in Fargo-Moorhead community beginning in the early sixties. One of our faculty members, philosophy professor Reidar Thompte, was invited by a local Catholic priest to join him in conversation with members of the Benedictine Order at St. John's University in Collegeville, Minnesota. At about the same time, President Knutson, a Lutheran clergyman, was invited to be the chair of the committee raising funds for the construction of a new Catholic hospital, St. Ansgar's, in Moorhead. In a real sense, ecumenism at Concordia and in the Fargo-Moorhead community pre-dated the daring ecumenical initiatives following Vatican II. In December of 1964, Bishop Leo Dworshak of the Fargo Diocese, spoke at a convocation at Concordia regarding the work of the Vatican Council. This event was reported to be the first time that a Catholic official had spoken on campus, and Bishop Dworshak would return in 1967 for an ecumenical service at Concordia. Another example of ecumenism was evident when a local Catholic layman who owned a construction firm that had done work at the college developed a friendship with President Knutson. Each holiday season, this individual would host a luncheon with Knutson, the editor of *The Forum*, and the bishop of the diocese as his guests. For all of these reasons, it was not a surprise when an ecumenical faith and life series was initiated by Concordia in the early sixties, to be followed later in the decade by the Charis Ecumenical Center under the direction of Rev. Wayne Stumme, which provided both formal and informal learning opportunities to lay and clergy of all denominations. Not surprisingly, the evolution of the college's ecumenical initiatives coincided with significant growth in the number of Roman Catholic students choosing to attend Concordia.

Another major academic development in the Fargo-Moorhead community was the founding of Tri-College University, a consortium that included Concordia, Moorhead State College, and North Dakota State University. The TCU was governed by a board that included the presidents of the three institutions, plus some citizens of the community. This consortium offered a number of benefits to students, including the opportunity to register in classes on neighboring campuses without additional fees, access to the libraries at the three schools, and a subsidized shuttle service among the campuses. TCU also featured joint programs in education, nursing, environmental science, and the humanities. Some of these programs were phased out over time, however. Initial funding for the consortium came from the federal and state governments and the participating schools. The leader of the Tri-College University effort was George "Bud" Sinner, who was then serving on the North Dakota Board of Higher Education and would later become governor of North Dakota. He was able to rally the leaders of the three schools as well as area legislators and community leaders around the Tri-College idea. The founding Tri-College provost was Albert Anderson, a member of the Concordia faculty and the former associate academic dean of the college. Anderson led the way in establishing the first joint programs, including the Humanities Forum, that was unique among consortia nationwide.

In addition to program innovations at this time, several facilities on the Concordia campus were expanded and renovated, including the construction of the East Complex, the Ivers Science Center, Lorentzsen Hall, and the Comstock Theater, plus the renovation of Academy Hall and Old Main. These developments were guided by master plans initiated in the fifties and updated in the sixties. Understandably, there was a real sense of momentum and excitement throughout the Concordia campus and beyond.

Concordia was in the midst of wide-ranging change. In 1969, a major curriculum study was launched under the leadership of the Curriculum

Commission, chaired by Walther Prausnitz (English). The prelude to this project began in 1965 when, as noted earlier, a study of curriculum was initiated by the Joint Faculty Administrative Planning Committee. This led to faculty wide discussions. Subsequently, the Curriculum Committee of the faculty engaged in detailed work and several ideas surfaced. Dean Bailey organized this work into a single document in the summer of 1968. Curricular change was in the air. At the fall meeting of the Board of Regents, four of us were invited to address key subjects of interest to the board. As the interim academic dean, I spoke about the faculty and curriculum; Paul Sponheim, chair of the Religion Department, addressed its role on campus; Vic Boe, dean of men, commented on the standards of individual and community life; and Larry Falk from the Sociology Department reported on a survey of the constituents of the college.

A word about my part in the presentation to the board: I began my presentation by noting the growth in the number of Ph.D.'s on the faculty. I also commented on their loyalty to the college. I described some of the recent innovations and then identified challenges related to faculty salaries, efficiency of instruction, academic facilities, and the cost price squeeze. Regarding curriculum reform, I reported that while many ideas were on the table, we were lacking any clear or widely shared view on the Core Curriculum and the present curriculum structure.

A lively discussion of my paper followed. One could sense in the board a very strong interest in the subject of curricular change. In the hours that followed, I imagined the possibility of asking the board to commission and fund a comprehensive study of the curriculum. It was clear that there was broad campus interest in comprehensive reform, but the effort lacked focus and strategy. Walt Prausnitz had become a close confidant, and I visited with him about my idea. Al Anderson was the acting associate dean, and I also sought his counsel. I walked across the parking lot to the physics lab where Carl Bailey was spending his leave, and he, too, was enthusiastic about the idea. That evening, I drafted a resolution establishing the curriculum commission. The first thing the next morning, I tested the idea and resolution with President Knutson, who thought it was a great idea and gave me his full support to continue my efforts. I also checked with Bill Smaby, the chief financial officer, to see if we could find some funding to enable the commission members to work full-time on the project in the coming summer, 1969. He was supportive and assured the necessary funding. With strong support in place from key players on campus, I brought the resolution to the business meeting of the board the next morning, where the resolution was adopted by a unanimous vote. It was, in retrospect, a cheeky thing to do—to somewhat step over the faculty in organizing its work and setting an agenda to move forward with setting in motion a process for curricular change. Because the faculty had been discussing the curriculum for some time, however, curricular change was not a new idea, and there was broad support for change. What was lacking was a defining momentum and a strategy to organize and focus this work. I was a rookie dean, who, in a real sense, didn't know any better.

The resolution authorizing the study was carefully constructed to make it clear that the responsibility and authority for the curriculum rested with the faculty. With major curricular reform, that's an important point. The first "whereas" in the resolution clearly stated: "Whereas, the Board of Regents acknowledges that responsibility for the curriculum and graduation requirements is specifically delegated to the Faculty of the college." The second "whereas" identified the key goals of the study: "Whereas the Board of Regents shares the concern of the Faculty for constant reexamination of curriculum and instructional methods which will enhance the educational program of the college and improve the efficiency and effectiveness of the instructional effort." The "resolved" section of the resolution authorized administrative officers to establish the commission to begin work immediately and to engage in full-time study of the instructional program in the summer of 1969. It was also made clear that the commission's recommendations were to be submitted to the Faculty Senate for action.

The board action commenced the most comprehensive curriculum review in the history of the college. The commission members included a mix of experienced and newer faculty under the extraordinary leadership of the indefatigable Walther Prausnitz. The reforms that were eventually recommended and adopted led to a new Core Curriculum that would be subject to periodic assessment, a reduction in the number of credits required for graduation, a shift from the credit system to the course system, the restructuring and review of all departmental majors and minors, and the establishment of an Office of Liberal Arts Studies that would be responsible for monitoring and refreshing the Core. This office, under the direction of Walther Prausnitz, would become a valuable resource to the faculty in coming years. The curriculum changes were fully implemented in the fall of 1972.

The Core Curriculum was at the heart of the changes we made. Instead of merely listing a set of courses available to meet Core requirements, the new curriculum listed the outcomes or goals for each Core area, and faculty were invited to submit proposals for courses that supported the Core. Once a course was accepted for the Core, the acceptance was on the condition that the course would be subject to intensive assessment and that it would come up for periodic review. This was to ensure that Core courses met intended objectives and were refreshed sometimes. Responsibility for implementing and overseeing the Core rested with the Core Committee, chaired by Prausnitz, who oversaw the assessment activities and held extensive interviews with faculty members who were teaching Core courses. Content from these interviews found their way into *Teaching at Concordia*, a publication that centered on the faculty and the curriculum. This whole approach to Core Curriculum caught the attention of the Bush Foundation, which provided substantial grants to assist in the implementation and assessment activities over a three-year period. Concordia's approach to the Core Curriculum was novel in higher education and garnered the college a good deal of attention regionally and nationally in ensuing years. Prausnitz was a "giant in the earth" for Concordia, and it is fitting that an endowed chair in the Department of English would be named in his honor.

As the college continued to transition from the sixties into the seventies, one of the conditions challenging the college in the early seventies related to uncertainties around enrollment. The college's student-to-faculty ratio had declined, and faculty salaries were behind those of peer institutions. As the dean of the college in 1972, I initiated a study of faculty loads. This study considered both the current enrollment and the impact of the newly adopted curriculum that had lowered the number of credits required for graduation. The study process was arduous and involved multiple consultations with the department chairs, both individually and collectively. The result was a decision to increase the student faculty ratio to 16.5:1, thereby reducing the size of the faculty by fourteen. This had not been done before. The decision was not easy for me personally since I knew many of those who would be affected by the reduction. The savings gained were reinvested in faculty compensation, and within a few years, faculty salaries were competitive with peer institutions.

Besides addressing student-faculty ratio as part of the college's overall careful budgeting, efforts were made to bring various programs into budget alignment as well. For example, at about the same time as the review of teaching loads, the college was experiencing transition in the leadership of the Concordia Language Villages (CLV). While not a major drain on college resources, the Language Villages were not yet self-supporting. In consultation with President Knutson and Bill Smaby, we agreed that CLV should be, and that building a self-supporting program would put the Language Villages in a stronger position in the long term. This goal was accomplished under the leadership of Odell Bjerkness and Al Traaseth, business manager for the Language Villages. Subsequently, in the eighties, administrative leadership determined that CLV, now self-supporting, should achieve a margin of ten percent in excess of expenses and that these funds would be assigned to a reserve for the repair and maintenance of Language Village facilities. This proved to be a good decision. Likewise, from the beginning of the May Seminar study abroad program, May Seminars operated on the principle that income should cover direct expenses. This is how Concordia was able to build a strong program without invading operating funds from the balance of the academic program. Administrative offices at the college provided strong support for financial management, marketing, and especially fundraising, for May Seminar programing. The Language Villages and May Seminars were successful, in part, because of prudent financial management.

BLUEPRINT FOR THE SEVENTIES

Planning and change at Concordia did not slow in the seventies. A decade had passed since the publication of the original *A Blueprint for Concordia College*, so the college's Long-Range Planning Committee commissioned preparation of an updated *Blueprint* for the seventies. Carl Bailey and I guided the process that involved scores of papers, presentations, and study groups over a two-year period. At the beginning of the study process, there was extensive reflection on what were called "basic instrumentalities," that is, the mission of the college, the liberal arts, the notion of community, and the role of the faculty. The result was both a new exegesis and a reaffirmation of the importance of these matters in the college's life.

The study process led to the publication of a new institutional planning document, *Blueprint II*, which contained a number of recommendations related to program, faculty, finance, facilities, and personnel. Among the recommendations was one calling for the appointment of a college-wide commission to "evaluate provisions and practices related to equality of opportunity." The commission led to several changes, including matters related to equity in compensation for women, special recruitment initiatives for women and members of minority groups, a committee on the status of women, and broader representation of women on faculty committees. As you might imagine, I was behind the recommendation to establish the commission. Having come from a family of strong, high achieving women, I knew how important this action would be for the college. At the very heart of the matter, it was a matter of justice. There was also a recommendation that the Faculty Handbook and policies related to appointment, tenure, and promotion be reviewed, so that too was accomplished by 1974. The *Blueprint II* process also led to the establishment of a formal faculty evaluation policy and the reformulation of Concordia's faculty leaves program.

In view of the uncertainties related to enrollment that were identified in the *Blueprint* study process, the commission recommended a review of the tenure process. At the time, nearly all faculty eligible were granted tenure, resulting in a high level of tenured faculty, which, in turn, limited the college's ability to adapt to changes in enrollment either in total or within the college. There ensued a study process that led to the creation of a new tenure category called "tenure eligible non-probationary." This category was created to accommodate persons who met the criteria for tenure but whose appointments were in departments that were heavily tenured. This was conceived as an interim strategy and was modified in the eighties and nineties before being essentially abandoned in the nineties as the college's tenure distribution leveled out. As I consider lessons learned over the years, I reflect now that my approach to the tenure distribution issue was naïve. As a faculty-oriented dean, I wanted to bring the faculty into decision-making on tenure-distribution issues. Most colleges did not do this at the time because most institutions didn't think of tenure-distribution issues as a faculty matter or because they recognized that faculty are very uncomfortable in dealing with these issues. Most colleges had, in effect de facto quotas that the administration maintained through non-tenure eligible and term appointments and the tightening of tenure criteria.

Back to the *Blueprint* process: The process and its product reflected the priority in the seventies that Concordia placed on Intercultural Affairs programming and minority students. An Office of Intercultural Affairs was in place, with various staff to support assigned responsibilities. *Blueprint II* underscored the significance of these issues and provided direction for both Student Affairs and Academic Affairs. Another recommendation of the *Blueprint* process in which I had great personal interest called for consideration of a program for high ability students. The idea was code-named "Project Phoenix" in reference to Greek mythology. Consideration of this idea was a bit of a stretch for a community like Concordia that held strong egalitarian values. A study group was subsequently established, and I devoted considerable attention to its work. The outcome was the creation and implementation of the Credo Honors Program, a program that has undergone numerous adaptations and revisions through the years. There was also a good deal of interest in accelerated learning programs. New programs were emerging by which students could earn credit by examination and thereby earn advanced standing. Academic leadership suggested that the faculty look into the matter, and, subsequently, provision was made for selected programs.

On the finance and facilities fronts, *Blueprint II* emphasized the importance of maintaining existing facilities and programs. The document was conservative with respect to new construction, arguing that fundraising should focus more on current programs than on additional facilities, though the planning for and the construction of new student-life facilities (the Knutson Campus Center and the swimming pool) were affirmed. The report also recommended that Concordia should seek to fund at least seven endowed professorships and the summer faculty growth and development program. While neither of those goals was achieved in the short term, the college was successful in obtaining foundation funding for several of the innovations mentioned earlier, including the new curriculum and various faculty development activities. As already noted, the Bush Foundation of St. Paul was especially supportive of new curriculum efforts and related faculty development and core assessment initiatives.

THE CIVIL RIGHTS MOVEMENT AND CAMPUS DIVERSITY

As Concordia moved into the seventies, it is important to understand the broader national context in which the college found itself. The sixties and seventies were a turbulent time in U.S. history, so here I am recalling my perspective on various people, events, and actions that impacted college campuses nationwide, including Concordia, at this challenging time. To understand this era for the college, one must consider the context from the fifties and early sixties regarding civil rights. Perhaps the emergence of broad public awareness concerning civil rights issues stemmed from the Supreme Court's decision in the Brown vs. Board of Education case in 1954 that outlawed the "separate but equal" basis for discrimination in public schools. This decision was followed in 1955 by the bus boycott in Montgomery, Alabama, which was triggered by Rosa Park's decision to sit in the "whites only" section of a public bus. Martin Luther King, Jr. was a prominent pastor who cut his eye teeth as a civil rights leader during the Birmingham boycott. He was party to the establishment of the Southern Christian Leadership Conference that began to coordinate protest activities using nonviolent strategies. There were sit-ins and boycotts in various areas of the South, all seeking equal accommodation for African Americans. While there were some exceptions, in the early phase of the Civil Rights Movement, northerners on college campuses like Concordia's were sympathetic advocates rather than engaged citizens.

Public consciousness over civil rights reached a high pitch at the time of the March on Washington in the summer of 1963. Thousands gathered from across the country to demonstrate solidarity with those who sang "We Shall Overcome." Martin Luther King, Jr.'s "I Have a Dream" speech would mark the day in history. The memorable speech was an eloquent call to peaceful action and had a broad base of appeal. Concordia history professor Martin Lutter participated in the March on Washington. Upon his return to campus, he addressed the community at a well-attended chapel service, where he conveyed both his experience and his passion. As a young professor in the Speech Department at the time, I recall assigning the King speech to my students as an example of rhetorical eloquence.

In the early sixties, leaders in the Lutheran church expressed solidarity with the Civil Rights Movement. (Note: While many readers may associate Concordia with the Evangelical Lutheran Church in American (ELCA), the ELCA wasn't formed until a three-church merger in 1988, so in the early sixties, Concordia was still associated with the American Lutheran Church.) David Preus, who would later lead the American Lutheran Church (ALC), was a parish pastor in Minneapolis and became a leading advocate on behalf of civil rights initiatives in that community. The civil rights cause was picked up in a public way on the Concordia campus following the violence that occurred in the summer of 1962 at Old Miss with the enrollment of James Meredith. Concordia student Marc Borg supported the government's intervention, and in an article in *The Concordian*, he called on Concordia students to develop a better understanding of both the Negroes and Southern whites.

In the early months of 1963, there was an article and editorial in *The Concordian* about voting rights and violence in Birmingham, Alabama. Sociology professor Raymond Farden was appointed to the ALC Commission on Research and Social Action and expressed concern about the ALC's past failures to act on civil rights matters. Following the church bombing in Birmingham in the fall of 1963, *The Concordian* editor Marc Borg wrote:

> This past week in Birmingham a bomb was thrown into an all-Negro church. Four children were killed, their bodies ripped by flying glass and crushed by falling mortar. ...the Negro is trying to obtain for himself the constitutional rights which we enjoy, and for the most part his efforts have been peaceful. What has been the reward for his efforts? More violence, more atrocities committed against his race, and this past week, the irony of Sunday School children killed while studying the text, 'Love your enemies.'

There was discussion among Concordia students about what the church ought to do, and there was also discussion by the church about what it ought to do. At the ALC national level, there emerged an emphasis on racial equality and church-wide initiatives. Naturally, the church looked to the colleges for leadership and action and provided some limited programs and targeted funding to that end. It would be accurate to say that the church's main role was moral and was given expression by church leaders and pastors across the country, including on campus. As ALC President Fredrik Schiotz put it, "Human rights take precedence over all other rights—be they property or state's rights." I recall the attention given to civil rights by campus pastor Carl Lee, a number of faculty members, and visiting dignitaries who spoke in chapel. For several years, students from all the ALC colleges gathered for an annual conference, and during these years, the agenda often included a discussion of civil rights and racism.

I recall various examples of how the broader national conversation about civil rights was part of the Concordia campus as well. During the period when a civil rights bill was being considered in 1964 by the Congress, *The Concordian* editor Marc Borg urged students to write their congressional representatives. On one occasion, the president of the college Young Republicans wrote an article in which he disavowed segregation but urged a moderate approach. In March of 1964, John Bennett, President of Union Seminary and a world-renowned ethicist, spoke on the Concordia campus and addressed the issue. In the winter of 1964, the Concordia choir toured in the South, and faculty member Ted Heimarck inquired about whether or not the choir would perform in segregated facilities. Choir manager Kurt Wycisk assured him that they would not. Choir members reported the value of their first-hand experience with these issues from the tour. In May of 1964, Jackie Robinson, who had broken the color barrier in baseball, was the speaker at the C400 spring banquet.

The Concordia community found its own ways to engage in the Civil Rights Movement. In March, the Student Senate endorsed the Civil Rights Act of 1964, a civil rights bill that was before the Congress. In addition, Student Senate made a financial contribution to the family of slain civil rights leader Medgar Evers. Student Dan Lee noted that few Black students were attending Concordia and raised a question about what Concordia could do to support the Civil Rights Movement. Another student urged fellow students to make contributions in support of the voter registration efforts in Mississippi. Concordia students and faculty participated in a local public demonstration in support of the march for civil rights in Selma, Alabama, that took place that spring.

One could say, in general, that the vast majority of Concordia students, faculty, and staff were sympathetic and committed to the cause, but we also experienced a certain kind of guilt or defensiveness over not doing very much. Subsequently, a number of specific actions were initiated in the early sixties. While we were geographically isolated from the issues, we were determined to do what we could do to inform ourselves, change our program, and welcome diversity. The Admissions Office redoubled efforts to recruit minority students, and there was strong student support for this initiative throughout the sixties and seventies.

Under the leadership of Eleanor Haney of the Religion Department and a former faculty member at Virginia Union University, a student exchange was initiated with that historically Black college in 1965-66. In addition, federal funding was sought and secured to support the exchange program, establish an urban seminar, and bring distinguished lecturers and scholars to the campus to speak on matters related to race, civil rights, and segregation. Among the speakers visiting campus in the sixties and seventies were Nathan Wright, who lectured on Black Power; Andrew Young, former aide to Martin Luther King, Jr.; Alexander Allen, Eastern Region Director for the Urban League; Vincent Harding, distinguished historian; Stokeley Carmichael, Black activist; Vine Deloria, Native American scholar and activist; Dick Gregory, comedian and civil rights activist; Dennis Banks and Russell Means, Native American activists; Nikki Giovanni, African American writer; William Kunstler, attorney for many civil rights defendants; and the list went on. The events were well-attended, and the campus lecturers participated in many classes in addition to their public lectures, increasing community awareness inside and outside of classrooms. The many guest speakers were an informative, consciousness-raising experience for the campus.

Black consciousness was on the rise and many Black students at Concordia became restive. I was the interim dean in 1968 and an advocate for the exchange program and the visiting scholars' program, so the Black students saw me as an ally. These students were informally organized and invited me to a meeting in the lower lounge (later to be named to honor Martin Luther King, Jr.) of Park Region Hall in January of 1969. About twenty students were present, and they teed off on me about their grievances: not enough Black students, lack of Black faculty and staff, inadequate recruitment, and the lack of curriculum in ethnic studies. The meeting was very long and uncomfortable. One discouraged Black student gave expression to her feelings in these words from an interview in *The Concordian*: "I am tired of showing Concordia their mistakes and of their not giving a hoot about how to correct them.... I have yet to see a happy Black person on this campus who feels he is a member of the Cobber family." There were responses to the letter, which verified that her critique had hit a sore nerve with some. Her honesty was a painful reminder that achieving equity in civil rights at Concordia would be a long, arduous, sometimes difficult process. All of this would lead *The Concordian* editor to opine that "the racial crisis that confronts America today is no longer isolated from the Concordia campus. Events of the last seven months have brought to this campus an awareness that something is happening between Blacks and whites these days, not just in the South nor in the cities but in Moorhead." It was clear that more needed to be done.

The students with whom I met that January evening correctly assumed that I would bring their message to the appropriate people. This led almost immediately to the creation of a Committee on Minority Students to give overall direction to the effort. There were several tangible outcomes to our work in coming months, including offering a concentration in African studies in the History Department, adding other courses related to minority studies in sociology and religion, expending new efforts in student recruitment, and seeking new recruitment strategies for faculty and staff. The minority program, renamed Intercultural Affairs, was broadened in its scope. With more funding, largely from grants, counseling and program staff were added. In 1972, under the leadership of Richard Green, who was director of Intercultural Affairs and a faculty member in the Chemistry Department, a program was initiated for at-risk students. James Coomber, professor of English, took a leadership role in this program known as PACE (Personalized Attention in College Education), which included thirty-nine students in its first semester of operation. In addition, a new emphasis was directed toward the recruitment of Native American students, with some success through the late seventies. The student exchange program was expanded to include Fort Lewis College in Colorado, which had special academic resources related to Southwestern Native American culture. Virginia Union, Fort Lewis, and Concordia each sponsored summer seminars that included students from all three schools and featured their respective regional cultures.

A host of other curricular, programmatic, and other changes in the seventies were related to issues of race and equality, building on the awareness and concerns that emerged from the early seventies. Just a few examples follow. A Human Relations Day was inaugurated in 1972 and continued for several years. There were special observances related to Martin Luther King, Jr.'s birthday, Black History Month, and Native American Month. A faculty committee was appointed to consider our offerings in minority studies, and they produced a useful resource for the community. As mentioned, courses were added in several departments, and beginning in 1969-70, the publication *Aspects of Women's and Minority Studies* that identified courses and class emphases related to minority studies was made available annually. It was noted that, rather than having a single major or department devoted to minority or women's studies, our attention to these subjects should be reflected throughout the curriculum. Depending on one's point of view, this was seen either as a strength or a weakness.

Other changes were afoot in the demographics of the campus in the seventies. During the early seventies, Concordia's Admissions strategy for increasing minority student began producing results. Since there were few African American students in the Fargo-Moorhead area and the region of North Dakota and Minnesota at the time, the college focused recruiting in areas in and around Washington, D.C., Saint Louis, Milwaukee, and Chicago. Concordia Admissions staff were welcomed into the high schools and the homes of prospective students, and their efforts yielded good results. We discovered that local colleges in those cities were not very active in recruiting Black students, and the students we often recruited were open to the adventure of a new culture and location.

Concordia's minority student population in the early to mid-seventies began to reflect the college's dedicated recruiting efforts. Those efforts included recruiting Native American students in the region. We had the most success in the Minnesota tribal communities, adding to our changing campus demographics. In 1972, Concordia enrolled ninety minority students, 101 in 1973, 102 in 1974, and seventy-three in 1975 (including fifty-one Black students). In addition, there were between 30-50 international students, many of whom were persons of color. Most of Concordia's minority students fared well. They became involved in campus life, worked hard in the classroom, and went on to meaningful careers. Several have been recognized by the college and been elected to the Alumni Board and/or the Board of Regents. In 1977, eighteen students of color received degrees, which was a major shift from previous decades. The momentum of the early seventies did not continue, however. By the late seventies, numbers had declined significantly as Black students had become more inclined to attend colleges closer to home, and those colleges, in turn, stepped up their recruiting efforts.

Similar to Concordia's efforts to diversify the student body in the seventies, efforts also extended to build more diversity within faculty and staff. The lack of minority faculty and staff was noted early in campus conversations. As a result, departments across campus were encouraged to make extra efforts to identify and recruit minority people. To this end, as noted earlier, a Commission on Equality of Opportunity at Concordia College was established to conduct utilization analyses of college employees and recommend hiring goals for women and minority members. We made special efforts to identify and advertise vacancies in publications that were accessed by minority persons. We used church contacts where possible. At one point, I sent a minority faculty member on a scouting trip to a group of universities with graduate programs that enrolled significant numbers of minority students. While Concordia's initiatives to increase the percentage of women faculty and staff were successful, our minority hiring initiatives were not. Colleges and universities across the country were looking for minority faculty, and demand far exceeded supply. Our region, with few minority persons, was not very attractive to emerging minority professionals, who had no difficulty finding employment in areas with greater diversity. The challenge to hire qualified minority faculty and staff continued for at least the next thirty years, and, even today, new recruiting strategies are being utilized to continue efforts to build a more diverse faculty and staff.

As a campus leader, I was in the middle of most of these developments, both in my position as dean and because of my commitment to the cause. I authored some of the initiatives and encouraged many more. Eleanor Haney, Religion Department, was a leader in her ethics classes and with the student exchange and the visiting scholars. Jim Hofrenning, also in the Religion Department, became a program leader and advisor as well as a curriculum developer. As noted earlier, Richard Green, an African American, Cobber, and faculty member, would assume leadership of what we called the Intercultural Affairs Center in the early seventies. Later, Carol Ann Hart joined the staff with responsibilities for the recruitment of Native American students. Green and Hart would be followed by other staff members over the years as the college maintained its commitment to minority students and related support programs. Ed Ellenson and Jim Hausmann provided leadership and imagination in Admissions and Financial Aid. Both Morrie Lanning and David Benson were significant players in their respective roles in Student Affairs.

Black students were active in organizing activities and participating in campus life at Concordia in the seventies. In 1972 a group of students on the exchange program from Virginia Union presented a musical, *Beware of the Young, Gifted and Black*. It was a real hit with the campus community and led to the establishment of a Black choir under the direction of student Arthur Treadwell. In addition to performing on campus, the Black choir appeared in several area churches. Around this time, the Black students also organized Harambee Weuse, an organization of minority students that sponsored events of various kinds, including a style show. Through many years, Harambee Weuse published a newsletter. The Intercultural Center, located first in Old Main and later in a house near campus, became the meeting place for both Harambee Weuse and other minority and international students.

Concordia's commitment to racial diversity involved risks for the college and, more importantly, for the minority students. For example, in the fall of 1973 there was a threat to the Intercultural Center, and some Black women received obscene phone calls. Understandably, this caused anxiety in the minority community, and immediate steps were taken to address the matter. President Knutson preached at a well-attended chapel on the topic, "When Will the Walls Come Tumbling Down?" He identified racism as a cultural, political, and spiritual problem. In this and other ways, the president was stalwart in his support of the initiative to support of civil rights and to diversify the campus.

Black students stirred us to action on many fronts, and while the campus might have taken some missteps on occasion, I believe Concordia was earnest and correct in its efforts to directly engage in the turbulent issues of the time. We were learning from each other, and I feel fortunate to have been a part of this time at Concordia. Some years later, in the spring of 1996, a Black student named Gene Poole, who had been involved in the 1968 protest, reflected on events at the time in these words: "Paul Dovre, who was dean at the time, was an effective administrator who listened to us and took action. Concordia responded to the faith and love we showed. I thank God for the opportunity to be at Concordia. A small campus is what I needed, and it gave me confidence" (*Alumni News*). Poole went on to a significant career, as did many of the minority students from the seventies.

STUDENT VOICES

In comparison to a decade later, the early sixties were quiet on most college campuses. *In loco parentis* was a reality that was accepted by most students, even those who thought the rules were antiquated. Concordia's social regulations reflected the culture in which most students had grown up. Indeed, except for not allowing social dancing and smoking at Concordia, most public institutions had similar rules.

With respect to the governance of the college in the sixties and into the seventies, Concordia was typical. Students' voices at the time were largely expressed through student government, discussions regarding shared academic interests, and campus-related social events. Student government was active in planning social activities, fostering political conversations, and overseeing the student honor system and campus publications. In other matters, college officials, students, and faculty would convene semi-annually to discuss matters of common interest. By the mid-sixties and into the early seventies, Concordia student government was exceptional in the sponsorship of concert appearances by the big-name popular entertainers of the time and sponsorship of fully student-produced and directed musicals. Among the visiting musicians were Blood, Sweat and Tears; Judy Collins; Bread; Pat Boone; Grass Roots; Mary Travers; Carly Simon with James Taylor; Dione Warwick; Dave Brubeck; Gordon Lightfoot; Bachman-Turner Overdrive; and Peter Yarrow, all considered to be major players in the national music scene. Regionally, Concordia had a reputation for attracting big-name musicians to Memorial Auditorium, usually playing to a capacity crowd of students and attendees from the region.

The key dynamic of social life at Concordia in the sixties and seventies revolved around societies, Concordia's version of fraternities and sororities, to which I made reference in Chapter 2. Dating back to the 1920s and multiplying in number by the 1970s, the societies generated social and entertainment events. Organized by gender, men's and women's societies were paired up, that is, each men's society was associated with a paired women's society. Most societies met weekly, and they hosted banquets, parties, and dances. Societies also competed with floats in the homecoming parade and skits at an annual winter competition, and, in general, participants had a good time being socially active on campus through societies. By the late seventies and early eighties, however, there was a noticeable decline in both the number of societies and their membership. Perhaps this change reflected the nation-wide change in student attitudes and the trend toward individualism. Whatever the case, the energy of students active in social societies on campus left a gap and was missed by many of us.

Controversy was relatively uncommon in the early sixties, although occasional topics garnered campus interest, providing additional opportunities for student voices to be heard. For example, in 1963, there was a lively give-and-take in *The Concordian* concerning the activities of the U.S. House Committee on Un-American Activities and the John Birch Society. There was also a dialogue on whether the Concordia campus should have a Young Socialists Club. There was only mild student interest in any of these matters, however. As campus enrollment grew from 1,725 in 1963 to 2,102 in 1965, there was campus discussion about the relationship between growth and academic quality. This would remain an issue throughout the decade, and, as noted earlier, several faculty shared these concerns.

The relative calm and lack of heated controversy of the early sixties would change over time. By the late sixties, the Concordia campus was alive with controversy on a range of issues, and similar to college campuses across the rest of the nation, Concordia students were beginning to find power in their voices. The backdrop for this was the national drumbeat heard around the country about civil rights, student rights, the Vietnam War, the relevance of the curriculum, and moral standards. In 1964-65, a national movement emerged from the Free Speech Movement at the University of California at Berkeley. The Free Speech Movement was initiated around the perceived lack of freedom of political expression on the Berkeley campus. Some of that movement's leaders had been leaders on the national stage of the Civil Rights Movement, so they brought with them to the Berkeley campus both organizational skills and passion for civil rights. Campus protests at Berkeley resulted in the occupancy of a major campus facility, followed by the arrest of many students. These events emboldened college students across the country. They came to believe that they ought to have a voice in the decisions and actions affecting their academic and social lives. Campus protests became commonplace across the United States, and governance arrangements were often modified as a consequence, with steps were taken to insure freedom of expression.

What had been a drumbeat turned into a crescendo as the baby boomer generation raised questions about nearly every aspect of their inherited traditions and current campus experience. The sexual revolution was heralded by Hugh Hefner and *Playboy* magazine's features and photographs. Nationally, between the early fifties and early seventies, there was a tremendous shift in attitudes about premarital sex, with seventy-one percent of the population believing it was acceptable by 1971 (Ashley Kahn, *Rolling Stone: The Seventies*). Consequences of this social change in attitude included the growth of co-ed housing and intervisitation across the country. Adding to the dissonance was students' growing opposition to the war in Vietnam. Throughout the second half of the sixties, anti-war protests and draft resistance were commonplace across the nation.

While Concordia was isolated geographically from much of the early and active student protest, that isolation was transcended by the power of the media and the passion of these social movements. As was true nationally, Concordia student voices were getting louder as well. For example, already in 1965-66, there was a series of editorials and articles in *The Concordian* on the war in Southeast Asia. Several editorials and student columns called for campus debate on institutional issues, including campus social policies. President Knutson gave a chapel talk defending these policies and noted that they were part of what made the college distinctive. In the spring of 1966, there was a major movement among Concordia students to eliminate the ban on dancing, and a survey indicated strong support for such a change among both students and faculty. In April, the Board of Regents reaffirmed the prohibition on dancing, but that would change in the future.

The pressure for change continued on the Concordia campus, and leaders were clearly getting the message. There continued to be a lively exchange of differing points of view. The title of President Knutson's opening convocation in September of 1966 was "Rebels of the Sixties." The president asked students to be responsible rebels, that is, to use legitimate channels and to be sure that their causes were worthy. In his address, President Knutson cited the statement by the dean of a large university that "anyone 21 years-old and intelligent enough to be in college is intelligent enough to control his own life." Knutson called this statement "bad theology, bad psychology and bad common sense." In his greeting to the students on that occasion, Student Association President Dan Lee said that "to differ is not to be disloyal." In another setting and in a meliorist tone, Dean Carl Bailey said, "To do our job better, we need support and we need criticism." At the annual student/faculty/administration retreat in the fall of 1966, there was extended discussion on the social dancing issue. Dean Boe and President Knutson said that changing the policy would be "embarrassing to the college." *The Concordian* co-editors Jim Nestingen and Jon Oleson wrote a series of editorials about college policies and the Vietnam War. Students and administration on campus were in the midst of working through a variety of challenging issues of the time.

One of the lighter moments in the ongoing conflict between students and the administration occurred following a meeting of the Board of Regents at which a decision was made to change the name of Old Main to Bogstad Hall in honor of one of the distinguished early presidents of the college. Student leaders had not been consulted and thought the renaming was a bad idea. They staged a sort of mock protest, preceded by a brief program at Prexy's

Pond—the small pond on campus between Old Main and the president's residence—during which students delivered tongue-in-cheek campaign speeches on the theme "Old Main Shall Remain." A trio of faculty wives, including my wife Mardeth, sang an appropriate protest song. Thereafter, in Biblical style, the students marched around Old Main seven times. It was all good natured and college officials took it in stride. College leaders realized that the students had a point, and the decision to change the name was rescinded.

I was the associate academic dean at the time, and I felt that easing some of the social policies was in order. Many of the student leaders were, or had been, my students. While I sympathized with their cause, I urged them to work through the structures in place and to build trust, and I worked to create those structures and ensure their credibility. My views were consistent with most of the faculty and a large percentage of the administrative staff. We were able to maintain civility and respect amidst disagreement on the issues. This was due to both the mediating role many of us of assumed and the deep respect students held for President Knutson. It is also worth noting that President Knutson, who freely expressed his opinions, respected the rights and voices of students to be heard as well. At several points during those years, student leaders and editors paid respect to President Knutson while also taking exception to his ideas. By the mid-sixties, it was clear that Concordia was out of step with most of our sister ALC colleges that had long since permitted social dancing, women smoking, and inter-dorm visitation. It was often said in those days, most students had come to the college for an education and were not taking part in expressions of protest. That was true on most campuses. While most students were inactive, that did not mean they were unsympathetic to the various causes, however.

As the year 1966-67 progressed, *The Concordian* editor Jim Nestingen kept up the pressure for change. He wrote an editorial on pietism, and student columnist Mark Chekola expressed concern about the image of Concordia as a fundamentalist college, which it clearly was not. The cleavage on lifestyle norms centered on the issue of trust. Students voiced that they could be trusted, and President Knutson responded that he could not even trust himself, that human-beings are broken, prone to sin, and in need of practiced discipline. By year's end, editor Nestingen had shifted his focus from college social policies to the war in Asia because he didn't see much chance for change with current campus policies. He wrote, "Right or wrong, the average student at Concordia thinks of the administration as a big brother who won't let him out of certain fences.... I think the real hope for Concordia (is) concentrating on her academic strengths."

The conflict over Vietnam was noted beyond the pages of *The Concordian*. Speakers opposed to the war, including one of the Berrigan brothers, American peace activists, spoke on campus. More than one chapel homily focused on the subject, including a defense of the war by a member of the Religion Department. In the fall of 1966, Army Chief of Staff Harold K. Johnson spoke on campus, and some students organized a small protest outside of the fieldhouse. Later that fall, some faculty and students from the college joined in an antiwar protest in downtown Fargo. Student Mark Bratlie wrote a series of columns in opposition to the war effort, and other students joined the chorus. On the other hand, Vietnam veteran student Robert Brunsvold took exception to the critical assessments of the war, but his was a solitary student voice in the public discourse of the campus.

The summer of 1968 featured the riots at the Democratic National Convention. *The Concordian* co-editors Wendy and Chris Ward led the continuing dual focus on the war and social change at Concordia. They announced in their opening editorial that *The Concordian* would continue the path of criticism on campus, national, and international issues. Two new campus publications appeared with the purpose of promoting debate on public issues. Subsequent editorials would attack college policies and argue that the college should permit students to make their own decisions about social behavior and politics.

In late 1968, a joint Student and Board of Regents Committee on Student Affairs was established. The purpose was to provide for better communication between students and regents on matters of mutual concern. Chief among these was social dancing. This committee would subsequently process recommendations concerning social dancing and women smoking. By this time, student leaders were pressing the smoking policy as an equity issue: If men could smoke on campus, why not women? Some 350 students participated in a torchlight parade in support of women's rights.

While student voices expressed opinions about the Vietnam War, the thrust of student protest on the campus continued to be directed at college social policies. At a tumultuous student/faculty/administration retreat in January of 1969, a small group of women students lit up cigarettes at the retreat in the presence of, among others, J. L. Rendahl and Dean Victor Boe, to visually express their displeasure with the smoking policy on campus. Both Rendahl and Boe maintained their composure. I was then serving as interim dean and recall the first meeting of President's Cabinet following that retreat. The tone was measured, but there was clarity about what we were dealing with. One of the students who had participated in the smoke-in, Wendy Ward, would write, "If the girls at Concordia aren't going to be allowed to smoke legally, they should then simply assume their right to start smoking—illegally." In the spring, student elections candidates for office almost tried to out-do each other in their advocacy for student rights, social dancing, more liberal dorm hours, intervisitation, and a student union.

The years 1969 and 1970 would be watershed years with respect to several student hot button issues. In the fall of 1969, student body President Donald Gaetz would say in his address to the student body that "Concordia cannot stand still. Concordia cannot be defined in static terms. Concordia must be a changing, living, flexing, moving institution that frees people instead of chaining them. Concordia must be a school in constant revolution." Clearly, the traditional defense of the smoking policy was crumbling campus-wide, and so, too, the prohibition on dancing. Dancing was already happening at events hosted off campus by societies, so why not allow dancing on campus? A poll was conducted by the Sociology Department, indicating that eighty-five percent of students supported a change in the dancing policy and sixty-one percent of the alumni. Bowing to the inevitable, the board approved in January of 1969 a policy for social dancing on campus. Within days, the first dance was held in the south gymnasium of the fieldhouse with live music provided by The Four Dons. Mardy and I attended the event. In January of 1970, the Board of Regents approved the right of women to smoke on campus. An anti-smoking campaign was initiated at the same time. Somewhat ironically, by 2010, the campus was declared smoke-free with broad student support.

While the lively debate about Vietnam played out nationally and on the Concordia campus, on other fronts Concordia students were making progress. They were involved in discussions regarding a revised faculty constitution, and students found faculty support for their proposal that students be included as voting members in the Faculty Senate and on nearly every faculty committee. President Knutson and Carl Bailey, the dean of the college, concurred. These changes were approved in 1968-69. On another front, Assistant Dean Morrie Lanning and I attended professional meetings on the student movement. We came home from those meetings convinced that we ought to review all of Concordia's student policy documents and prepare a new policy statement on student rights and responsibilities. This document would both guarantee the right of students to protest and spell out the appropriate institutional procedures to safeguard protesting students and ensure the orderly operations of the college. The document was approved in 1969 by President Knutson and served the college well. As I reflect, I'm glad campus leadership was pro-active in recognizing the changing needs and demands of students. Overall, perhaps our foresightedness in finding constructive ways to empower student voices helped head off what could have been even more challenging problems or situations.

About the same time, to further opportunities for direct student involvement, Assistant Dean Lanning proposed establishing a student internship program for students who were coming into leadership positions in student government. This involved 18-24 students in a month-long series of seminars and work projects through which they became acquainted with college leaders and campus governance. The program's main benefit was creating effective working relationships between administrative staff and student leaders. I believe it is one of the reasons that change proceeded in an orderly way through the late sixties and early seventies. Another helpful change was the establishment of the College Council in 1969. The Council brought together members of the Faculty Executive Committee, the Student Cabinet, and the President's Council for monthly discussion on matters of mutual interest. This was another effective way of keeping the lines of communication open.

As dean, I actively supported student rights and the inherent value of having student voices provide input on matters that affected them, whether academic or social. I outlined these views in "The Community of Common Interest," a presentation I made in 1969. I spoke to various student and administrative groups about the concept of collegiality and its applications in the Concordia community. The basic ideas were that we should be honest in expressing our opinions and be respectful and accountable to one another. Strongly associated with this idea was the principle that people affected by a policy or plan in discussion or question should have the opportunity to be part of the conversation. The editor of *The Concordian* wrote that while I may not have coined the word *collegiality*, I had been "the major figure in hammering out the basic outline for the concept as a working instrument at Concordia." This discussion was salutary in the formation of the new faculty constitution and several joint student-administration committees. Of course, these expressions of shared governance did not lead to agreement in every matter, but the discussions modeled civility and led to mutual understanding and respect.

As the 1960s drew to a close, the Vietnam War continued to impact national conversations. The same was true at Concordia as we started a new decade. In the spring of 1970, campus opposition to the war effort continued, this time focusing on the commissioning of ROTC graduates at spring commencement. The Student Senate opposed the practice, while President Knutson supported it. Some students and faculty threatened to walk out of the commencement ceremony if the commissioning took place. The issue was complicated for President Knutson because his son was one of the two students who were to be commissioned. After extensive and quiet negotiation in which I was engaged, a compromise of sorts was fashioned. The commissioning would occur at the end of the commencement service. A hymn would be sung immediately before that the commissioning, so persons opposed to the practice could exit the auditorium. The number of students and faculty exiting the event was small, but significant enough to make an impact. As soon as the commissioning was completed, the audience rose for an extended ovation in support of the new officers. With respect to future practice, President Knutson asked for a recommendation from the Student Affairs Committee. They recommended that commissioning occur at a ceremony separate from commencement, and the president accepted the recommendation.

Concordia's social policies continued to draw controversy. Women were still under hours restraints in their campus residence halls, and pressure continued to build on this issue in the 1970-71 school year. In October, somewhere between 50-150 women staged an after-hours walkout in protest of women's hours, and an editorial focused on the discriminatory college policies. Letters were directed to *The Concordian* on the issue. A campus poll of women students supported change, and by end of November 1971, women's hours were extended, and by the end of 1972, hours for women had been abolished.

The rate and extent of these changes in campus rules exceeded anything experienced in the school's history. These changes were a challenge to both the experience and convictions of President Knutson. He had lived most of his life as pastor and college administrator in a society that expected the college to provide discipline and oversight in several areas of student life. To be sure, there was theological grounding both for suspicion of the human capacity for self-control and the role of discipline in living a sanctified life. The president was passionate about these matters and expressed his views frequently, sometimes cautiously and sometimes emotionally. The president's equanimity was framed by the view that while he might hold strong opinions on some of these matters, they were not for him determinative of the moral framework of the school. While he did not favor the changes made, he bowed to the opinions of some of his colleague administrators and, eventually, the will of the Board of Regents.

While President Knutson may have acquiesced on a number of issues, there remained for him some limits about what was acceptable on a campus like Concordia, and he wanted to make those matters clear to the students and constituents of the college. This led to the publication of *The Concordia Communiqué* in the summer of 1970. In this publication, he noted that "the convictions, values, mores, and regulations which hold together the thin veneer of civilization are fast being discarded." He went on to draw a line in the sand indicating that Concordia would not permit interdorm visitation or the use of alcohol and drugs. This document was approved by the Board of Regents and widely distributed throughout the constituency.

A major test of the power of student voices occurred in the fall of 1970 with the advent of the new editor of *The Concordian*, Omar Olson. In addition to his continuing critique of college policies, Olson managed the paper as he saw fit, including decisions about advertising. In the fall, the paper included an advertisement for an agency in New York that provided abortion counseling in these pre-Roe v. Wade years. It turned out that such advertisements were proscribed by Minnesota state law, but the law was not enforced. After consulting with the college's legal counsel, the President Knutson closed down *The Concordian* in December 1970. The publication of the student newspaper would not be resumed until March of 1971. The immediate campus response of some faculty and students was strong, but cool heads prevailed, and no formal protest occurred. The closing of the campus newspaper led to national coverage, with people weighing in on both sides of the issue. As publisher of the newspaper, the president had a right to close it down, and the abortion related ads were clearly a violation of Minnesota state law. People who were anxious about or opposed to the student power movement sided with the president, and their number was large. Support for the student editor was confined to the academic and journalistic communities. After this event, the Student Affairs Committee developed a detailed publication policy that was approved by President Knutson. I was on leave at this time, but it is my opinion that for President Knutson, this issue was the culmination of his accumulated distress over the direction of campus life. This event took him over the top, so to speak. The expressions of support extended to him far exceeded the critiques, and, as a result, I had a sense that he experienced a renewal of confidence.

Students seeking the extension of hours for intervisitation were hardly mollified by the changes in other policies that had been so difficult for the president and his resolve to go no further. In the spring of 1973, he met with several hundred students in Grant Commons to discuss the subject of intervisitation. Campus physician Dr. Borge spoke first of the dangers of sexual permissiveness. President Knutson warned against any outbursts or intimidation. Following a volley of questions, he dismissed the meeting by saying, "People strongly against the dorm policies held by the administration could consider going somewhere else."

As this section on student voices of the sixties and seventies ends, you might believe that the entire campus was absorbed in social and public issues, but that was not the case. The work of the college continued at this time, despite the periodic challenges, intense conversations, or minor protests that were underway. With respect to campus-based social issues, there was strong support for change, even though the public actors were fairly few, but included student government leaders and *The Concordian* staff and editors. With respect to more public issues like the Vietnam War and civil rights, most Concordia students could generally be described as interested by-standers. This was not unlike most social movements for change that are led by the few, but eventually supported by the many. Under President Knutson's leadership, like much of the nation at the time, Concordia weathered a number of storms, but the mission and work of the college continued.

RELIGIOUS LIFE

When I returned to the college as a faculty member in the early sixties, the religious life of Concordia had changed somewhat. Lutheran Students in America (LSA) was not as significant, and one or two of the smaller groups interested in religious life on campus had disappeared. Campus ministry still reported to the president, a common practice in religious colleges then and now. By this time, the college had called Reverend Carl Lee as campus pastor. He managed daily chapel, had oversight of various campus ministry activities, and was the primary counselor on campus. Carl had a unique capacity to adapt to diverse student needs and preferences. Campus worship under Carl's leadership was eclectic, sometimes formal, other times folksy and informal. He had a gift for hospitality, and students of a variety of religious styles, commitments, and preferences were comfortable with him. Once into the student protest years of the late sixties, Carl made sure that campus ministry was a place where everyone's voice was respected and welcomed, so activist students were free to express their social slant on the gospel, and evangelical students were free to express their convictions about mission. It was, in short, a big-tent ministry.

In the mid-sixties, there developed on the Concordia campus what some described as a religious awakening. This direction started among evangelically inclined students, who regularly met together for prayer and study. According to some reports, the number of participants in early 1966 was about twenty. By 1967, there were fifty students and the following year, eighty. Reverend Arthur Grimstad, a member of the Religion Department faculty, was their advisor. He was a natural choice because Art came out of an evangelical background, and he was an outstanding Bible teacher and an inspiring preacher. Through study and prayer, this group developed a passion for spreading the Gospel and their numbers grew dramatically. In order to accomplish their mission, they organized into teams. The teams visited congregations in the region, providing programs of worship and praise. The students on the teams were well-received, and each summer a team was formed to tour the region where the college served, which included the states of Montana, North Dakota, and northern Minnesota. Early tours were sponsored by the Commission on Evangelism of the ALC. Seeing the value of the outreach program to the college, Concordia became a sponsor as well.

Eventually, there would be upwards of twenty teams, and they called their program "The Outreach Ministry," continuing the practice of outreach teams. From an organizational perspective, this ministry resembled the LSA ministries of an earlier time. Most of them were worship teams going to area congregations, and a few of them were called "fellowship teams" and served needs in the Fargo-Moorhead area by visiting nursing homes and detention centers. The outreach program was organized and led by students. Each team met three times a week, twice to practice and once for Bible study. In addition, team leaders met at Pastor Grimstad's home every Friday night for fellowship and study. There was high demand for the teams throughout the territory. One of the leaders reported that they turned down as many as 40-50 invitations in a given year.

The movement on campus toward a religious awakening, of sorts, was not without its problems. It was easy for decision theology, that is, the belief that individuals must make a conscious decision to accept and follow Christ, also known as being "born again," to slip into the message for some of the students who were sincere, but theologically ill-formed. For that reason, the advisor developed an evaluation form that host pastors would complete and return to the president's office following each visit to a congregation. These evaluations were overwhelmingly positive, with occasional criticisms of either the theology or the music. This feedback was passed along to Pastor Grimstad and the student leaders for appropriate remediation or commendation. One consequence of general assessment of the teams was the hiring of a music coach who taught in the Music Department.

On balance, the outreach ministry was viewed very positively by the college. On one occasion, President Knutson reported that "the Holy Spirit continues to work among our students in a most unusual way. Interest in prayer and Bible study groups and outreach teams continues unabated." Of course, not everyone agreed with President Knutson's assessment. Some students believed that the theology of the outreach teams was fundamentalist. Others felt that campus ministry, in its various expressions, should be focusing on inequality and social justice. Some of the Religion Department faculty were critical, while others were supportive. On the music side, some felt that the quality of the outreach teams' gospel music fell well-below the choral standard of the college, while others felt there should be room for some variety, so long as the performances were of high quality. In the late sixties, some student government leaders objected that the outreach teams enjoyed financial support from the college. Why shouldn't other groups and activities on campus enjoy that kind of financial support as well, they asked. Roger Swenson, vice president for Development, who represented the college, responded by saying that the teams were serving the college in a unique and positive way by visiting area congregations and representing the college. He suggested that if there were other college activities that could do the same, they would be considered for financial support as well, so that seemed to quell the objection to the team ministry.

Another project of the Outreach Teams Ministry was hosting the annual New Horizons Conference, initiated in 1970. The conference featured two or three speakers and various musical groups or soloists. These conferences were three-day events and included classroom presentations, chapel presentations, and an all-day evangelistic event open to both Concordia students and constituents from congregations around the region. Hundreds of people gathered for these events, which featured a combination of praise music, inspirational preaching, and teaching. One of the earliest of these conferences featured George Forrell, a highly respected Lutheran theologian from the School of Religion at the University of Iowa; Hal Lindsey, author of the controversial book *The Late Great Planet Earth*; and Ralph Bell, an evangelist with the Billy Graham organization. Lindsey's views were outside of mainstream Lutheran theology and caused quite a stir in the community. Subsequent conferences avoided speakers quite so far out of the mainstream, and while many of campus visiting speakers were evangelicals, the programs were anchored by Lutheran clergy and scholars like James Burtness, Carl Johansson, James Hanson, James Bjorge, and James Scherer. These conferences were a major event in the religious program of Concordia and had a run of perhaps fifteen years.

The Outreach Team Ministry was a vital element in campus ministry into the nineties. Arthur Grimstad had a charisma that appealed to students who were devout and committed to providing a Christian witness to the world. This ministry was a hospitable place for students whose roots or inclinations were evangelical. Many students tended to move out of active team ministry in their upper-class years, however, as they developed other interests or a more complex theological perspective. The teams produced many candidates for ministry over the years, including some distinguished leaders. Following Grimstad's retirement, alternative arrangements were made for staff advisement of the team ministry, but his charisma was irreplaceable.

SECULARIZATION AND LUTHERAN IDENTITY

The paradox at Concordia in the late 1960s and 1970s was growing secularization, on the one hand, and religious renewal on the other. I have previously noted evidence of secularization, such as students striving for independence in matters of lifestyle and the challenges of building a Christian faculty. I believed that strengthening of the academic credentials of the faculty was good, necessary, and Lutheran. With our commitment to what Martin Luther called the "earthly kingdom" where natural laws prevail, securing well-prepared faculty and strengthening the academic program were faithful activities. Within the academy, however, the scientific method was the coin of the realm and the humanities, where matters of heart and soul reside, were under pressure. Most of the faculty hired in the sixties and seventies took the scientific method as axiomatic. The humanities strived to be as scientific as possible, with new methods of analysis and criticism, which, it seemed to some, was drawing the blood from the humanities. The challenge was reconciling the quest for meaning with the quest for knowledge. I will address that matter more comprehensively in succeeding chapters. At this point, I want to focus on the teaching of religion, which is where the paradox between secularism and Lutheran identity first manifested itself at Concordia in the sixties.

In the fifties and early sixties, the role of the Religion Department was faith formation. Every member of the department was a Lutheran who brought experience in the parish. Most had master's degrees and nearly all were above average teachers. As noted earlier, in the fifties, religion faculty members led chapel, advised religious groups, attended chapel, and preached frequently both on and off campus. The religion curriculum was extensive and included required courses in Bible, church history, and theology. A few elective courses were available in the junior and senior years, but the shift to a Religion Department with a more academic focus was on the horizon.

In the early sixties, two or three Ph.D.'s fresh out of graduate school and with only limited parish experience joined the Religion Department faculty. They worked well with their department colleagues and brought an increased level of academic knowledge and rigor to the classroom. The role of the Religion Department in nurturing spiritual development still held, although the emphasis was shifting from spiritual nurture to intellectual nurture. Then, in the mid-sixties, due to enrollment growth and retirements, the department experienced a decided shift to a more academic role. Now populated with Ph.D.'s from places like Chicago,

Princeton, Union, and Yale, the Religion Department was one of the strongest academic units of the college.

The shift toward an increasingly academic Religion Department impacted the campus in subtle ways. For example, opening class prayer almost disappeared. In the fifties and early sixties, most religion faculty were faithful chapel participants, whereas in the late sixties and seventies, there were far fewer. Most members of the Religion Department, while possessing some pastoral experience, did not see themselves in a pastoral role with their students. Indeed, some faculty members saw their role in terms of challenging what they viewed as almost childlike faith of their students, literally seeking ways to shake up students' thinking about their faith. There was tension within the department as well, because, not surprisingly, the two non-Ph.D. faculty members came to feel marginalized.

The ongoing challenges with the Religion Department irked President Knutson, who preferred the days when religion faculty members were more pious and nurturing. Despite his personal feelings, however, Dr. Knutson approved all the new appointments to the department because, one by one, he was impressed by their experience and competence. The process of selecting new faculty had gone through a sea change since the early days of leadership President Knutson's in the fifties and early sixties when the process was informal and largely directed by the president, dean, and department head. In the sixties, however, departments took charge of the hiring process under the leadership of the department chair.

In the late sixties and early seventies, searches took on more structure. In the interest of building broader and more diverse pools of candidates, positions were announced, and vacancy notices were distributed widely through professional publications and informal networks. Applicants were then vetted by departments or committees within departments. This process essentially determined the candidates who would be brought to campus for interview, so, in a real sense, the president's participation came at the end of the process and focused on a set of pre-selected candidates. President Knutson was often frustrated by the results. In the case of the Religion Department, President Knutson became concerned about the cumulative effect of the many new appointments made in the late sixties and early seventies. He was concerned about the drift away from piety and religious nurture and toward a more critical, intellectual framing of the professional roles of the faculty and the curriculum's academic direction.

Late in his presidency, Knutson gave voice to his concern in an interview with *The Concordian* (4/18/75):

> My big criticism of the theology and theologians of America today is that they're talking to one another. The typical theologian in the institution of learning doesn't seem to know how to talk to the average person. That is one of the reasons why students in the general population turn to some of these revivalists that the theologians are so quick to criticize. If they only spoke a language that people understood....

Some religious leaders in the region and some members of the faculty and staff shared these concerns. And, not surprisingly, several students in the renewal movement were highly critical of some department members. The president found sympathy for his concerns from some members of his leadership team as well. The academic deans, myself included, thought the direction of the department was, on the whole, constructive, so we essentially ran interference for the department. At the same time, we were sympathetic to his concerns about faculty who used what seemed to be shock tactics on conservative students. By the early seventies, the president had had enough. He decided not to renew the contracts of two Religion Department faculty members to send the department a message. The department responded that there had not been adequate consultation on the matter, and the president, with my encouragement, rescinded his action, hoping that his message had been received. But subsequent events did not reassure him. In 1974, President Knutson refused to grant tenure to a member of the department. So, on the eve of my presidency, I thus inherited the issue and proceeded to set up a consultation process involving selected faculty, regional church leaders, and selected board members. This led to the granting of tenure to the candidate.

These actions in the late sixties and early seventies created a sort of fortress mentality among many members of the Religion Department. This took on a life of its own and persisted for decades, well into the 2000s. Early in my presidency, I contacted the department to improve relations and work together on matters important to the college. In general, this was well-received, and we cobbled together a satisfactory working relationship. In the eighties, however, some students filed a complaint with the dean, alleging that a faculty member in the Religion Department was promoting false teaching. Some members of the Board of Regents took a strong interest in the complaint. After the dean had completed a comprehensive review of the charge, the results were shared with the faculty member. The dean and I reported the findings to the complaining students and the Board of Regents. Not everyone was pleased with our report, which concluded that the issue was pedagogical rather than theological or doctrinal in nature. As noted earlier, the tension between the administration and the Religion Department was a long-term reality. While I did my best to assuage the tension, I came to understand that I could only do so much, and that the department had to find its own way to get beyond the history. From that time forward, I spent much less time concerned about the department.

Based on this history, I took an active role in the hiring process for religion faculty with respect to the mission of the college and the department's role in the faith formation of our students. In this way, I was exercising my role as both president and spiritual leader of the college. In my mind, faith formation and the academic study of religion are inseparable, which makes the teaching of religion one of the most strategic and high priority academic functions of the college. I still adhere to that position, and I rejoiced in the members of the department who shared that belief and exemplified the practice.

Another of my convictions was, and is, that Concordia ought to provide an approach to religious studies that is rooted in and formed by the Lutheran tradition. After all, it was upon the Lutheran tradition that the college was formed. It is the tradition that continues to sponsor us, and it is a tradition that has a great deal to offer the academy, the church, and the world. I also believe the Lutheran tradition challenges us to examine all things, including our own faith tradition and the traditions and practices of other denominations and faiths. In my years, Concordia established itself as a strong ecumenical center and partner in the region, and we welcomed non-Lutherans to our faculty, so the matter of leading from our Lutheran identity and drawing from other traditions was never an either/or proposition.

Over time, the Religion Department has transitioned from a department of religion to a department of religious studies, seeing its function as almost exclusively academic. Few members participate in chapel. The Lutheran content and identify of the department are more muted, and the composition of the faculty is more ecumenical and inter-faith, including at least one Muslim. I believe it continues to be a strong department academically. In all of these respects, I believe Concordia's Religion Department is in the mainstream of the academy. While I don't find that particularly virtuous, I concede the reality. Furthermore, I affirm the academic commitment of the department and its members, most of whom are active in their faith communities and, in their own ways, supportive of the religious aims of the college.

THEOLOGICAL AWAKENING

As academic dean in the early seventies, I began attending meetings of the Lutheran Educational Conference of North America (LECNA). The membership consisted of nearly all Lutheran colleges, universities, and seminaries in the United States and Canada. The presidents—and, in some cases, the deans—of the member institutions attended these meetings. The agenda related to matters that were specific to Lutheran institutions, such as enrollment trends, academic program initiatives, and Lutheran identity. Other agenda items were more generic, such as trends in higher education, governance, public policies, and legal issues. I found these meetings very helpful and through them, I developed a rich network of colleagues, both deans and presidents.

One of my most significant experiences in LECNA occurred at the 1974 annual meeting organized around the theme, "What's Lutheran about Higher Education?" The principal speakers were Sydney Ahlstrom, professor of history at Yale University, and Robert Bertram, professor of theology—first at Concordia Seminary and then at the Seminary in Exile (Seminex). These two speakers literally awakened me to a new awareness of, and an appreciation for, some of the distinctive academic and confessional resources of Lutheran higher education. Ahlstrom spoke of the critical tradition that was framed and encouraged by early church reformers Martin Luther and Philip Melanchthon as well as their championing of freedom of inquiry. Bertram spoke of the Lutheran scholarly tradition of public accountability and the willingness to re-examine received traditions. Christian scholarship does not subscribe to unique methodology, but Christian scholars do bring their faith and world view to their work and this may influence their uses of the knowledge they discover. Christians also come to the scholarly task in the knowledge that sin is real but not ultimate.

These presentations made an immense impact on me. I had been nurtured within a Lutheran ethos, and its impact was more implicit than explicit. That is, I appreciated that one goal of a Lutheran college was to provide opportunities for students to grow in their understanding of the faith and the world, that worship and community were fundamental resources and expressions of faith, that faculty and staff were primary faith mentors and exemplars, and that we are called to use our talents in behalf of God's mission in the world. These fundamentals were well and good. What happened as a result of the St. Louis meeting of LECNA, however, was an awakening to the intellectual tradition of Lutheran higher education, an awakening that would impact my leadership for the rest of my career. A third major influence on my emerging theological awareness was David Lotz, a professor at Union Theological Seminary. Lotz focused on the connections between Lutheran theological principles and learning. I first heard him at a LECNA conference in 1978. He subsequently lectured on the Concordia campus.

The impact of these experiences was manifest in several ways. First, I became a more intentional student of Lutheran theology and practice, and I discovered my study and growing depth of Lutheran theology to be an invaluable resource. Second, I began to envision, encourage, and implement strategies for faculty and staff development around these ideas, which I believed would directly and indirectly influence the college. The first of these ventures occurred in the summer of 1974. With financial support from the American Lutheran Church, Concordia hosted a week-long seminar called "The Context and Mission of Lutheran Higher Education." We invited two people from the faculties of each of the ALC colleges to join seven of our faculty members. The primary lecturers were, not surprisingly, Sydney Ahlstrom and Robert Bertram. The event was a glorious endeavor.

Because of my growing interests and participation in LECNA, I moved into leadership roles in LECNA, which gave me an opportunity to advance various projects related to the identity and mission of Lutheran higher education. And, on the Concordia campus, there would be more seminars and workshops related to the subject—more on that in coming chapters.

LEADERSHIP TRANSITIONS

The mid-seventies were a time of transition for many at Concordia. Most members of the leadership team who had served from the fifties forward either were retired or had plans in place: J. L. Rendahl, Vic Boe, and Dorothy Olsen had retired. Loren Anderson succeeded J. L., but in a somewhat altered role. David Benson and Morrie Lanning split up the jobs previously assigned to Vic and Dorothy. Roger Swenson had moved from vice president for Development at Concordia to a similar position with the Fairview Health System in Minneapolis. Ed Ellenson had moved from Admissions and Financial Aid to Development, and Jim Hausmann had replaced him as dean of Admissions. Bill Smaby, vice president for Business Affairs, indicated that he would stay for a year of my presidency as we sought his replacement. And, of course, there was need to find a replacement in the office of the vice president for Academic Affairs. Even with all these changes in place, leadership transition at Concordia in the mid-seventies was most impacted by President Knutson's retirement.

In the spring of 1974, President Knutson announced his retirement plans. Academic year 1974-75 would be his final year of service to the college, and was perhaps the best of times for him as president and the worst of times for him as an individual. Let me start with the last comment. In May of 1974, President Knutson and his wife Beatrice accompanied the Concordia choir on a tour of Norway. Since his retirement was imminent, the Knutsons were honored wherever they went in Norway. Toward the end of the tour, they received the tragic news that their son Fredrick had been murdered in a domestic situation in California. The shocking news was devastating for the family, and the event hung over them like a cloud all through the year. Their grief was exacerbated by the front page and sensational press coverage in *The Forum*. Of course, their friends, family, and the college community surrounded them with love, support, and hospitality.

To note some of the best of times for the Knutsons, the college's Development Office had declared the 1974-75 school year "The Year of the Knutsons." Among various and events to that end, friends and alumni of the college could contribute to a scholarship named to honor the Knutsons. Alumni gatherings were held across the country to honor the distinguished couple. The Board of Regents decided that the newly expanded student commons would be named to honor the Knutsons. Various community clubs and organizations honored Dr. Knutson with plaques and expressions of appreciation. In the spring, *The Concordian* devoted an entire issue to the Knutsons. The edition was a very gracious tribute to the Knutsons, especially considering the tensions between President Knutson and *The Concordian* in the past. The newspaper also featured him in a friendly way in its annual issue of *The Discordian*, an annual version of the paper that spoofed people and events on campus, all in good fun. When the new swimming pool opened in April of 1975, the president swam the first lap. for the new pool was a project in which he had especially strong interest. Governor Wendell Anderson of Minnesota appeared at a C400 meeting that year and extended state honors to our very own Prexy Joe. It turns out that at one time, Dr. Knutson had ministered to the governor (or a family member) when he was a pastor prior to becoming college president at Concordia. The Knutsons also had an especially close bond with members of the Concordia choir that year, so every once in a while, you would see President Knutson receiving a hug on the sidewalk or a special handshake after chapel. The annual Founders' Day celebration in May 1975 was centered on the Knutsons and featured a number of tributes and heartfelt expressions of honor and thanksgiving. The last of the celebrations occurred in the fall of 1975 at the dedication of the Knutson Center. The event was a full house, and, upon being introduced, Dr. Knutson received a standing ovation. In response, he said, "Concordia students are the finest group of young people you can find on this side of heaven." In short, 1974-1975 was a year of gratitude and celebration for the larger-than-life leader who had done so much to articulate the mission, shape the campus, and lead Concordia to prominence among the Lutheran colleges of the American Lutheran Church and the private colleges of Minnesota.

In the years following his retirement, Joe and Beatrice would reside in a college residence not far from the campus. They attended campus concerts and events, socialized with longtime friends, and volunteered to assist with development calls and as honorary leaders of our fund-raising campaigns. They were an honored and welcome presence at homecoming, C400 meetings, and Founders' Day events. In the eighties, a life-sized bronze statue of President Joseph L. Knutson by artist J. Paul Nesse was commissioned and placed in the center that bears his name. Located in the main rotunda where hundreds of students pass by it each day, the students lovingly refer to the statue as "the Chocolate Man" because of the deep bronze tone's resemblance to chocolate. Years later, I would earn a certain inadvertent claim to fame when there was rumor that a new and bigger student center was contemplated and that it would have a new name. I ended up serving as interim president at about that time and urged the board to take action reaffirming the Knutson name for the expanded structure. I am happy to report that the name stands.

5. Transition to Leadership: 1975-1980

In the late sixties, people began to speculate about President Knutson's successor, assuming that he was perhaps in his last term. The speculation focused on Lloyd Svendsby, a former faculty member. Lloyd was highly regarded by the faculty and college community. He left the college to join the staff of Augsburg Publishing House and then moved to the deanship at St. Olaf College. The next logical step was a college presidency. While my name was being mentioned in some circles by then, it was generally assumed that Lloyd would be the choice, and I shared that expectation. But then a funny thing happened on Lloyd's way to our presidency. He was called to the presidency of Luther Seminary the year before President Knutson was to retire, so my name was in the mix after all.

I was personally unsettled about the prospect of assuming the presidency of Concordia. I did not feel a strong sense of call to the work, but I assumed that the search process itself would influence my disposition. I told the search committee that I did not know if I would accept the position were it to be offered, but that I was willing to participate in the process. This ambiguity frustrated the search committee and my advocates. There was a feeling among many that after twenty-four years of Knutson's leadership, Concordia needed someone from the outside. I could understand their point of view. Others believed that Concordia ought to stay with the tradition of having an ordained person in the presidency. All of this would be processed in the search itself and at an extended board meeting. After something like six ballots, I was elected.

When the Board of Regents chair Carrol Malvey and the search committee chair Noel Fedje called on me at home on a Saturday afternoon to tell me the outcome, I asked them to let me wait until Monday to respond. Mardy and I wanted an opportunity to reflect again on this significant decision in our lives. We also wanted to consult with several trusted friends. In addition, I wanted to seek the counsel of some key faculty members. I do not recall all of those conversations, but I do remember a meeting at the Moorhead Holiday Inn on Sunday night with a number of the newer faculty. After telling them about the invitation to lead the college, I asked them for their counsel and if they were willing to join me in building the future. The following day I accepted the position:

> I accept the election of the Board of Regents to the office of president of Concordia College with a sense of wonder, thankfulness, and humility—wonder at the ways of God; thankfulness for the support of friends, colleagues, and students—a veritable cloud of witnesses; and humility in the face of profound responsibility. The years ahead are most often described as a period of uncertainty for higher education—uncertainty about enrollment, about finances, about program. I prefer to describe the days ahead as a time of special opportunity—opportunity to affirm the special place of a church college, of liberal arts education, and of Christian community. This college endures by the grace of God and the company of His servants who care for this place and to them I make these pledges:
>
> To the Christ whose advent we now celebrate and who is the Lord of this college, I pledge my talents of leadership and teaching and administration.
>
> To the constituents of this college—alumni, Lutheran congregations, those who support the place in word and deed and prayer, and the Regents who are their formal representatives—to all of these I pledge constancy with the mission of the college.
>
> To the faculty and staff of the college—those who teach the students, clean the buildings, tend the boilers, counsel the students, prepare the food, and mow the grass—to all of you I pledge my support for your ministries.
>
> And to the students who carry out our mission in society I pledge myself to quality education and a caring, listening community.
>
> And to fulfill these dimensions of my servanthood I solicit support and understanding; from students, I ask your best effort as learners—for that is your fundamental calling during your years on this campus. I ask your assistance in building community here—for thereby we all grow richer.
>
> From faculty and staff, I ask you to continue to do your best in the classrooms, laboratories, committee meetings, boiler rooms, counseling sessions, offices, and kitchens on this campus. I ask for your criticism, your imagination, and your continuing care for and commitment to the purpose of this college.

From the constituents of the college, I ask for continued support for the needs and mission of the college and I ask that you extend to me the same opportunities to lead and serve as you extended to my predecessors.

And from the Lord of us all, I ask that His Spirit will bring the gifts of patience, wisdom, grace, and strength to me and to all of us. For with His strong arm to sustain us we shall go forth with joy. It is with that assurance that I accept this election.

Soli Deo Gloria. To God alone the glory.

Paul J. Dovre, December 17, 1974

With these words, I embarked on the calling of my lifetime. My transition to the presidency began with the election, but from that date forward, there were several new tasks to attend to, including the search for a dean to replace me, speaking requests from several area congregations, and outreach to key individuals in our constituency. President Knutson was gracious and supportive at every turn in the transition process.

I was well-prepared for this new calling in several respects. The mentoring of Joseph Knutson and Carl Bailey had provided me with first-hand experience in leadership, and my friendship with Roger Swenson had given me some comprehension of my coming role in fundraising. My previous relationships with several of the presidents of Minnesota private colleges at whose meetings I had often represented President Knutson provided me with a strong network of support, and through varied roles and experiences over the years I had developed problem-solving, planning, and speaking skills. But most important, I had the unwavering support of Mardy and my family. I was fully confident that I could do this work.

I was inaugurated as the eighth president of Concordia College at homecoming in October of 1975. The inauguration was a significant gathering of alumni, church leaders, academic leaders from the region, members of the Concordia Corporation, faculty, staff, students, and local community representatives. Reverend Carl Lee, senior campus pastor, delivered the invocation and benediction, and Reverend Dr. Cecil Johnson, bishop of the northern Minnesota district of the American Lutheran Church, presented me for inauguration and offered the inaugural prayer. Reverend Dr. David Preus, presiding bishop of the ALC, brought greetings from the church and conferred the oath of office, and Dr. Roland Dille, president of neighboring Moorhead State University (now Minnesota State University Moorhead) brought greetings in behalf of the community. Carrol Malvey, chair of the Board of Regents, presented the corporate charter authorization of election, and Reverend Wade Davick, a pastor from Minot, North Dakota, brought greetings from the corporate area. The Concordia choir presented a short program.

The title of my inaugural address was "Look to the Rock," based on the text of Isaiah 51:1-2 (see Appendix A). I spoke about the dimensions of the rock: the Gospel of Christ, theology, the liberal arts, and a nurturing community. These four themes allowed me to identify what I believed to be essentials of the college in pursuing its mission. In closing, I said:

> ...in remembering the rock from which Concordia was hewn, we find our hope. I pledge myself to the rock from which Concordia was hewn, to the God and Creator of all things by whose grace this college is an agent of reconciliation. And I make this pledge in joy and confidence because He has promised to bless us with His love, His spirit, and His power.

In this address, I was identifying with the mission and tradition of the college out of my own exegesis, thus informing people of my values, principles, and intentions. The address was a bit long, but the friendly audience of two-thousand people was patient.

Getting started with my presidency called for more than giving a speech with such lofty goals. In other venues, I spoke to the more pragmatic goals of the immediate future, which were five in number: communication with constituencies, long-range financial planning, program development, strengthening community, and accommodating and adjusting to leadership changes. The first goal was related to the fact that I was new to the constituents of the college and the first non-clergy president anyone could remember. Furthermore, I believed that there might be a promising synergy between the college and the churches of our region. With respect to the second goal, for most of its history Concordia had been anxious about money and budgets, and I was convinced that we needed to take a longer view and develop new fiscal strategies. Concerning the third goal, we had some new programs at the implementation stage in communications, computer science, cooperative education, and food and nutrition sciences that needed attention. The fourth goal relating to community reflected the reality of a decade-long period of protest and change in the society at large, which had reverberations on our campus. In addition, we needed to mend some of the strains that had developed over time between the administration and students. Finally, there were many leadership transitions, either completed or pending, including my own.

There was also a subtext emphasized in both formal statements and informal actions. The themes of the subtext were about change that would be evolutionary rather than revolutionary, about a future anchored in tradition, about being mission driven, and about reconciliation. The last theme was especially prominent in my early years as I sought to move us away from the acrimony that had marked so much of the previous decade, particularly with respect to students and somewhat with respect to faculty. I wanted to set a pattern of welcoming dialogue, respecting differences of opinion, and processing issues in a fair and rational way. That last theme would be tested early with the Black student strike the coming spring of 1976.

There were, as I said above, many leadership changes. Gerald Hartdagen became the new academic dean after a difficult search, difficult because we hadn't undergone a search for an academic dean in a while and difficult because the college community was divided in its preferences. Since I was an inside appointment, I was strongly urged to appoint someone from outside of the campus to the deanship, so I took the advice into account. Hartdagen was a conscientious and hardworking dean, fair and thorough in all matters. He was attentive to academic integrity and the new programs that needed to be fully implemented. Although he worked hard, Hartdagen's temperament created unease among the faculty, of which he was aware, and he accepted a new position as dean of Wilkes College in Pennsylvania in 1979. His successor was Associate Dean David Gring, who had arrived in the fall of 1976. He quickly won the respect and cooperation of the faculty. He had an eye for academic quality and possessed a winsome style of interaction with both faculty and students. Gring chose as his associate dean senior faculty member Olin Storvick, who was universally respected. Gring would leave Concordia in the late eighties when he accepted the presidency of Roanoke College in Virginia.

On the business side, Bill Smaby stayed on through my first year, which was a big help. Then, following a lengthy search, Don Helland was appointed vice president for Business Affairs. He had served in a similar position at Occidental College in California. Don's roots were in the Midwest, and he had at one time been a pastor in the Lutheran Free Church. Don brought good experience and new strategies to the office. He helped the college shape a new long-term financial strategy and new budget disciplines.

While I was dean, Loren Anderson had joined my staff as director of institutional research, a title that did not entirely fit because he was looking after a variety of planning and staff development matters. When I became president, we shifted his title to assistant to the president, and his duties came to include board liaison work as well as planning and general institutional trouble shooter. A few years into my presidency, Ed Ellenson moved to a more specialized role in Development as we moved into a major fund-raising campaign. Loren moved into the vice president for Development spot with the expectation that, once the campaign was over, Ellenson would, as executive vice president, move into what had been Loren's old spot. However, Ellenson and his wife Ann subsequently purchased a business and he left his position with the college. We had a strong friendship, so his departure was both a personal and professional loss to me. On the other hand, the Development spot was an exceptionally good fit for Loren because of his planning skills and his almost innate strategy sense for fundraising.

This transition discussion would not be complete without mentioning leadership changes in the Board of Regents. Carrol Malvey completed his term of service in 1978, and Noel Fedje became the chair. He termed out in two years and was followed first by Norman Jones and then by Norman Lorentzsen. These four men were an exceptional quartet of leaders. Carrol Malvey was closely associated with the local business community and had great common sense. He was a highly respected, credible man. Noel Fedje came into the chair after extensive work as a volunteer, having served as the national chair of the C400 club. Norman Jones was national chair of Concordia's major fundraising campaign and knew his way around the college, the community, and the region. Norman Lorentzsen had been an effective two-term board member, and because everyone saw his leadership potential, he would successfully serve as board chair through most of the eighties.

Taken together, these changes represented a generational shift from leaders schooled in the 1920s and 1930s to leaders schooled in the 1940s and 1950s. While there was continuity around mission, church, and culture, there were also differences in outlook, style, and strategy. For example, the preceding generation of college leaders tended to compare Concordia to more well-off colleges like St. Olaf, which had nicer facilities, wealthier and more generous constituents, a stronger endowment, and a more robust academic program and reputation. My attitude, however, shared by of our other emerging leaders, was that Concordia should be measured against its mission and potential, not some other institution's track record. While St. Olaf had a longer history and a wonderful tradition of support, Concordia had a vast geography to serve and incredible potential among its people. I believed Concordia's sweet spot was serving the sons and daughters of farmers, small town professionals, and business people. Ours was a somewhat laid back, informal constituency of hard-working and well-meaning people. While Concordia students may have lacked cultural sophistication, most of them were above average academically, with many all-stars in the mix. Cy Running once said that Concordia was like a man with a bit of hayseed on his sleeve, and very comfortable about it.

Concordia was doing an excellent job of serving its constituents and everybody knew it. The new leaders at Concordia had self-confidence built on this reality, and we were optimistic about our ability to grow in service, quality, and reputation. As I had said when I accepted the presidency, some people looked to the future with foreboding, but we looked to the future in terms of its possibilities for strengthening the quality of our liberal arts approach to Christian higher education, our service to church and region, and our sense of community. Beginning in the seventies, we began to rally the college and our constituents around this vision and these themes. At public occasions both on and off campus, I would emphasize Concordia's strengths and achievements, seeking thereby to build pride, esprit de corps, and confidence. It wasn't a matter of glossing over our challenges; rather, it was a matter of seeing them in a context of confidence and positive momentum.

Some years later, sociologists would refer to ours as "the Silent Generation." We had been born and educated in the Depression, had seen our friends and family experience a great war, and then had experienced the recovery of the post-war years. While most of our parents were not college graduates, we were the beneficiaries of their hard work and commitment to a better life for their children. We were said to be silent in the sense that we did not make great waves politically or culturally even though most of the leaders of the civil rights and women's rights movements came from our ranks. Schooled in the realities of the Depression and the recovery of the fifties, we had good work habits, and we believed in ourselves and our future. Nurtured in caring families and a robust faith, we were clear about our values and our ultimate goals. All of this would play out in the leadership we would give to Concordia College for the next twenty-five years.

FAMILY AND TRANSITION

While this reminiscence focuses on my reflections in relationship to events at the college, it is impossible to isolate my calling from my family. Indeed, my wife Mardy was pivotal in all of this. She was, and is, a reliable source of counsel, a steady and steadfast compass. Mardy was a trailblazer of sorts, in that while I assumed the presidency at Concordia, she was a community volunteer and a member of the business department at Fargo South High School. During these years, her volunteer activities were centered in the Fargo-Moorhead Junior League and included work in the schools and the Nokomis Childcare Center in Fargo. On the professional side, Mardy taught half-days at Fargo South, always in the morning, thus freeing her for occasional college functions at the lunch hour and the rest of the day. She was able to arrange her schedule to accompany me to selected donor and alumni events.

In the early years of my presidency, we developed a strategy for major college events—we would go our separate ways to meet and greet guests to ensure that we connected with as many people as possible. Mardy's natural warmth, friendliness, and genuine spirit of hospitality were major assets to me and to the college. Her professional work was important, both as an expression of her vocation and as a balance wheel for her personally. That is, it was important that she had a life beyond the college. For Mardy, the transition to the presidency meant taking on a new agenda while sustaining her former interests and commitments as volunteer, teacher, and mother to our two teenage children, Erik and Louise. For our children, the changes were less obvious. That is, my assuming the presidency didn't mean that they would have to move to a new town or school. Life in the president's residence at the northeast corner of the campus was a good experience for them, with lots of room to roam and be creative. Their social relationships were undisturbed, and Erik and Louise continued to thrive both academically and socially, just as they had before my presidency.

Mardy and I retained our circle of friends, and then expanded our friendships exponentially as we were introduced to a new circle of professional colleagues, regents, and other leaders in our constituency. Just as my relationships with faculty changed when I became dean, so my relationships with administrative colleagues changed when I became president. I don't want to overstate these changes. We retained good friendships and shared hopes and dreams. The change was in the agenda; there were things about the work that I could not share even with good colleague friends. I found that to be challenging, and it took me a while to accommodate this change without feeling embarrassed, but I came to understand that my colleague friends accepted the need for confidentiality. Through my years as dean and president, I always relied on the steady and reliable counsel of Pastor Carl Lee. Given his professional commitment to confidentiality, he was the one professional colleague in whom I could and did confide. He was a source of grace and strength to me all through the years. Now, years later, one of the joys of my retirement is that those occasional boundaries are no longer present, and I count among my very best friends several former administrative and faculty colleagues.

Not only was there necessary transition and adjustment to my personal and professional relationships once I assumed the presidency at Concordia, but also there was heightened awareness of the words and language I chose in various situations. There is a passage by Dag Hammarskjöld, the much-admired Secretary General of the United Nations, that always reminded me of the importance of words, especially as my leadership role at Concordia changed:

> Respect for the word...is the first commandment in the disciplines by which a man can be educated to maturity.... Respect for the word—to employ it with scrupulous care and incomparable heartfelt love of truth—is essential if there is to be any growth in a society or in the human race.

Christians use *word* to refer to sacred scripture and the person of Jesus Christ. While Hammarskjöld's motivations were religious, his use of *word* in this passage was secular rather than religious. He was referring to the responsibility that we each carry for the responsible and ethical use of language.

While the use of language is common to nearly all human enterprises, precision in words and language is especially important to leaders. I often think about the critical role of words in the leadership of teachers, pastors, community officials, and college leaders. The ability to express ideas effectively helps inform, shape, and inspire a community. In the case of a college, the office of president confers special responsibility to maintain traditions of quality and integrity, keep the mission alive, and nurture the welfare of faculty, students, and staff. I, too, assumed those responsibilities when I accepted the call to become president at Concordia.

I observed first-hand the effectiveness of Dean Carl Bailey and President Joseph Knutson in utilizing words to carry out the responsibilities of their respective offices. Both leaders were thoughtful and prudent in their selection of words to enlighten their listeners and convey passion. Each possessed a charisma unique to their personalities and appropriate to their responsibilities. They respected their audiences and spoke in words that were at once clear and meaningful. Dean Bailey and President Knutson modeled excellence in their communication, and I learned from their examples but also brought my own gifts to the task. My disposition and rhetorical skills were not the same as either Bailey's or Knutson's, though I learned a good deal from each of them.

Over time, I also came to understand that various public speaking opportunities offered me occasions to express important ideas on behalf of the college. The presidency is, after all, to use Teddy Roosevelt's language, a "bully pulpit," an essential tool for leadership. For example, the annual fall opening student convocation event provided an excellent venue in which to articulate mission and envision the future. The annual state of the college address to the faculty and staff was an important opportunity to celebrate achievements, to refresh our strategic direction, to appraise the changes in our environment, and to rally around our future possibilities. Homecoming sermons provided an opportunity to explore the will and ways of God for those who sought to carry out our holy calling as individuals and as a college. Chapel homilies were similarly strategic opportunities to explore our sacred calling in the context of real life. There were multiple opportunities to employ words beyond the campus at alumni events, in legislative and professional gatherings, and at an innumerable number of friend and memorial celebrations. Throughout my service to the college, I embraced this range of opportunities to effectively use my voice, especially as president.

In view of the important place of words in my role as president, I cultivated some habits of preparation. Even when the speaking assignment might have been incidental, often under the category of remarks or greetings, I set aside time to prepare. I sought to connect with my listeners, offer something of substance, and do this with an economy of words (i.e. "keep it brief"). Preparation for a major speech, however, occurred over weeks and involved research and rewrites. I would often ask people to review my drafts. I maintained files with notes and resource materials that I revisited and added to frequently. I prepared a manuscript for my major speeches and homilies to ensure that I was writing for the ear and disciplining the speech's development. I undertook every invited speaking occasion with the seriousness in preparation that it deserved.

The history of Concordia College was one of my primary resources in presentations on campus and among constituents. As with any history, there are certain people who stand out as particularly important or colorful, and Concordia's history is no different. Several past presidents were influential. Rasmus Bogstad, first hired as a professor in 1891 and later college president in 1902, was an innovator and advocate in the early years. J. A. Aasgaard, fifth president of the college (1911-1925), led the transformation from an academy to a college, and later, J. N. Brown, who was elected president of Concordia in 1925 and served for twenty-six years as the institution's leader, presided over accreditation in the twenties and the vagaries of the Depression and WW II in the 1930s and 1940s. Also worth noting, of course, was J. L. Knutson (president from 1951-1975), who took the college to new levels of growth and stature.

Not only did I draw on the lives and stories of former college presidents as part of my research and resources, but there also were others whose contributions I could draw upon as I shared the Concordia story and my perspectives. For example, Professor Carl B. Ylvisaker was a favorite teacher both on and off the campus, and in the midst of the Depression, he would describe Concordia as a "college of destiny." I thought this to be an insightful distinction for the college, one I shared at various speaking occasions. Others, such as early and long-serving board members Lars Christianson and J. M. O. Ness, would somehow rescue the college from more than one crisis, also gave me stories from the college history worth sharing. These stories and others from a long list of college heroes could go on for additional paragraphs. After all, the history of the college is about people and how these and other key figures illustrate the drive, creativity, persistence, and dedication that have both sustained and invigorated the college for more than a century. In my experience, people loved to hear memorable anecdotes and examples from the past and often were inspired by them, so as I spoke at various public functions, I sought to connect audiences with the power of Concordia's history. I believed that this public work was one of the most important roles that I assumed as president and was worth the investment of considerable time and effort. This was work I found deeply satisfying for its mix of creativity, discipline, and introspection.

FACULTY AND PROGRAM

In the late seventies, the academic focus of the college and the faculty was on modifying and living with all of the changes that had been implemented in the early seventies. The late seventies saw successful implementation of new programs in communications, computer science, food and nutrition sciences, and cooperative education. To this list would be added programs in long-term care administration and healthcare financial management. The Concordia Language Village program continued to grow in numbers and expand in facilities with initial construction on the German village. The May Seminar program, led by highly qualified leaders Dell Bjerkness and Al Traaseth, continued to expand.

There were two high-visibility observances in this timeframe, each with academic components. The first major observance occurred in 1975-76 when Concordia observed the sesquicentennial of Norwegian immigration to America. This historical event was of particular significance to the college because of Concordia's long, deep ties to early Norwegian immigrants. Throughout the academic year, the campus hosted several events. In the fall of the year, the bishop of Norway visited campus, and there was a community worship service with special music. Several civic and religious leaders were in attendance. The Scandinavian Studies program sponsored noted scholar Einar Haugen, emeritus professor from Harvard with Midwestern roots, presented a series of lectures on campus. Also, the famous Norwegian explorer Thor Hyerdahl spoke on campus to a capacity crowd. After that event, we hosted a reception honoring him at our home. With fondness, I still recall his entrance. As Hyerdahl came in the back door from our driveway rather than the front door, the more customary entrance for guests in our home, his first words were, "Where's the bathroom?" Another honored guest during the celebration that year was Trygve Bratlie, the prime minister of Norway, who was honored at a luncheon in the Grant Center. We had some free time before the event, so I asked the prime minister if he would like to take a walk, to which he replied yes, so we took a short walk outside of the building. Upon our return, I was chastised by his secret service (that is, U.S. Secret Service) for this unannounced, unplanned activity. Little did I know.

The second major observance that impacted the campus was in 1976 because of the celebration of the Bicentennial of the United States. Concordia observed the celebration in a series of events and lectures featuring such luminaries as Congresswoman Shirley Chisholm, theologian Langdon Gilkey, historian Eugene Hollan, classics scholar Paul McKendrick, physicist (and Cobber) Rein Uritam, and journalist Carl Bernstein. These events, coordinated by James Hofrenning of the Religion Department, were well-attended.

Although the mid-seventies recognized historical milestones and celebrated in many ways, throughout the seventies there were other issues and practices worth noting. Two issues relating to academic practices took center stage in the mid-seventies, one related to grade inflation and the other to academic integrity. The campus had seen a rise in grade inflation over time, which was met with growing concern by many faculty members. Upon reflection, part of this was our own creation in implementing pass/fail options for students in the late sixties. Dean Gerald Hartdagen identified this as an issue that needed attention, and most members of the faculty agreed. There were meetings, hearings, and features and interviews in *The Concordian*, all for purposes of enlightenment and persuasion. Although there were good intentions with analyzing the problem of grade inflation, the issue largely disappeared in the eighties—not because grade inflation was solved, but I think because people simply gave up on the matter, although many faculty would say even today that grade inflation continues to be a challenge.

The focus of the academic integrity discussion centered on the Student Faculty Academic Responsibility Code, a code that had been in place since the early sixties. Each time students took an exam, they would sign (or not sign) a statement affirming that they had not practiced any kind of dishonesty nor had they observed anyone doing so. If students failed to sign the statement, they would be invited to meet with the SFARB (Student

Faculty Academic Responsibility Board) for a follow-up conversation. This system worked effectively until the early seventies when students began to voice unhappiness about the responsibility of policing the moral conduct of others. This was consistent with their opposition to *in loco parentis* and the general mood that each person should be responsible for his or her conduct. A special committee was elected to review the code. The process took a long time and involved numerous public events and news stories. The outcome was a revised code that reduced student responsibility and increased faculty responsibility.

In addition to grade inflation and academic integrity, concerns were apparent regarding issues related to women in particular, matters such as equity, representation, inclusion, salary, advancement, and so on. Our campus reflected the broader national conversation about women that emerged in the late sixties. At Concordia, attention to women's issues began principally among students, and by the seventies, several Concordia faculty members brought leadership to these matters. To support the effort and engage the conversation on campus, there were several guest speakers, frequent articles in *The Concordian*, and creation of a designated space called The Women's Center. A Women's Studies program would also emerge from this effort. The result of all these efforts, stretching over a decade, was growing sensitivity and awareness. Attention was being paid to women's issues in college policies and practices, in scholarly and pedagogical matters, and in the community-wide focus on human relations. The results were salutary. I would add that these issues were important to me personally. My mother, two sisters, and wife had been, or were, teachers, and our daughter was a talented student with high aspirations. It was my personal conviction that these were matters of equity and justice.

Another area of growing interest and discussion in the seventies was connected to Concordia's relationship with the local Jewish community. Perhaps owing in part to the strong ecumenical focus of the college and surrounding community, Concordia pursued an interfaith connection with the Jewish community in Fargo-Moorhead. There were established links with Temple Beth El through the Communiversity (explained in more detail in the next section), and members of the Religion Department were interested in pursuing an academic initiative related to Jewish studies. Consequently, we entered into conversation with the Alex Stern Foundation of Fargo, and this led to a multi-year grant that brought to the campus a series of visiting scholars in Jewish studies. Grant funded activities led to a fairly long-term arrangement whereby the rabbi of Temple Beth El would teach a course in Jewish studies on the Concordia campus. In addition, existing curricula was refreshed by adding insights gained from visiting scholars. The importance of interfaith conversations and connection opportunities for the Concordia community has continued over the decades.

In the previous chapter, I described the changes made to Concordia's tenure system in response to both enrollment and economic uncertainties and to our then-high percentage of tenured faculty. By the late seventies, a number of new faculty had been added under the so-called tenure quota system. While they had known that there were limits on tenure opportunities when they were hired, they liked the place and wanted to see the policy change. By the late seventies, there was conversation and increasing pressure, so we were beginning to think about how we might address the matter. In the late seventies, Dean David Gring would begin working with the standing faculty committee on tenure and promotion in devising changes that would be reviewed and approved in the eighties.

OUTREACH INITIATIVES

The outreach initiatives on behalf of Concordia had three focuses. First, in an effort for outreach early in my term, I needed exposure to our constituents and them to me. This included alumni in various communities around the country, constituents of the member churches of the Concordia Corporation, and members of the local business community. The need for increased exposure meant that I was on the road a lot in my first year, establishing a pattern of personal outreach that would continue through the years. In the first winter, I accompanied the Concordia band on their tour of western North Dakota and Montana. For me, the tour involved several alumni receptions as well as gatherings with area pastors. I also accepted as many preaching invitations as I thought I could manage, about one a month. In addition, I joined a local service club and had many informal conversations over coffee or breakfast gatherings with local leaders, thereby connecting to the local community. It was good work, work that I enjoyed, and I felt well-received all around.

Another focus of outreach related to congregations in the region, both

Lutheran and others, and to the broader communities. In the sixties, the college initiated a program for the local community called the FM Communiversity. Communiversity was an ecumenical, community-based initiative that was incredibly well-received. This was the work of James Hofrenning of the Religion Department. Jim had a special charisma for gathering people, engendering enthusiasm, and forging partnerships. Throughout most of its history, the Communiversity sponsored a variety of study opportunities, everything from buying and selling stocks to end-of-life planning. Enrollment in various Communiversity opportunities averaged close to 1,000 annually. At the beginning, the courses were offered in the month of February for many years and featured an opening convocation with a speaker of national recognition like Martin Marty, Garrison Keillor, Senator Paul Simon, Robert McAfee Brown, Krister Stendahl, Elisabeth Kubler-Ross, Harland Cleveland, Carol Bly, Bernice King, Joan Mondale, and more. Over time, the Communiversity program was expanded to a nine-month calendar, with courses offered both on campus and in the community. The program continued to thrive into the 2000s.

In addition, in the late 1960s, with assistance from the American Lutheran Church, Concordia established an ecumenical center for theology called Charis, named for the Greek word meaning a reflection of God's grace. Once again, Jim Hofrenning was instrumental and shepherded the planning process. Wayne Stumme was named as the first director of Charis. This center enjoyed broad ecumenical support in offering continuing education courses and credit arrangements for clergy in the area. In short, Concordia had some very strong initiatives in place, something to build on.

In the seventies and eighties, Concordia also started outreach programs to serve health care and education professionals in area communities. Professor Ted Heimarck, creator of the programs in hospital administration and healthcare finance, led the formation of an annual conference for health care professionals in the Upper Midwest. Hundreds would gather each spring to hear national scholars and health care professionals share their wisdom and experience. It seems a fitting honor that decades later in October 2023, Concordia recognized Ted's passion for teaching, his commitment to students, and his love for Concordia by naming the new high-tech campus facility for health professions the Sanford Heimarck School of Health Professions.

Another successful broader community outreach program that came into its own in the 1970s through the 1990s was the summer reading conference housed in the English Department. The original summer reading conference, the first of its kind in the surrounding states at the time, was started in 1956 by Professors Dorothy Johnson and Walther Prausnitz. Professor Dorothy Johnson was named director of the conference, whose leadership was followed by Professor James Coomber (English) for many years. Again, like many other outreach programs of this era, Concordia's outreach brought hundreds of teachers from across the Upper Midwest to the Concordia campus to participate in these events, which featured leading scholars, authors, publishers, and practitioners from across the country. The last Concordia summer reading conference was held in 1999.

Campus leaders also sought to broaden Concordia's reach beyond the Fargo-Moorhead area by exporting some of our Charis programs to the outlying area and by developing a world class theological conference that would bring in prominent theologians and scholars, thus attracting pastors from throughout the region. It was Jim Hofrenning who had the vision for this kind of project, so I named him director of continuing studies. His responsibilities included Charis, Communiversity, and the annual summer theological conference. The summer conference annually attracted hundreds of pastors from our region and was widely recognized as the finest program of its kind.

The third focus of outreach was the strengthening of the bonds between the college and the congregations of Concordia's corporate area. While the activities certainly connected the college and congregations in the immediate area, we also wanted to strengthen the relationship with all of the nine hundred-plus congregations in Montana, North Dakota, and northwestern Minnesota that legally owned the college. These relationships had been somewhat casually attended to in the past, so now we meant to cultivate them more actively and systematically. David Benson, previously in the Student Affairs division, became the director of college relations. Among his responsibilities were coordination and cultivation of outreach to congregations. David began to systematically get facetime for representatives of the college at district conventions and conference meetings throughout the corporate area. Perhaps the highlight of these early years was when Concordia hosted the national convention of the American Lutheran Church in the fall of 1978. This conference brought one thousand delegates to the campus from all over the country, plus another five hundred visitors and staff. The event provided a chance to feature the colleges in the ALC church's life, and one evening program was devoted to that purpose. Another feature of the convention was the appearance of Vice President Mondale, a Minnesota native with many Lutheran connections. The place of Lutheran colleges in the life of the broader church as a whole was strongly affirmed at this event.

Don Rice assumed responsibility as Concordia's first full-time director of Church Relations in the early eighties, and the church relations outreach continued to expand. We initiated a pastor-in-residence program that brought area pastors to Concordia for four or five days. We selected pastors from throughout the corporate territory, thus spreading the word of Concordia. Through these activities, we both gained feedback from constituents and shared with them something of the life and mission of the college. In addition, for years Concordia sponsored a church youth day in the fall of each year, which regularly attracted over a thousand teenagers from the region. To this effort the Koinonia Academy was added, a summer program for young people, which annually enrolled around one hundred students during the years of the program's existence. Our outreach also added organ workshops on and off campus in response to the growing shortage of church organists. In partnership with congregations, we initiated the CORD scholarship program, in which congregations and church women's groups supplied scholarships to students from their churches who attended Concordia. The college would match these funds. Don Rice had his ear to the ground and developed a tremendous level of trust and confidence in congregations throughout the region. Indeed, through the eighties and nineties, Concordia's church relations program was without peers in Lutheran circles.

THE GROWTH NARRATIVE

While a retrospective on Concordia enrollment suggests that the seventies, eighties, and nineties were decades of enrollment stability and growth, the early seventies did not feel that way. Fall enrollment numbers in 1970, 1972, and 1974 showed slight declines in student numbers. A national scholarly study described "the new depression in higher education" in foreboding terms and predicted the demise of many private colleges. While Concordia experienced some minor enrollment declines in 1979 and 1981-1984, the trend over the late seventies, eighties, and nineties was growth and stability. Enrollment stood at 2,640 in the fall of 1975, and later reached a high of 2,999 in the fall of 1993 and stood at 2,979 in the fall of 1998, my last year as president.

Returning to the 1970s, the climate in the early seventies led us to be cautious. When we experienced a one-year gain of 159 students between the fall of 1974 and the fall of 1975, we were not prepared. This was especially noticeable with respect to student housing, which led us to lease motel rooms in Moorhead to house the overflow. The college policy required that, except students who lived at home, all first- and second-year students were to live on campus while upper-class students could live on or off campus. While students were reasonably good natured about the overcrowding in the fall of 1975, they expected more by 1976. The college intended to do better. Bogstad Manor, an apartment building for upper-class students, was built on land Concordia already owned just north of Park Region Hall on the old music hall site. Yet, even with the additional one hundred or so living spaces available in Bogstad, 180 students were on the waiting list after spring sign up for fall housing in 1976. This led to a student petition of complaint signed by 1,500 students. The petition effort preceded by only a few weeks the Black student strike, which made 1975-76 a rather inauspicious beginning for a new college president.

By the summer of 1976, administrative leaders had sorted and solved the needs of wait-listed students, and that fall welcomed a record-setting 1,004 new students to campus, which, in turn, gave Concordia a record-setting enrollment of 2,678. Within a few years, another student apartment building, Bogstad East, was constructed. Concordia constructed these two apartment buildings according to commercial standards so that in the event that enrollment declined and they were no longer needed, the apartment units could be rented out to the public. That day didn't arrive; in fact, in the early 2000s, the townhouse complex was added on the east campus.

In addition to housing, other growing pains came with enrollment growth. Concordia's retention rates were not strong, perhaps because faculty and staff were stretched thin, and we had to hire a number of part-time faculty. In addition to dormitories filled to slightly beyond capacity, the academic facilities on campus were feeling the pinch. By the eighties, we had a handle on most of the space issues with the remodeling of Grose and Bishop Whipple Halls and the construction of a new science facility to house the departments of biology and home economics. In addition,

Concordia purchased residential property adjacent to the campus as eventual parking to accommodate more vehicles as enrollment expanded.

While there were pains accompanying the college's growth, the benefits exceeded the dislocation. Growth reflected positive perceptions of Concordia in our region. The growth also provided an opportunity to add strength to the college faculty. Much of the additional income from a growing student body was available for compensation, program improvements, and upgrades in existing facilities.

The effectiveness of Concordia's Admissions and Financial Aid programs was a key to sustained growth. We had solid leadership in Jim Hausmann and several long-term field staff members in a profession that is marked by burnout and high turnover. We also modified the college's marketing materials and strategies to better fit the changing expectations and habits of potential students. Most notable of these efforts was The Concordia Equation, which outlined specific student outcomes. These new, more sophisticated outreach efforts contributed to strong enrollment from our regional corporate area. There was a sense of momentum that will be more fully identified later in this narrative.

FINANCIAL PLANNING

In the sixties and seventies, most private colleges in the Upper Midwest lived on the edge financially. While they did not have much capital debt and perhaps little operating debt, remaining whole financially involved a tenuous balancing act. In comparison to other schools, Concordia did fairly well in that our budgets were balanced, enrollment income was growing, and salaries were paid on time. William Smaby, chief business officer, was a kind of genius in managing the budget. Still, at the end of most years, we were experiencing only modest surpluses on the order of forty to fifty thousand dollars, which meant that we were just a broken boiler or an unexpected decline in enrollment away from a fiscal problem. This bred an underlying anxiety about finances that I thought the college needed to address. As a result, those in financial leadership adopted four strategies to address potential financial challenges.

First, in the spring before my inauguration, I appointed a Budget Planning Committee. Their task was to review the college's financial condition, economic and enrollment trends, and institutional needs. The committee developed a set of recommendations related to institutional budget priorities, overall budget guidelines, and tuition and fee levels. Their recommendations went to the President's Council for consideration and action. This planning committee included representatives from the staff, faculty, and student body. Accompanying this annual budget-planning process were two public meetings of the faculty and staff, one in the fall and one in the spring. In the fall, administrative staff would review financial results from the previous year, the priorities and guidelines that would frame the coming budget, and the recommended tuition and fees. Members of the Budget Planning Committee participated in this meeting. I recall David Moewes, professor of economics, and his thoughtful economic analyses. In the spring of the year, a second meeting was held to share enrollment projections, the budget recommendations that would be going to the Board of Regents, and, of most interest, the anticipated adjustments in faculty and staff compensation.

These planning and public sharing activities were powerful in establishing confidence and trust in the college's fiscal management and priorities. The transparency was welcomed and led to a well-informed faculty and staff. When times were good, attendance at these public events tended to tail off. On the other hand, when there was an enrollment or other economic issue on the table, attendance was strong. The effectiveness of this planning and public information strategy is best indicated by the fact that the process was still in place some forty years later.

The second strategy to address potential financial challenges was the initiation of a long-range budget planning process. The college had been doing long range program and facilities planning since the early sixties. To strengthen Concordia's financial health going forward, however, we determined that a financial plan should accompany the program blueprints. The first financial blueprint was commissioned by the college's Long-Range Planning Committee. Again, a group of faculty, staff, and students were given the responsibility for leading the process. This committee's work involved a comprehensive analysis related to enrollment trends and demographics, regional economic trends, federal and state funding policies, facility needs and plans, and compensation goals. While the resulting document was not a best seller, it became a valuable resource to the college in terms of short-term budget planning, fund raising needs and goals, and coming challenges and opportunities for the college. This document's value is indicated by the fact that this planning activity was repeated in the eighties and nineties.

The third strategy involved a series of steps designed to strengthen Concordia's current budget and related practices. Part of the strategy had to do with setting goals and part had to do with identifying and implementing new budget disciplines. Chief business officer Donald Helland took the lead in building this strategy. First, we determined that, over time, we wanted to develop a reserve equal to ten percent of the operating budget. Consequently, we began budgeting an annual contribution to reserves, a process that continued throughout my years as president. Second, budget leaders determined that we would build annual budgets assuming seventy-five students fewer than expected. Again, this strategy was implemented over time, which turned out to be a short time because our enrollment was growing rapidly. The result of these steps was a strengthening of Concordia's current budget, balance sheet, creditworthiness, ability to adjust to short-term surprises, and sense of well-being. For example, the need for short-term borrowing during the summer months disappeared. In addition, by budgeting below enrollment, we often had resources at year-end to address extraordinary building maintenance and improvement needs. This approach to financial planning was a pacesetting set of strategies in higher education, and these strategies were the key to the growing financial strength of the college in the eighties and nineties.

The fourth strategy emerged in the late eighties as financial leaders at Concordia arranged financing for the construction of a new science building. Although the cost of the facility was to be funded through pledges, we wanted to initiate the project before those pledges were paid. This led us to borrow money through the Minnesota Higher Education Facility Authority, a state agency created to provide tax exempt bonds for projects like ours. The bonding agreement required that the college establish a sinking fund into which the pledges would flow and from which the bond payments would be made. It turned out that the interest we paid on the bonds was significantly less than the interest we earned on the fund. The result was that Concordia developed what was, in effect, an investment vehicle that would assist in funding future capital projects.

A NEW DAY IN FUNDRAISING

When the C400 Club was formed, this approach to financially supporting the college was unique. Consider how the C400 Club responded to key facility needs of the college in the fifties, sixties, and seventies: The first project, construction of the Ylvisaker Library, had a goal of $400,000. Subsequent projects provided funding for Lorentzsen Hall, the expansion of the library, Comstock Theater, and the renovation of Old Main and Grose Hall. Club members also contributed to the construction of the Christiansen Stadium and various Language Village projects. The C400 Club was both a fundraiser and a friend-raiser effort, with its frequent monthly meetings that featured well-known speakers and entertainers. Consider this array of speakers at various C400 events: Tom Brokaw, Carl Bernstein, Bud Grant, Art Linkletter, Victor Borge, Carl Sagan, John Wooden, Arthur Godfrey, Tom Netherton, Ed Bradley, Jack Anderson, Abba Eban, Nobel Laureate Norman Borlaug, and more. In short, the C400 Club created a lot of buzz and was an effective strategic marketing tool as well.

In addition to the funds raised by C400 members, the college received funds from the church, from alumni through the annual fund, from a share of funds contributed to the Minnesota Private College Fund contributed by corporations, and from funds provided by the federal government and designated for financial aid. Funding totals in the decade of the seventies were as follows:

Fiscal Year	Funding (in Millions)
1971-72	$1.83
1972-73	$2.33
1973-74	$2.10
1974-75	$1.75
1975-76	$2.27
1976-77	$2.74
1977-78	$3.02
1978-79	$3.02
1979-80	$4.32

Concordia's fundraising practices were effective in that we were meeting capital expenditure needs, drawing substantial federal and some state funds for financial aid, and raising adequate funds for general operating costs. In the late seventies, however, two realities indicated the need to step up fundraising activities. First, Concordia needed an additional science facility to accommodate the biology and home economics programs, which eventually would be named the Jones Science Center, with an estimated cost about five million dollars, a figure well more than any C400 project in the past. Second, the federal grants, which had been the source of most of the funding required for capital projects in the fifties, sixties, and early seventies, were no longer available. While we had been good at raising one-thousand-dollar level C400 gifts, and we would continue to need them, it was clear that we would need many larger gifts if we were to meet Concordia's needs going forward. Added to our need for significant growth in gifts for construction projects was the reality that Concordia's two-million-dollar endowment did not provide much financial security.

The pressure to expand major fundraising practices led to some intensive study and planning in 1975-76. We did a close analysis of Concordia's needs and hired a consultant to assist in determining the college's fundraising potential. The analysis results were mixed. People had confidence in the college and would do what they could, but few were capable of the large gifts that would be needed. It was clear that major work had to be done. We concluded we needed to develop a three- to five-year comprehensive campaign. The centerpiece of this effort would be the science hall. In addition, we identified goals for both annual operating needs and endowment. The goal of the campaign was $10,750,000. To work toward this goal, financial leadership established planning and study committees, we envisioned a campaign among the congregations of our area, and we identified volunteer leadership. Next, we enlisted the C400 Club to sign-on support for the campaign, with a goal of two thousand new memberships. The C400 Club had been the backbone of Concordia's fundraising for the previous two decades and would be again.

Strategic financial leaders felt the approach was a good plan, the first such comprehensive campaign in fifty years. But would it work? Our consultant was guarded. I recall the board meeting in Frida Nilsen Lounge, December 1977, when the Board of Regents was considering the campaign. James Krause, Investment and Development Committee chair, was tapping on the shoulder people who had not yet pledged, inviting them to the outer lobby for a private conversation. Soon, everyone was signed on. The normal prerequisite for the public announcement of a campaign was having fifty percent of the goal pledged, and it was clear that was not going to happen. In most major fundraising cases, board members provide substantial lead gifts, but Concordia's board was not built for this. While every one of twenty-seven board members had made a pledge to the campaign, which was a positive step, the total commitment at the beginning of the campaign was only $111,000. I was asked how I felt about other college boards of directors contributing more substantially at the early pledging stage of a major fundraising campaign, to which I responded by saying that people had to do what was going to work for them without regard to the experience or capacity of other boards. At my recommendation, the Board of Regents authorized the campaign. It was like taking off (not landing) on a wing and a prayer (actually, many of them). By February 1978 when the campaign was announced, we had pledges of only $250,000, so we said very little about the specific amount that already had been raised and simply proceeded with a great deal of faith in the effort.

In a pivotal step, a faculty and staff committee invited their colleagues to sign-on and well over ninety-five percent did so. I felt good about this level of support from faculty and staff, so pushed forward with cautious optimism. Campaign leadership organized campaigns in seventy-five communities that had concentrations of alumni, family, and friends. Howard Osborn, a faculty member in the Biology Department, took leave from his teaching duties to lead several of these area campaigns. Howard was full of energy and very effective in telling the story. The congregational phase of the campaign included presentations by Concordia faculty and staff members in ninety-six congregations. The progress of the campaign is reflected in the following data:

Progress	Total (in Millions)
Winter 1978	$3.7
Spring 1979	$5.1
Summer 1979	$6.9
Fall 1979	$7.5
Spring 1980	$9.0
Spring 1981	$10.3
Summer 1981	$12.1

A total of 7,761 people contributed to the campaign. By the end of the campaign, board members had contributed $247,000; faculty and staff $255,000; area corporations $1,400,000; foundations $1,100,000; and the church $785,000. In addition, we received state and federal funds for financial aid more than $1,100,000. There were no gifts of one million dollars or more, one gift in the $750,000 range, and twelve in the $300,000 range. In addition to fully funding the science project and meeting current budget needs, the campaign led to the doubling of Concordia's endowment, from two million to four million dollars, which some might think was not much, but it was a start.

Announcing a major campaign with so little up front and no history with an effort at this scale was high risk. We learned a lot, and our constituents learned a lot. At the end of the day, we had a celebration for not only meeting but exceeding the campaign goal. More than that, however, I believe Concordia established the confidence and momentum for what would be a series of successful campaigns in the future.

MINORITY CONCERNS

Amidst fundraising and campaigns in the seventies, other concerns equally held my attention. In my first year as president, 1975-76, we had a substantial number of minority students on campus and a record number of Black students at fifty-one. In early April of that year, two of our Black students were suspended for disciplinary reasons. Although this was the spark for a protest that came to be called "the Black student strike" at Concordia, there were several broader issues of concern to Black students across the country at this time. Black student protests on college campuses were a common occurrence, dating from the mid-sixties, and the agendas varied from campus to campus. In the case of Concordia, among the topics at issue were that students didn't think Concordia was making adequate progress with hiring faculty of color, and they were hoping for a stronger minority studies program. In addition, they thought the counseling functions needed to be strengthened on campus, and they were critical of some of the athletic coaches. Also on this list of concerns, the Black students believed *The Concordian* was not providing sufficient coverage of their activities, and they wanted to see better efforts in new student orientation, especially for students of color. In total, the students raised seventeen points of concern. These were grievances over largely familiar matters that we were addressing, but not always with the success we would have liked, for example, the hiring of minority faculty to the degree that would meet the expectations of our African American students.

In April of 1975, the Black students at Concordia initiated a strike to negotiate their demands for change. The student organizers of the strike received counsel from professional organizers from the Twin Cities. The strike generally entailed boycotting classes and holding occasional peaceful demonstrations. The protesting students also held daily news conferences in the early days of the strike that led to extensive coverage both regionally and nationally. Fortunately, Concordia had established the Student Rights and Responsibilities policy in the early seventies that included provisions that framed our response to the strike. While we could not comment about the student disciplinary matters that were in the background, within hours of the strike, we assured striking students that we would meet with them to discuss their grievances.

The campus was very uneasy about the Black student action. A team of staff members including Associate Pastor Ernie Mancini, my assistant Loren Anderson, director of Intercultural Affairs Gloria Hawkins, and Associate Director Dominick Sillitti met with students in each dormitory. These meetings were strategic in clarifying the issues and maintaining a sense of calm. We administrators were cautious in our actions and comments, and the student leaders were too. I presented a homily titled "The Reconciling Community" at a chapel service that week. In the homily, I addressed sins that divide communities and the spiritual and community resources to address them. I also offered my assurance that the college would preserve its practices. I concluded in these words:

> I shall preside over a community that honors its processes and, at the same time, is open to changing and improving itself when necessary. We shall not make decisions in this community by headlines or press conferences, by intimidation or coercion. No, we shall make them in the established context—where brothers and sisters in Christ reason together, respecting one another's human needs and our common need for reconciliation. And we shall do this within the certainty that this college's mission is unchanging.

Within a few days, the local media quit covering the daily news conferences; in fact, some media said they thought they were being used. Some of the striking students realized that their activities were costing them academically because the Faculty Senate had made it clear that all assigned work would need to be completed, strike or no strike. In addition, at a meeting of the executive committee of the Board of Regents early in the week, Chair Carrol Malvey and the other members made it clear that I had their full support.

For help in resolving matters, I turned to Richard Green, formerly a faculty member and now a Board of Regents member. Many students had known and worked with Richard when he was our director of intercultural relations, so he had high credibility. Richard led a series of conversations, and following a community-wide meeting on a Sunday afternoon a week into the strike, Black students resolved that they would return to class. Later, I distributed a summary of follow-up actions related to each of the seventeen issues raised by the students. In the introduction to the communiqué, I wrote:

> We have the internal resources to deal with the concerns which have been expressed by our Black students. As the following report indicates, the college has addressed, or is in the process of considering, most of the concerns raised by our students this past Monday. We are willing to discuss these topics and responses with all members of the Concordia community.

Not surprisingly, there were repercussions to the strike, both on campus and in the community. Some of the other students were critical of the Black students and felt the college had done more than enough to support them. Various constituents wondered if we were holding a firm enough line. The president of the ALC, David Preus, made comments to the press that were not helpful. As a result of these and other post-strike tensions, I spent some time putting out fires and reassuring loyal friends of the college. I made it clear that, on the one hand, we would not be intimidated by protesting students, but on the other, that the minority student initiative was an essential element of Concordia's mission.

In the years following the Black student strike, Concordia experienced continuing fallout. Black students tracked progress on the issues they had raised and were generally dissatisfied, particularly with respect to the lack of a freestanding minority studies program, the slow progress in hiring minority faculty and staff, and the racial homogeneity of the Fargo-Moorhead community. While Concordia's situation was not unlike other campuses, the strike had framed a set of critical attitudes that were difficult to address, much less overcome.

The college community made prodigious efforts to address myriad human relations issues. There were Human Relations Days, sometimes involving the dismissal of all classes so that we could reconvene around various topics and issues of importance. For the purpose of expanding knowledge and understanding, a who's who of civil rights and African American scholars continued to be featured during the observance on campus of Black History Month and Native American Month. Campus guests included comedian Dick Gregory, theologian Miles Jones from Virginia Union University, sociologist Robert Staples of the University of San Francisco, American Baptist Church leader Barry Hopkins, U.S. Representative Walter Fonteroy, and Native American Phillip White Hawk. In addition, U.S. Representative Shirley Chisholm, correspondent Ed Bradley, and baseball star Hank Aaron were featured at C400 events. We took steps to engage the broader campus community in a range of disciplines, conversations, and perspectives to help expand understanding of human and civil rights.

The decline in the enrollment of Black students was noted by both majority and minority students, and, like colleagues at similar schools, the enrollment staff was stymied in efforts to turn the numbers. Black students with few congenial educational opportunities in their home environments in the sixties and early seventies now had attractive regional options, options that included colleges with a significant enrollment of minority students. Chicago, St. Louis, Milwaukee, and the area in and around the District of Columbia had been important sources of minority student enrollment for Concordia in the late sixties and early seventies, but from the mid-seventies, those numbers declined. In December 1978, the president of the minority student organization, Harambee Weuse, wrote an article in *The Concordian* bemoaning the declining minority enrollment, the lack of Blacks in the immediate community beyond the campus, and the pressure on Black students to represent the "Black point of view." Campus leadership could sympathize with the writer's concern. In the fall of 1979, Harambee Weuse requested funds from the Student Senate for their annual program of activities to include minority speakers. Their request was denied. A Black student, Eric Grey, wrote a hard-hitting letter to the editor of *The Concordian*, complaining about this decision. He noted the decline in the number of Black students and implied that student government disapproved of the attitude of Black students and their presentation to the Student Senate. This led to a spirited response from the Student Association vice president, Robin Larson. Among other points, Larson wrote, "To say that Concordia College doesn't try or that it is the core of the problem is an inaccurate, immature, and thoughtless response."

This was a hard and sad time for those of us who had invested our hearts and minds in the minority student program. As a measure of the college's ongoing commitment, staff and program resources continued to support the Intercultural Affairs program. Excellent leadership was provided, first by Richard Green in the sixties and early seventies, and, subsequently, by Gloria Hawkins, Spencer Roberts, and Walt McDuffy. Despite concerted efforts, Concordia could not reverse the enrollment decline.

In retrospect, I believe that the myriad approaches put forth during this challenging time for Concordia were absolutely the right things to do. The students, the awareness-raising initiatives, the exchange programs, and other efforts to support civil and human rights on campus and to attend to the needs of *all* students shaped the college in ways that were constructive. Upon reflection, to be sure, we were naïve in thinking we could create a sustainable critical mass of Black students. We were also naïve in seeming to promise too much. Ours was a somewhat misguided idealism. We should have been more realistic with ourselves and more forthright with our minority students by promising them opportunity and support, while at the same time, pointing out that Concordia could not overcome the handicaps of our location.

By the 2000s, diversity was becoming more of a regional reality due to increasing social mobility and the immigration of many refugees and foreign nationals. That yielded the new challenge of successfully integrating and serving these new citizens on the Concordia campus. Hopefully, the lessons of the seventies and eighties will prove helpful.

IN RETROSPECT

I believe the student strike of 1976 should be seen as a coming-of-age experience for the college and the Black students. For the college, there was a new awareness of both our capacities and limitations in responding to social and cultural change. For the students, there was a new self-awareness as individuals and as African Americans. Their expression of opinion and demand for action were, in that sense, signs of growing maturity and an assumption of responsibility—values we affirm as a college. Was it a bumpy ride for them? Yes, and for the college, too, but in the trajectory of history, this was a seminal time for all. In the years that followed their graduation, many of the students involved in the strike became very involved in the life of the college as volunteers, members of the Board of Regents, and Alumni Board, assuming leadership roles in several instances. Clearly, their continuing engagement in the life of the college reflects their support for and commitment to Concordia.

As this reflection is written decades later, the persistence and increasingly flagrant practices of racism are sobering. Understanding and acknowledging the long-term, multi-generational impact of racism leads to a new humility about the white population's position of privilege, the institution's good intentions, and our strategies for positive change.

CHANGING CAMPUS CLIMATE

As with any major institution, especially one whose work centered on a majority of individuals who were 18-22 years-old, the Concordia campus climate shifted over time. The protest years of the sixties and seventies had produced an underlying atmosphere of unease. It is difficult to put student morale in perspective because of the exaggerated influence of leaders, advocates, and critics. To read *The Concordian* in the period from 1975-78, one would think that students were unhappy, frustrated, and oriented around issues related to *in loco parentis*. Editorials, columns, and news articles conveyed this impression, and it was a reality to which college leaders like Dean Morrie Lanning and I had to relate. A succession of *The Concordian* editors and columnists seemed to try to outdo each other in their critiques of the college. In the closing years of the seventies, however, there was an evolution in campus climate. Several factors contributed to the change. First, the intensity of the national collegiate protest movement gave way to some combination of achievement, fatigue, and reality. That is, many of the goals of the broader student movement were achieved, including changes in governance to include students and the relaxation of *in loco parentis*. The emerging generation was refocusing on the more traditional academic goals of building a solid record and finding employment in a competitive economy or placement in high-quality graduate and professional programs. These national trends were reflected at Concordia as well.

Another set of factors leading to change in the Concordia campus climate was local in origin. In the fall of 1975, we celebrated the opening of the Centrum and the addition of a second campus pastor, Reverend Ernest Mancini. These two changes had a profound effect on campus ministry and campus climate. The Centrum provided a flexible and congenial worship space and quickly became the center of campus life. Ernie Mancini's outgoing personality was the perfect complement to Carl Lee's reflective approach. Attendance was strong at daily chapel and the Wednesday evening communion service, a new addition to the worship schedule. The communion services were usually informal and celebrative, and often attracted more than a thousand students, with standing room only. I attended communion services frequently and always came away energized and thankful. In addition to worship, campus ministry provided rich and varied opportunities for study and service, including the continuing strength of the Christian Outreach Program. All these events and activities led to a deeper sense of community on the Concordia campus.

Among my many other commitments to Concordia, my letter of call to the presidency included responsibility as the spiritual leader of the college. While I understood that to be an oversight responsibility, I took seriously my personal role, but I wasn't alone in this effort. Campus pastors Carl Lee, Ernie Mancini, and I formed strong bonds, which helped create an atmosphere of trust in our spiritual leadership. Among the many ways I played a direct role in the spiritual life of the college were that I opened meetings of the faculty, the Faculty Senate, and the Administrative Council with reflection and prayer. In addition to preaching off-campus as part of Concordia's outreach, I also spoke in campus chapel about once each month and occasionally at the Wednesday night communion service, opportunities I enjoyed. I usually presented the opening convocation address, which included reflection on the religious character of the college's mission. With only a few exceptions, I annually preached at homecoming services. The campus pastors reported to me, and we met weekly to discuss the needs of the campus, specifically, the spiritual dimension. There also was ongoing communication with the board regarding such matters, since the campus pastors met regularly with the board's Committee on Student Life. Carl and Ernie were attuned to the student pulse on campus, and their input was valuable to me. While my role in campus ministry was subordinate to theirs, my part in spiritual reflection and development at Concordia was one of the most satisfying and challenging dimensions of my calling as president.

Another factor in the changing climate was the contribution of several campus leaders and opportunities for regular, ongoing conversations among students, faculty, and others. For example, Dean Lanning and I were always in dialogue with student leaders, and we avoided being defensive in these conversations to keep the lines of communication open. By the mid-seventies, the College Council, the Student Affairs Committee, the student/faculty retreats, and the summer internship program were well-established institutions and provided venues for frequent conversation on a range of issues. Students knew they were respected and that their opinions were taken seriously. Indeed, the extensive participation of students in the governance of the college set Concordia apart.

In addition to providing opportunities for open, ongoing conversation on campus, there were lighter sides to my engagement with students as well. Beginning in 1978, Morrie and I did a skit each year at the opening gathering of new students in the fall. Our skit usually was built around a currently popular movie or song. The first skit featured us as The Blues Brothers and was a great success. On other occasions, Morrie and I impersonated Rambo and Crocodile Dundee, Wayne from *Wayne's World*, Batman and Joker, and more. While some on the faculty may have been unhappy with such frivolity, the students loved it. Somehow, such opportunities established a rapport and set the stage for good relationships with students by demonstrating that we did not take ourselves too seriously and were ready to have fun, even at our own expense.

Once into the academic year, both Morrie and I were regularly out and about with students. For example, on most Wednesday nights, I would stop at the offices of *The Concordian* for their weekly pizza event. The next week's newspaper might take a shot at me, but at least they knew I was a human being. There also were student dinners, carnivals, and fundraisers of various kinds that also provided opportunities for direct engagement with the students. In fact, I recall getting "pied" at the annual dance marathon. In addition, I followed athletic teams and attended concerts and theater productions, often with Mardy as her schedule allowed. I enjoyed all these activities, and students enjoyed my presence at them, so beneath the sometimes-critical rhetoric of some student voices, there was an underlying rapport.

The late seventies saw a noticeable shift in the attitudes of student leaders, a noticeable change from the wary unease that often-reflected students' attitudes in more turbulent times. I recall the shift to constructive and well-reasoned editorials of *The Concordian* editors Brad Edin and Mary Ann Waalen; columnists Dan Hofrenning, Brent Reichert, Peter Thrane, and Anne Keir; and Student Association Presidents Hemchand Gossai and Dan Hofrenning. During Gossai's term, there were adjustments in the dorm visitation hours because of a series of conversations involving student and administrative leaders. As Hofrenning completed his term of office in 1980, he wrote, "...thank you to administrators and faculty who, although not agreeing on every issue, always kept the lines of communication open." In short, we treated each other with respect and genuinely enjoyed and trusted each other.

Let me add that it was not the case that students were no longer interested in issues like intervisitation; rather, it was that they had their eye on other issues as well. For example, in the fall of 1979, as part of a national focus on energy conservation, the Student Association organized a "no gas to class" day, urging students, faculty, and staff to walk or use bicycles instead of cars. The event started with a parade from downtown Moorhead to the campus. I participated by riding the bicycle I had received as a ten-year-old, big balloon tires and all. My bicycle became the central attraction of the day. In fact, at the communion service that evening, the Clipper, as my bike was called, was suspended from the balcony and, subsequently, placed in "protective custody" until I would ride it around the football field after we scored our first touchdown at the homecoming game, a tradition initiated in 1976 when Pastor Ernie Mancini, dressed in Viking costume, would chase me around the field. In this and other ways, it was evident that students and administrative leaders enjoyed each other.

THE RHYTHM OF TIME

As I reflect on my long tenure as president at Concordia, I see a natural rhythm of time, that is, an ebb and flow to the interests, issues, concerns, and highs and lows over the years, whether related to education, politics, global relationships, athletics, celebrations, the arts, or other matters. This was true for Concordia as the decade of the seventies ended for our campus. There was a natural rhythm to how we were engaged with the world and each other.

The late seventies continued to bring national guests to the college. For example, the national convention of the American Lutheran Church in 1978 brought nearly one thousand delegates to the Concordia campus from all over the country. This gathering was a great chance to feature Lutheran higher education and Concordia College. Students were also interested in national issues beyond energy conservation, and as the presidential campaign of 1980 warmed up, the campus hosted candidates John Connolly and George H. W. Bush. These events were well-attended and created a buzz on campus.

Global relationships continued to be important to Concordia. The college's Norwegian heritage had been celebrated in 1975 in connection with the Sesquicentennial of Norwegian immigration. There were additional campus celebrations with the Concordia choir's tour of Norway in 1978 and the royal visit of Crown Princess Sonia in the fall of that year. During the Concordia choir's time in Norway, the group participated in the dedicatory concert of the Grieg Concert Hall in Bergen, an event attended by the prime minister and the royal family. Mardy and I spent several days with the choir on its tour, and also had opportunity to meet King Olav V. These experiences increased my awareness of the richness of the relationship between Concordia and Norway, the importance of international exchanges, and the prominent role of the royal family in Norway and the United States. Let me add a brief word about royal protocol. When the Concordia choir performed with royalty in attendance, the college was technically the host, even when the concert took place in Norway. Accordingly, I met the king at the entrance to the concert hall and accompanied him to his seat. His aide accompanied us, walking a step or two behind. At intermission, King Olav and I retired to a reception room for conversation and refreshments, usually champagne (with or without alcohol content, I did not inquire) and cookies. Following the intermission, we returned to our seats, and at the end of the concert, I would accompany the king to his waiting car and bid him farewell. Visiting with King Olav was pleasant. He was royal without being formal, and the conversation was about ordinary matters such as the number of singers, the tour schedule, the state of the college as well as our families.

As far as athletics in the late seventies, Concordia seemed to be on the rise. In the fall of 1978, the Concordia football team started surprising people. The team had a habit of allowing the opposing team to score first, but then pulling off a number of come-from-behind wins. The offense emphasized the running game, and the defensive secondary always seemed to outsmart pass-oriented teams. The 1978 team won the national NAIA championship, which hadn't happened since 1964, so this was certainly a high for Concordia football. I attended each of the playoff games and experienced the agony and ecstasy of that remarkable season. In basketball, the coaching baton was passed from long-time head coach Sonny Gulsvig to John Eidsness. Sonny was a revered figure on campus and in the community, and he continued his duties as assistant coach in both football and baseball.

In athletics, as in life, there are highs and lows. My most disquieting experience in athletics occurred in the winter of 1979 when our men's hockey team was competing for the conference championship. The championship was decided in the final two games of the year with Augsburg College. Augsburg won the first game, and Concordia seemed to come unglued when the team fell behind in the second game. In the process, two of our top players and our head coach were kicked out of the game. The following Sunday, we received word that, even though the team had lost the conference championship to Augsburg, the hockey team was invited to participate in the national tournament. In the meantime, reports had reached me about the conduct of our team and coach in that Augsburg game. Subsequently, the athletic director Armin Pipho, our faculty representative to the conference, Carlton Paulson, and I agreed that the two players who had been disqualified in the final game, along with their coach, would not be permitted to coach or play in the championship tournament. This was a great blow to the players and coach, but it seemed the only course in upholding institutional standards and values. Concordia's part-time assistant coach took over the team and initiated a whole new game strategy. In the quarterfinal game of the national tournament, Concordia exacted revenge by defeating Augsburg. We also won the semifinal game before losing in the championship round. So, with a somewhat patched together team, we were second in the nation. Who would have imagined it?

The rhythm of time on a college campus is marked by commencements, always a festive occasion, and graduation was always a highlight at Concordia. It was not unusual that over time, several siblings from the same family attended Concordia. For example, during the late seventies, we celebrated two of those families: the Jepsons from Elbow Lake, who had seven children graduate from the college over a period of twenty-two years, and the Knutsons from Great Falls, Montana, who had five graduates. And while baccalaureate and commencement speakers would come and go over time, one of the most memorable years was 1980 when William Lazareth of the Lutheran Theological Seminary in Philadelphia gave the commencement address and one of our own, James Hofrenning, preached at the baccalaureate service. Lazareth, speaking without notes, received a standing ovation at the end of his address. The title of Hofrenning's sermon was "Easter People in a Good Friday World," which gained sufficient acclaim that led to the publication of a book with the same title.

Homecoming at Concordia was always something special as well, a reality observed by President Knutson early in his presidency. Hundreds and even thousands of alumni would return because, in President Knutson's words, "They loved the place." Homecoming was a festive time with reunions of many kinds. In the fall of 1977, alumni of the Concordia choir gathered in observance of the 40th anniversary of Paul J. Christiansen's service as conductor. In addition to the concerts, there was always a lighter side to the observances centering on a Saturday evening show that featured both serious music by the Concordia Band and entertainment provided by students, faculty, and staff. I was a frequent participant in the frivolity of that event. The centerpiece of homecoming was the worship service on Sunday morning, an event that centered all generations of Cobbers in the promises and calling that brought the college into existence. Perhaps the evolution of student attitudes noted earlier was best illustrated in the fall of 1978 when three students—Phil Hatlie, Sue Schmidt, and John

Snustad—asked and received permission to repaint the dome of Old Main, saying, "We did it in the spirit of homecoming for the alumni."

The rhythm of time was also marked by artistic works added to campus in the late seventies. In the same year as the newly painted dome of Old Main, two new pieces of sculpture were added to the campus, one in the library by artist Paul Granlund and named *The Founders*, offering a beautiful and powerful expression of Concordia's founders, and another sculpture between Old Main and Academy Hall by Raymond Jacobson and named *The Arvegods*. Both were funded by a substantial gift from the estate of Cobber Clarence H. (Chris) Berg. On the base of *The Arvegods* are printed these words from Ephesians 2:19-20: "So then you are no longer strangers and sojourners, but you are fellow citizens with the saints and members of the household of God, built upon the foundation of the apostles and prophets, Christ Jesus himself being the chief cornerstone." As artist Raymond Jacobson described this work, "These two figures...have a bearing of grace and nobility buttressed by self-confidence and commitment. These forms project a straightforward simplicity and direction of purpose." I was moved by the sculpture and the inscription, and the piece provided text for many subsequent messages. The statement from Ephesians, in my mind, gets it just right—for the college and for me.

6. The Golden Years: 1980-1990

In the summer of 1977, work was completed on A *Financial Blueprint for Concordia College*. This analysis of trends and identification of financial needs and strategies would be helpful in the eighties. The college and higher education were operating in uncertain times in the face of double-digit inflation, uneven enrollment, and predictions of increasing difficulties in the eighties. Yet, in 1977, the lead paragraph in the closing section of A *Financial Blueprint* reads as follows:

> Concordia College is, in many ways, approaching 'the golden years.' The college's mission is clear and relevant, the academic program is vigorous and promises to remain so, the faculty is strong and loyal, students indicate considerable satisfaction with their experiences at Concordia, and the constituency of the college is maturing and growing in numbers. These factors must inform our attitudes and shore our confidence as we plan for the 1980s. In light of the pessimistic forecasts for higher education, it is important to be cognizant of the college's strengths.

There was a clear sense that Concordia was on the brink of an exciting and productive decade. New administrative leadership was now well in place. We were young, all of us in our thirties and forties, but with the benefit of good mentors, we were ready to go! To complement the leadership team, the Board of Regents was solid as well. The planning process was well-oiled, and, most importantly, Concordia had strong faculty talent ready to move the academic program to new heights. To accomplish such curricular goals, I recall the veteran faculty who were near the zenith of their careers and other future leaders still relatively new on the scene. These people worked well together, respected each other, and had confidence in the institution—a veritable powerhouse. Given this abundance of talent, a vision for the future, and unexpectedly good conditions in the environment, the eighties did indeed turn out to be golden.

PLANNING REDUX

Continuing the tradition of *Blueprint* I in the sixties and *Blueprint* II for the seventies, in 1981 the Board of Regents commissioned the preparation of *Blueprint III* for the eighties. The study process that would shape the report featured a year-long series of lectures, papers, and discussions. The study process was organized around four topics:

- The Nature of the Future
- Dimensions of Institutional Mission: The Nature of the Church College
- Dimensions of the Educational Program: The Nature of the Liberal Arts
- Dimensions of the Community: The Nature of Life in the Academy

Loren Anderson, vice president for Development, provided overall project direction, and four study commissions were formed to give direction to each of the study areas. A grant from the Northwest Area Foundation supported the study and publication expenses.

The study process was both extensive and intensive. To that end, members of the faculty prepared papers, nationally recognized scholars and practitioners addressed the community, and campus leaders organized between 8-10 campus-wide forums committed to each subject. Each commission then prepared a summary and a set of recommendations that were eventually integrated into a draft report that was presented to the community for further input before the final report was submitted to the Board of Regents. The undertaking to address each study area and the eventual report was a monumental task involving faculty, administrative staff, and students. The quality of the papers prepared by Concordia community members was (and remains) impressive.

In the foreword to the published study *Blueprint III*, I remarked, "We are not merely to be a good college but the best college that we can be, the best students and faculty that we can be. Thereby, we will be able to serve and glorify God on this campus and in the world beyond it." This statement summarized the missional/theological underpinnings of *Blueprint III* and the college. The document identified several specific recommendations that shaped our trajectory in the eighties, including the following:

- Foster self-knowledge and knowledge of our tradition and mission

- Strive for global and technological literacy
- Look for ways to expand our clientele by serving adults, both mid-career and retired
- Undertake a review of the Core Curriculum
- Enrich and diversify faculty development activities
- Enrich religious life by reflecting on the role of worship and the process of religious formation
- Emphasize lifelong learning

In a closing section, the study also identified more practical tasks ahead, including the following:

- Complete major capital projects: renovation of Fjelstad Hall, a new art facility, expansions to the Concordia Language Villages near Bemidji
- Implement subsidiary capital projects, including those related to energy conservation, the outdoor track, and completion of stage rigging in the Comstock Theater
- Increase gifts to the endowment
- Increase gifts to the annual fund
- Maintain an enrollment of 2,400

All of these recommendations would be pursued in one fashion or another, providing the college with a forward-looking agenda for the eighties.

The practical tasks were important, but the heart of *Blueprint III* included the lead recommendations noted above that focused on curricular matters. It had been just over a decade since the monumental changes of *Curriculum Reform* had been implemented, and it was time to revisit and, where indicated, make amendments and improvements on those changes. To support and carry out *Blueprint III*, this curricular reform effort was titled *An Agenda for Concordia's Academic Life: A Curriculum Plan for Concordia College*. In keeping with effective planning traditions of the college, this year-long effort was inclusive and thorough. The study led to several changes:

- The goals for academic life were made more explicit
- The foreign language requirement was reinstituted
- A common first-year student introduction of the liberal arts, Principia, was implemented

- Writing across the curriculum strategies were introduced
- Issues related to ethnic, global, and women's issues were to be integrated in course work across the curriculum

In addition to the work itself, the major planning activities undertaken in the creation of *Blueprint III* and *An Agenda* strengthened community. There was strong and willing participation on the part of the Concordia community in these endeavors. The in-depth planning process had another benefit in that people new to the faculty had an opportunity to participate in significant conversations, providing engagement across disciplines.

Decision-making in curricular matters was still largely a function of respected faculty elders' leadership. When this group rallied around a proposal, it was fairly certain to be approved. As both dean and president, I stayed in contact with these leaders, looking to them for wisdom and counsel on a variety of matters. On the other hand, in meetings of the faculty and Faculty Senate, I rarely took a public position on pending business in keeping with the tradition that the president was to be seen but not heard. I recall one exception to this rule during the discussion of the recommendations of *An Agenda for Concordia's Academic Life*. The discussion had become stalled in the Faculty Senate, and a member of the commission authoring the study stopped by my office and urged me to give an endorsement to the recommendations at the next senate meeting. I thought a long time about her suggestion, so I also conferred with Dean Gring and decided to make a statement in which I commended the faculty for the time and seriousness with which they had considered the report. I went on to say that I thought it was time to act and that these proposals were reasonable and would have a salutary effect. I did not get any negative feedback about my testimony, and the proposals were adopted by a vote of 43 to 6, as I recall, at the next Faculty Senate meeting.

THE ACADEMIC AGENDA: QUALITY AND NEW PROGRAMS

The eighties were brimming with projects and programs of innovation and enrichment. Under the leadership of Dean David Gring, the introduction of a nursing program through Tri-College University was a major strategic move. Since the sciences were one of Concordia's core areas of academic strength, the addition of a baccalaureate program in nursing was a natural. Through this program, we attracted good students and a whole new group of strong faculty. Under the continuing leadership of Dean Gring and Department Chair Lois Nelson, the nursing program grew, prospered, and quickly gained national accreditation. Our Tri-College partner in this venture was North Dakota State University, so nursing students completed some of their coursework on each campus. The program eventually led to two separate departments, one at each institution, but the consortium was an excellent launching pad.

As readers will note in each of the initiatives covered in this section, there were several key players in this era, but none more important than our dean, David Gring. He was bright, deliberate, and patient. Dean Gring also had a clear sense of what quality looked like, and he was congenial in his relationships with faculty and staff colleagues. I enjoyed the work we did together, from brainstorming about future strategies to figuring out ways and means. In addition, Mardy and I enjoyed the friendship of Dave and his wife Susan. When the Grings left for David to assume the presidency at Roanoke College, their son Chris lived with us during his senior year in high school. Our friendship endures.

But back to the work on the academic agenda: In the mid-seventies, Concordia initiated a comprehensive program of institutional research under the leadership of Walther Prausnitz, the director of Liberal Arts Studies. This research activity included the periodic completion of something called the Institutional Goals Inventory, a survey instrument created by the Educational Testing Service. This survey was completed by all members of the faculty and staff plus a sample of students. The survey indicated a growing commitment of the faculty and staff in the direction of higher academic standards, self-directed learning, lifelong learning, and intellectual growth. We also surveyed seniors in their final year and a retrospective survey four years after graduation. These surveys provided excellent data by which to assess student learning and student attitudes toward their college experience. Walt Prausnitz clearly loved this work; he was the glue that held the Core Curriculum together. His regular over-dinner interview chats with faculty members were good for both the curriculum and the faculty culture.

Another initiative was *Teaching at Concordia*, a quarterly publication edited by Prausnitz that featured the work of the faculty, the life of the Core Curriculum, and reports on various institutional research activities. I believe the interviews Prausnitz conducted with members of the faculty were one of the most valuable features of the publication. Another focus was faculty research activity. The collective impact of this publication and the activities it featured was a heightened sense of confidence in and commitment to the academic quality of the college.

The agenda for change in the eighties continued in other ways. A cluster of area studies programs was launched in the late seventies and eighties, including programs in East Asian Studies, Women's Studies, and Scandinavian Studies. These were interdisciplinary programs and, in the case of East Asian Studies, involved shared program resources with NDSU and Moorhead State University. The East Asia Studies program gave Concordia students access to language study in both Chinese and Japanese. The Women's Studies program was developed by members of The Women's Center. The program was built carefully over time and enjoyed strong support from the faculty and students. Similarly, the Scandinavian Studies program was also interdisciplinary. Leaders of the program were Verlyn Anderson (History), Joan Buckley (English), Stan Iverson (Classical Studies), and Robert Ronken (Education). Once the program was established, Rune Engebretsen, a recognized scholar, joined the team and directed the program. Through the eighties and nineties, the program hosted several distinguished Norwegian scholars, government officials, and artists. Enrollments were strong in both the Scandinavian Studies major and in Norwegian language courses.

One of the building blocks of the Scandinavian Studies program was an exchange program with a teachers' college in Hamar, Norway. Students and faculty moved between the two institutions to Concordia's considerable benefit. I had the privilege of visiting the Hamar campus on at least three occasions. Another dynamic element of the program was *Updag Amerika*, a program that recruited Norwegian students to study at Concordia. At one point, well over twenty Norwegian students were enrolled, some for only a semester but many for a longer period of time. The vitality of this program was made possible when the Norwegian government decided that students attending Norwegian heritage colleges were eligible for state funding. This funding support program was phased out in the nineties, and with that change came a dramatic reduction in enrollment of Norwegian students at Concordia.

In the 2000s, the fortunes of the Scandinavian Studies program waned for several reasons. Not only did the shift in Norwegian national policy lead to the decline in enrollment of Norwegian students, but also the Hamar exchange lost key leaders in both institutions, and Concordia's longtime leaders Anderson, Buckley, Iverson, and Ronken retired. Somehow the buzz was missing, and despite the best efforts of many, enrollment in Scandinavian Studies declined. While core elements of the program remained in place for another decade, I count it as a leadership failure that we did not create an endowment for the Scandinavian Studies program, a step which would have given some long-term stability to a program that is both a key expression of the institution's heritage and a strategic opportunity for Concordia's future. In addition, there were failures in program leadership to which we did not respond promptly and effectively.

Other initiatives of note that helped bring change to the campus in the golden age of the eighties included the Chicago Urban Seminar led by the Sociology and Social Work Department. Concordia students joined with students from other liberal arts colleges for a semester of living and learning in the heart of Chicago, a life-changing experience for many. In addition, the departments of business and economics, French, Spanish, and German initiated a study abroad program in business that placed Concordia students in international business settings for a semester.

The establishment of the Institute for German Studies was a monumental program innovation in the eighties. Following a pilot summer program in the context of the Concordia Language Villages, grant funding was secured from the National Endowment for Humanities to assist in the formation of this program. Leadership came from Elwin Rogers from the German Department and Al Traaseth and Odell Bjerkness from the Language Villages program. The program was built on the immersion pedagogy of the Language Villages and was located in Waldsee, the German Language Village near Bemidji, Minnesota. The students and faculty lived and learned together for a year in this somewhat remote, wooded setting on a lake. The buildings in which they lived and studied, the food they ate, and the recreational and cultural activities in which they engaged all reflected German life and culture. The program was rich with a variety of cultural activities and field trips, and the students gained great language fluency. Students who participated in the program were recruited from liberal arts colleges, but this market turned out to be small because most college German departments did not recommend that their students attend another institution where they would basically earn a major in a year of intensive study. The Institute for German Studies commenced in 1983 with an enrollment of twenty-three students; the program peaked in 1986 with an enrollment of fifty-three students. Most of the students were first-year students, but fewer than half of them returned to Concordia for their second year. Clearly, these students had come only for the year of immersion studies.

Despite excellent work on the part of the faculty and evaluations that documented substantial learning outcomes, the Institute for German Studies never lived up to its enrollment goals. The program was very expensive, and the financial model did not work. In addition, there was faculty/staff burnout, and the effects of the isolation of a campus in the north woods were difficult to overcome. The German Department on the Concordia/Moorhead campus also lost interest in the program, and the faculty and staff of the remote campus were never effectively integrated into the Concordia faculty. The undertaking had been a noble effort, but closing the program in 1995 after a thirteen-year run was a necessary decision.

One of the recommendations of *Blueprint III* was that the college consider expanding educational opportunities to "serve adults, both mid-career and retired, as well as pre-college students." There were two principal responses to this recommendation, both of which commenced shortly after the completion of the *Blueprint*. In 1983, the college offered its first Elderhostel. Elderhostel was a national brand, and institutions across the country could apply for use of the franchise in offering courses for adults over the age of fifty-five. Concordia's first offerings were in 1983, and by 1992, there were ten offerings, six at Maplelag located north of Detroit Lakes, four at the Bemidji Concordia Language Villages, and one on the Moorhead campus. While Concordia offered courses in many subject areas in the early years, by the late eighties and nineties, the course offerings were primarily related to language and culture, drawing on the strength of the Concordia Language Village tradition. Michelle McRae coordinated this program. She was both enthusiastic and level-headed in creating and administering our participation. By the late nineties, however, Elderhostels more or less had disappeared as a national brand and suffered a similar fate at Concordia.

The other major response to the suggestion that Concordia serve new student constituencies was the creation of the ACCORD program (Adults Continuing at Concordia) in 1984. This was an effort to enroll and support adult students who might have dropped out of college at an earlier age or who had never had an opportunity to begin college. The original strategy was to offer classes in the late afternoon and evenings for people who were employed and could not attend college full-time. Michelle McRae, the coordinator of continuing education, was the director of this program as well as the Elderhostels. Again, she proved to be very creative. It was hard to determine an exact count on ACCORD students because some adults simply registered through the normal process and did not avail themselves of the support and financial aid services available through ACCORD. We estimated that we had about seventy-four students enrolled in 1994-95. In addition to the counseling and support services, the ACCORD program provided workshops on topics like career choice and study skills. In addition, there were social events, receptions, and an annual recognition event that honored, among others, the Adult Learner of the Year award.

The Office of Continuing Education sponsored other events and workshops on campus, including an annual conference on health care that attracted health professionals from the region. This office was all but eliminated in the late nineties, however, as Concordia was forced to prioritize its resource needs. In retrospect, I believe Concordia should have expanded and restructured the program, thus capturing a larger share of the emerging market in degree completion programs.

The Concordia Language Villages program was a consistent source of innovation and growth. Consider the following changes from 1971 to 1989:

- The summer enrollment grew from 1,180 in 1972 to 4,263 in 1988 (plus an additional 2,300 in school year programs).
- The number of languages offered increased from 5 to 10.
- The FTE staff grew from 2 to 41.
- The budget grew from $275,000 to $3.6 million.
- New facilities were completed for French, German, and Norwegian and a Finnish Village was in the planning stages.
- Several major gifts were designated for various facility and program improvements.

In short, the Language Villages had an incredible record, and by the late eighties, the CLV was the most widely recognized program of the college, owing to its quality and national constituency. Odell Bjerkness was the creative genius behind this incredible growth, and Al Traaseth was the steady manager. The significance of their leadership accomplishments can hardly be overstated.

Surprising to many, the Language Villages were not a significant source of student enrollment for the college for many reasons. First, the typical villager was between 10-14 years-old and not yet giving serious consideration to selecting a college. Second, the constituency of the villages was very diverse, coming from all across the country and with little first-hand knowledge of Concordia. Finally, few of the staff had any direct tie to Concordia. Over the years, Concordia and the CLV tried many strategies to change this curve but with little success. We also discussed ways in which Concordia might seek greater integration between programs at the Moorhead and Bemidji campuses. There was no shortage of ideas, but there was a scarcity of agents. That is, any given department might imagine a form of collaboration with CLV, but when the time for implementation came around, there were neither available funds nor personnel. To use a figure of speech, there was a lot of romance but few marriages. It was not a natural partnership, and I note this continued to be the case in the next decades.

On the financial side, thanks to Al Traaseth, the program paid its way. In keeping with guidelines established in the early seventies and later amended, the CLV yielded a margin of ten percent over and above expenses, set aside in a reserve for the property's maintenance. In retrospect, the policy should also have provided for an additional transfer to the general college budget for overhead expenses. Fundraising, marketing, oversight, management, and liability expenses incurred by the college were considerable, and an additional transfer would have been reasonable. Many of my presidential colleagues across the country assumed that the CLV was a considerable source of income to the college when, in fact, it was not. Again, in retrospect, the college gave more autonomy to the Language Villages in financial management than was healthy, and doing so led to an assumption of entitlement.

In the eighties, the college continued to experience growth in the number of students majoring in business and economics. This was due in part to declining career opportunities in education and a broader awareness of career options among Concordia students, particularly among women. Our Business and Economics Department was light on management courses except for healthcare, where we had a regional and even national reputation thanks to the genius of Ted Heimarck. In the mid-eighties, two members of the Board of Regents, Mike Barrett and Jim Onstad, began to ask penetrating questions about the quality and offerings in the business management area. One board member had a son studying business at Concordia, and other board members simply had a deep interest in preparing business leaders. Barrett and Onstad urged Dean Gring and me to take a deeper look at the program, and they provided the necessary funds to do so. A member of the faculty and I visited with some faculty members at the school of business at Stanford University. While the visit was stimulating, there were few points of comparison between their program and Concordia's. More fruitful were the campus visits of two consultants who quickly sized-up Concordia's situation and recommended that we make leadership and program changes. This was not an easy message for Dean Gring to deliver to the department; however, most members acquiesced, a few with enthusiasm.

Thereafter, Concordia engaged a consultant to help find a new department chair to develop the business and economics program. That person turned out to be Clifford Harrison, a man with both a Ph.D. in management and extensive experience in the corporate world. He was an amazing choice in that he possessed strong interpersonal skills and a clear vision of where we needed to go. In addition, he had the strong support of Dean Gring and me. Among the innovations that followed were the establishment of a Council of Business Advisors, the Center for Ethical Leadership, and an Executive in Residence program. Some key adjustments were made in the curriculum, and several new appointments were made to the faculty. The result was a program more closely attuned to the business community and a program of more depth and quality. Following Harrison's retirement in the mid-nineties, the department went into a swoon, setting the stage for the next renewal effort in 2005-2007 and leading to the establishment of the Offutt School of Business in 2010.

The renewal of the business and economics program in the eighties was a lesson for me in the appropriate oversight role of the board. While Dean Gring and I had concerns about the program, I doubt that we would have taken such deliberate action without the oversight and encouragement of the Board of Regents. They asked the right questions and held us accountable for the answers without any micromanaging or heavy handedness.

FACULTY MATTERS

Administrative leadership entered the eighties with awareness that we needed to revisit the tenure quota policies that had been in place since the mid-seventies. Under those policies, we established a quantitative framework to determine how many people would be eligible for tenure. This policy was implemented when a high percentage of the faculty was tenured, but in the face of various uncertainties in the marketplace of higher education, we believed we could not risk adding to the tenure cohort. Faculty who were already in place were given an opportunity to remain beyond the tenure eligibility period, assuming they met the criteria, but they did not have the same assurance of continuing employment. This, of course, grated on faculty over time. In addition, the policy limitation hurt departments in recruiting new faculty and made it unlikely that the college would be able to retain some high-quality people.

Dean Gring led the faculty in a thorough review of the tenure quota policy. Through that process, we discovered that in view of predicted retirements and enrollment growth, there would be less stress on the tenure numbers. The result was that Concordia abandoned the quota system while retaining a target ratio of tenured to non-tenured faculty. Faculty in the limbo of tenure eligible but untenured were now granted tenure. One policy stipulation was that tenure ratio targets would be considered in making tenure decisions. That is, a tenure eligible person in a department with a high ratio of tenured faculty might not be tenured, and new appointees were to be apprised of this fact. The effect of these policy changes was salutary, although there would still be pressure when tenure decisions approached for qualified persons in departments with many tenured faculty. In the 1990s and 2000s, the policy would be revisited and revised again.

Another salutary change related to faculty in the eighties was modification in the target student-faculty ratio. In the late seventies, the ratio had been set at 16.5:1. Following the curriculum changes growing out of *An Agenda*, the ratio was adjusted to 15:1. Coupled with steady enrollment growth, this led to additional faculty appointments in the eighties.

With the assistance of the Bush Foundation, in the seventies the college had made excellent progress in expanding opportunities for faculty growth and development. The momentum continued into the golden era of the eighties with several grants and initiatives, including the following:

- A matching grant of $45,000 from the Council for the Advancement of Private Education (CAPHE) to assist faculty in integrating global content across the curriculum
- A $46,450 matching grant from the National Science Foundation for research in cellular biology
- Grants from the Bush Foundation and the National Endowment for the Humanities to assist faculty in implementing writing across the curriculum
- A $194,900 grant from the Bush Foundation to fund research for faculty-student teams, research related to improvements in classroom instruction, and workshops related to expanding the use of technology and in collaborative learning
- A commitment of $100,000 to expand campus technology and computer lab space

In addition, there was a broad array of ongoing summer workshops, a vital sabbatical leaves program, and additional support for attending professional meetings. The campus was figuratively aglow with faculty development opportunities, a testament to the college's growing stature and the effectiveness of leadership from both Dean Gring and the Development staff.

Another key element in strengthening the academic program was the introduction of new assessment activities. As noted earlier, elements of the Core Curriculum were assessed beginning in the early seventies with instruments of the college's own creation. New assessment activities were introduced after the adoption of recommendations from *An Agenda*. Walt Prausnitz took responsibility for implementing this initiative. He worked closely with a campus committee and the Educational Testing Service in selecting instruments that would be most useful in assessing student learning at Concordia. We began this assessment work long before accrediting agencies began requiring evidence of this kind of assessment, and I recall how impressed the accrediting agencies were with the college's work. More important, the assessment data became a valuable tool in refining and strengthening Concordia's curriculum and pedagogy.

ENROLLMENT

In most private colleges, enrollment is always on the agenda since tuition income drives the enterprise. Most schools, including Concordia, saw enrollment bounce around in the sixties and seventies. The eighties and nineties, however, would be different because of generally favorable demographics, although campus leadership took nothing for granted in the fight for market share. As noted earlier, Concordia's Admissions enterprise was on the cutting edge, one of the most successful in the region. Concordia began the eighties with an enrollment of 2,625 and ended the decade with an enrollment of 2,884, a number that would grow to 2,999 in 1993. In each year of the eighties, the college produced the second or third largest enrollment of new students at any private college in the region, a significant accomplishment given the college's location.

Under Jim Hausmann's leadership, the staff, strategies, and programs in Admissions would be strengthened in significant ways in the eighties. Three striking changes were initiated, the first of which involved staff. Concordia diversified, expanded, and strengthened the credentials of our staff. Among other changes, we created the position of director of Admissions to parallel the position of director of Financial Aid. Lee Johnson was appointed as director of Admissions and proceeded to create new systems and disciplines. This gave Jim Hausmann the opportunity to focus on the big picture and to expand his involvement in public policy and institution-wide projects.

A second initiative in the eighties, as noted earlier, was the development of new marketing materials around the theme, The Concordia Equation. The equation was developed after careful research, and the approach emphasized Concordia's goals and values as a college. The Concordia Equation was, in a sense, a sort of contract with our students. A third initiative was the development of a limited number of merit-based scholarships designed to attract students of high ability in academics, the arts, and forensics. There was plenty of competition for these students, and this program helped Concordia get their attention. In addition, we reached out to the congregations of our corporate area through the Cord matching scholarship program, whereby the college would match funds that local congregations provided for their students who chose to attend Concordia. This program had the added benefit of strengthening ties with Concordia's key constituents. A related project was Christian Scholars Day, through which pastors in our service region would identify students who were making significant contributions to their home congregation and showed promise for future leadership roles. Taken together, these initiatives permitted the college to grow its market share in the decade of the eighties.

EXTRACURRICULAR ACTIVITIES

The golden era of the eighties was extraordinary in terms of athletic achievement. Coach Jim Christopherson's Cobber football team dominated the conference for much of the decade, winning the national co-championship in 1981 after tying Austin State of Texas in the championship game. The women's basketball team under the coaching leadership of Mark Langseth dominated the MIAC and won the national AIAW national championship in 1982. The Concordia women's basketball team made the NCAA Tournament in seven straight seasons in the 1980s and was the NCAA national runner-up in 1987. The women's basketball team also won the NCAA Division III championship in 1988 on Concordia's home court with Duane Siverson as coach. Also that year, Cobber Jessica Beachy was named NCAA Division III National Player of the Year. The hockey team under Coach Steve Baumgartner was co-champion of the conference in 1986-87 and went to the NCAA Final Four. Coach John Eidsness' men's basketball team won the conference championship in 1982 for the first time in fifty-two years and repeated the feat in 1983. Coach Finn Grinaker's wrestling team had several student-athletes earn All-American honors, including Malcolm McLeod, a four-time All-American award winner and the national runner-up in 1983. Indeed, Cobber athletics were a powerhouse in the eighties.

The forensics program was likewise a force throughout the decade. Led by Fred Sternhagen, Concordia fielded the strongest forensic teams in the region and was a national player. The zenith was perhaps the 1988-89 season when two teams qualified for the national debate tournament, another team won the National Novice championship, forensic participants earned second place at the national tournament of Pi Kappa Delta, and students earned fifth place in the national individual events tournament

The art, music, and theater programs engaged large numbers of students and earned positive reviews. Under the direction of Rene Clausen, Paul J.

Christiansen, J. Robert Hanson, and Russell Pesola, the choir, orchestra, and band toured in the United States each year and sometimes internationally. The choir had spectacular tours of Norway in the early and late eighties, first under the direction of Paul J. Christiansen and then under the leadership of Rene Clausen. The choirs participated in the Bergen Music festival in Bergen, Norway, on both tours. The 1983 choir participated in the inaugural event in the new Grieg Hall, attended by King Olav V, Crown Prince Harald, and Crown Princess Sonia. Mardy and I accompanied the choirs on these tours as a way of both recognizing and strengthening the strong ties between Norway and Concordia. We had a great time with our choir students, whether sightseeing in Oslo, playing cards on the bus, or attending a royal reception. These are wonderful memories.

Concordia's theater program was focused on the campus community in the 1980s. Jim and Helen Cermak (Speech and Theatre Department) emphasized the education and empowerment of students in all aspects of the program. They worked closely with the English and Music Departments in the selection and production of plays. Students had extensive opportunities to act, direct, produce, and create. The annual musicals brought together the resources of the music and theater programs and were performed to sold-out houses.

CAMPUS ESTHETICS

The emphasis on campus esthetics accelerated in the eighties, an intentional focus that enjoyed wide support. This was evident in the expansion of campus beautification activities under the husbandry of Arden Toso, who was featured on the cover of *The Alumni News* and in more than one feature article in *The Concordian*. The completion of the Jones Science Center made way for the demolition of the old science hall and the development of an outdoor amphitheater. This work was completed in 1981. As the amphitheater was being constructed, the growing mound looked somewhat ominous, and the naysayers came out of the woodwork. I recall walking the site with Ansel Haakenson, director of buildings and grounds, and we literally gave instructions to the landscape engineers about how much elevation should be shaved off the emerging landscape feature. Once the work was completed, however, the sod laid and the trees planted, the community laid claim to the newest feature of the campus landscape. A writer for *The Concordian* suggested that amphitheater mound be named "Mount Saint Helland" in honor of our then chief business officer, or "Cliffs of Dover" in honor of me. Others referred to the landscape feature as Cobber Mountain. With the subsequent construction of Olin Hall, however, the name that seemed to stick was Olin Hill.

Other elements in the developing campus esthetic included murals in the library and Grant Center by Cobber alumnus David Hetland. Paul Nesse, another Cobber alumnus, created a bronze life-size statue of Joseph Knutson, which was installed in the Knutson Center. Nesse also created relief portraits of Professor Carl B. Ylvisaker and C400 founders Gene Paulson and J. Luther Jacobson, which were placed at the entrance to the library, and another of Dr. Jack Spier was placed in the Jones Science Center. Nesse created bronze bust portraits of Ed Fuglestad, Cyrus Running, Paul J. Christiansen, Martin Luther, and King Olav V. I took a personal interest in each of these projects and assisted in obtaining funding for many of them.

The primary esthetic project of the eighties was the development of the Centennial Mall on campus. The goals were to create a "front door" to the campus, move some parking to the perimeter of the campus, and create a defining and centering symbol for the college in observance of its centennial. The mall was some years in the planning under the able leadership of a campus committee chaired by Jim Hausmann. Sovik, Mathre, and Madson, the architectural group that had designed most of the buildings surrounding the mall, was engaged to design and oversee the project.

The idea of a campanile was included in a campus master plan completed in the 1940s, but was never constructed. The campanile idea surfaced again in planning for the Centrum. In fact, in the early plans, a tower was envisioned just beyond the southeast corner of the building. Although that was an attractive idea, funds were not sufficient to include a campanile in the project, but the idea gained legs and would emerge as the central element in the Centennial Mall project. The cost estimate for the project, which included parking lots and a substantial amount of landscaping, was $1.4 million, one element in the $46.5 million-dollar Centennial Campaign. The project had some early critics, who thought the money could be better spent on financial aid or the academic program. Not to be mentioned, of course, was that the Centennial Campaign goals were heavily weighted toward endowment, which would support scholarships, faculty, and program.

My favorite anecdote in support of the campanile relates to an occasion when one of our groundskeepers, Joe Marvik, was working near the campanile site during construction. A faculty member engaged him in discussion, complaining about the frivolous use of college funds. This got Joe's back up, and he told the faculty member how important it was to have a beautiful campus. He told the faculty member he thought the project was so important that he was going walk over to the Development Office to pledge $1,000 to the project. And Joe did just that—he literally "walked his talk."

The mall project included the removal of thirty-nine mature trees, some of which were diseased elm trees, and the planting of 154 new ones. When the trees were removed in the spring of 1990 immediately following commencement, however, there was an outcry among some, and graffiti messages were inscribed on tree stumps and sidewalks decrying the slaughter of trees. I always went to our family lake cabin for a couple of days of rest and relaxation following commencement, so I had already left town after graduation. Seeing the reaction to the tree removal, my assistant, Esther Allen, called me to say that I might want to get back to campus, which I did. I sent a communiqué to the campus community, outlining the details of the plan and the necessity over time to replace trees and renew the campus for future generations. The hubbub passed quickly, and with the completion of the mall later that summer, the project gained thousands of supporters saying, "Wasn't that a great idea!" The plan was to ring the campanile bells at the commencement of the centennial celebration in the fall of 1991, but members of the senior class, some of whom had been vocal critics of the project, petitioned to have the bells rung at their graduation that spring, a petition I was pleased to grant.

ADVANCEMENT

As previously noted, Concordia successfully completed the Founders' Fund campaign in the early eighties. Reflecting the success of that campaign was the two hundred percent increase in gift income between 1972 and 1982, another mark of this golden era for the college. Following on the success of the Founders' Fund, the C400 Club initiated Project 9, the goal of which was to raise a million dollars for financial aid to students. This turned out to be a successful project. Then in the fall of 1983, we announced another major campaign, Founders' Fund II. The goal was to raise $21.5 million for current fund needs and the endowment, half in cash and half in the form of planned or deferred gifts.

Over the course of the late seventies and the early eighties, Ed Ellenson, John Pierce, and David Benson from the Development staff had been active in explaining and promoting deferred giving in the forms of trusts, annuities, or bequest commitments, work originally initiated by Roger Swenson in the sixties. Increasingly, Concordia's constituents were motivated to establish such gift instruments, and this explains much of the growth the college experienced in its endowment fund in the late 1990s and early 2000s.

It is perhaps impossible to overstate the impact of John Pierce and David Benson on the Advancement effort of the college. Among all the frontline Advancement people I worked with, the two of them stand out. Both knew their stuff in terms of deferred and planned giving. John and David formed strong relationships with prospective donors, each in their unique way, and both were attentive and pleasantly persistent in building relationships. Advancement is primarily about relationships, and both gifted men understood that. The three of us put on many, many miles together and had congenial working relationships.

Dave and John were self-starters and self-directed, and they worked in harmony with others and recognized that no major gift commitment was a solo performance. In my work with the two of them, we each played our respective roles. Usually, I was the one who told the college story and set out the case for giving. John and David would follow up by exploring some of the ways one might transfer assets to the college. That would eventually lead us to a figure for consideration, and by that time, in what was sometimes a long process, even extending into months or years, we usually knew what the number would be.

Another outstanding member of the Development team was Rosalie Lier. She joined the staff in the late sixties and was the principal in obtaining significant funds from the Bush Foundation, the Kresge Foundation, Stanley and Dorothy Kresge personally, and E. W. Hallet, a highly respected contractor in northern Minnesota. Rosalie had an aura of quality and presence about her that was remarkable. She was able to make friends for the college that perhaps no one else could have made. In addition, we frequently sought her counsel on matters related to campus esthetics. Rosalie was self-confident, and I could always count on her to speak her mind.

I had the privilege of working with two of the best Advancement executives in the business in the eighties and nineties, Loren Anderson and Linda Brown. They were big picture people who had a combination of administrative and human relationship skills. In addition, each of them carried a portfolio of major donors and donor prospects. Loren and I, in a sense, came of age together in the Development world. He was a natural at organization, planning, and human relations. Linda came to Advancement by virtue of her expertise in deferred giving and her great ability to work well with a variety of personalities. I enjoyed the Advancement dimension of my job and the time the three of us spent strategizing, assessing, and planning. Good people, great talent, outstanding results.

Having said all of that, my role in fundraising evolved over time. In the early years, while I was good at cultivating relationships and telling the story of the college, I was uncomfortable asking people for a gift. I seemed to assume that if we drank enough coffee together, the prospect would volunteer a gift. My attitude and practice changed as I came to understand that every person needs a larger cause in life, whether they know it or not. My work in fundraising was to provide people with an opportunity to acknowledge and exercise their call to stewardship. When I saw fundraising in that light, raising money on behalf of a college and mission I believed in became much easier. In fact, fundraising came to be one of the favorite aspects of my work as president.

I worked with a diverse group of people over the years. On the one hand, I sat at Charlie and Jesse Grant's kitchen table as he made flour biscuits and she fried chicken. The Grants gave a series of gifts to the college for over a decade, and the home of the Offutt School of Business is named in their honor. I came to know Milton Bergsjo, a North Dakota farmer who established a $500,000 unitrust for the benefit of the college. The Grants and Milton were representative of a broad rural constituency, most of whom did not have the benefit of a college education but were motivated to share their largess with the college. On the other hand, there were conversations with Gabriel Hauge, chairman of Manufactures Hannover Trust, in his New York office. Hauge was a distinguished graduate of the college, who always made time for Concordia visitors like me. Another frequent call was with Humphrey Doermann, CEO of the Bush Foundation, from which the college received many substantial and strategic grants over the years. I enjoyed the range of these associations and was constantly learning new things about the worlds of these diverse supporters, their ties to the college, and their ultimate values. It was a great privilege to know and work with such dedicated, successful, yet humble people.

I recall wonderful stories related to my association with generous supporters of the college. A couple of favorite stories involve the Grants, in fact. Charlie and Jessie had lived a hardscrabble life through the twenties and thirties on their dry land in northeastern Montana. They also had a tendency to argue with each other a lot. On one occasion, I noticed the locked gun cabinet in their rather remote ranch house. I asked Charlie why they would need a lock and key on the cabinet. He replied that it was because he didn't want his wife to have access to the guns when she had one of her temper tantrums. We shared a good laugh over that. The Grants also built a mausoleum on the edge of their building site. When I asked why, Charlie reported that he had looked for lots in the cemetery of the largest town in the area, Plentywood, Montana. When he discovered that the lots available for purchase were surrounded by Republicans, he announced that he would build his own cemetery rather than be buried next to any "blankety-blank Republicans." Although their Grants were quite conservative, their Democratic loyalty was based on their appreciation for the New Deal programs of the 1930s.

Another anecdote from my fundraising travels also occurred in Plentywood, Montana. One fall day John Pierce and I came to call on Tom and Mary Lidahl, a prominent young couple in the community, and Tom was a Cobber. We wanted to meet them, so John and I, dressed in sport coats and ties, rang the doorbell, but there was no answer. I thought I heard noise in the back yard, so I went round the house and came upon two children playing on a swing set. I asked if their parents might be home, so one of them hastened to the back door and beckoned her mother. It turns out that Mary Lidahl had seen us approaching the house and assumed we were some of the missionaries who had been making the rounds in the neighborhood. She was initially embarrassed, but soon we all turned to laughter. Mary would one day become a member of the Board of Regents and the young daughter, Lisa, who was part of this story, became a Cobber and followed her father into the profession of dentistry. Their second daughter, Linn, also became a Cobber, who became an elementary school teacher.

Another of the stories I cherish involves the second man on the moon, Buzz Aldrin. A Cobber named Cliff Enger lived in California where he specialized in oil development and entrepreneurship. He had engaged Aldrin as a consultant and brought him along to a fishing outing on the Lake of the Woods along the Canadian border in northern Minnesota. There were several Concordia people on that outing, including former President and Mrs. Joseph Knutson and me, among others. One evening a group of us, including Buzz Aldrin, rowed to a neighboring island, climbed to its summit to view the full moon, and then listened as Aldrin shared some memories with us. The experience was a scintillating, once in a lifetime event.

Another interesting story related to support for the college was connected to the construction of the Olin Building. Shortly after I became president in 1975, a presidential colleague at Roanoke College in Virginia shared news that they had received a grant from the F. W. Olin Foundation. The Olin Foundation was created from capital earnings of the Federal Cartridge Company, a manufacturer of munitions and ammunition. Mr. Olin was not a religious man, so colleges with a strong religious affiliation were largely excluded from their grant-making activity. Then Mr. Olin died, and a grant was made to Roanoke College, a self-identifying Lutheran college. My friend suggested that we take a look, so we hired his former development officer who had secured the grant for Roanoke to serve as our consultant. The chair of the foundation was Lawrence Milas, an attorney based in New York. I made an appointment with him in 1978, and thus began a continuing relationship. In 1980, and operating on an entirely separate track, I received a call from United States Senator Rudy Boschwitz of Minnesota. He had read about the Olin Foundation and thought we ought to look into an association with them, plus he volunteered to help by arranging to visit with Mr. Milas. Subsequently, Senator Boschwitz went to visit Larry at his home, where he was doing yard work on a Saturday afternoon. The senator lent a hand with the yard chores and a helpful relationship was thus established.

As is often the case, relationships of this sort take time. I made regular calls on Mr. Milas as well as two of his foundation board colleagues who had their offices in Minneapolis. Since they lived in the region, we discovered people and causes that we had in common and so the relationships grew. The Olin Foundation only funded buildings and oversaw all their projects. Concordia's proposal was to build a new home for the Art and Communications/Theatre Departments. While we had estimated that the building would cost $2.75 million, the final cost was $3.4 million. The relationship with the Olin Foundation continued to grow and led to a site visit in 1984, followed by an early morning telephone call from Mr. Milas announcing their decision to fund Concordia's project. It was a great day for the college—the largest gift in the history of the college from a nationally prominent foundation. Only Macalester, Carlton, and Drake had received such grants in our region of the country.

The fundraising successes of the eighties were unprecedented. In addition to the Olin Grant, Concordia's fundraising efforts exceeded the Founders' Fund II goal by five million dollars, raised over $1.6 million for construction of the German Village, and obtained several grants for program and faculty development. In addition, there were C400 projects in support of financial aid and classroom and office renovation projects. As the eighties ended and the college's centennial drew near, we turned our attention to an appropriate stewardship project for that occasion. We secured outstanding volunteer leadership and set a goal of $46.5 million around the themes of "access and quality." With respect to the access theme, fund raising goals sought to raise fifteen million designated for endowment and $12.2 million for the annual fund. Regarding the quality theme, we sought $6 million for endowment of faculty positions, four million dollars in scholarships, and $8.3 million for facilities, totally $18.3 million. These were ambitious goals, but previous success in fundraising and a belief that Cobbers would continue to generously support the college inspired our efforts. By the conclusion of the campaign, we had exceeded the $46.5 million goal with a final figure of fifty-eight million from seventeen thousand contributors.

MISSION MATTERS

The title of this section could be read in two ways. That is, the section addresses matters related to mission, and, in fact, that mission does matter. To fully understand my interest in and commitment to the mission, I reflect on my earlier, formative days in leadership at Concordia. As a young faculty member and dean, I affirmed and took for granted the mission of the college and the Lutheran tradition. Most of my colleagues had come from the tradition, and those who did not adapted and/or respected the historical roots and Lutheran tradition of Concordia. My understanding of the mission and tradition, however, was very rudimentary. I had never explored its biblical and theological foundations in a rigorous way. As I have written elsewhere, my identity with the mission was more about *ethos* (e.g., the community) and *pathos* (e.g., my dedication) than it was about *logos*, (e.g., my understanding). I recognized I had more to learn to deepen my understanding of the Lutheran tradition and my leadership at Concordia.

As noted in the previous chapter, the event that led me to what would become a career-long avocation in faith and learning was the 1973 annual conference of the Lutheran Educational Conference of North America (LECNA). The theme of the conference was "What's Lutheran about Higher Education?" and featured Robert Bertram, professor of theology at the Seminary in Exile (Seminex), and Sydney Ahlstrom, professor of history at Yale University. Ahlstrom gave a stunning exposition on the significant role of Lutheran theologians in the formation of the critical tradition, and Bertram explored some of the distinctive ways in which the Lutheran theological tradition can shape academic life. I was very impressed by their presentations. Deeper understandings and new revelations about Lutheran higher education left me determined that I would initiate systematic reflection on such matters at Concordia.

Again, as noted in the previous chapter, I shared this expanding interest of mine with Norman Fintel, director of higher education for the American Lutheran Church at that time. He was receptive to the idea and promised funding for a faculty workshop on the Concordia campus that would bring together two representatives from each of the eleven ALC colleges. The workshop featured daily lectures by Bertram and Ahlstrom plus speeches by area Bishop Roy Gilbertson and Concordia President Joseph L. Knutson. It was a very stimulating week of conversation and hastened the growth in my own understanding of and fascination with mission and Lutheran identity. That fall, I wrote a brief paper on the subject, which appeared in the ALC's *Lutheran Standard*. I anticipated that my passion for mission and Lutheran identity would continue to shape my leadership in the coming years.

Moving forward in time, in my first year as president at Concordia, I was elected to the board of LECNA. At the first board meeting, conversation turned to planning for the 1977 conference program. Shedding any new-kid-on-the-block inhibitions, I suggested that we focus on mission. And we did. In fact, those matters became the center of LECNA programs for more than a decade. At the 1978 annual meeting, I spoke to the assembly about the significance of identity issues. I noted that we didn't all see identity issues the same way, which made the conversation both lively and valuable. This idea gained traction in both LECNA and the ALC family of colleges, which initiated a program of theological development for faculty, including a week-long workshop.

In 1979 David Lotz, a professor of church history at Union Seminary whom I mentioned in an earlier chapter, spoke at the annual meeting of LECNA about the theological foundations of Lutheran higher education. This was another significant moment in my ongoing theological development. At the 1980 conference, over which I presided as president, the conference theme was "Lutheran Higher Education in the Eighties: Heritage and Challenges." The presenters included the sage Arthur Olsen from Augustana-Sioux Falls, South Dakota; Harold Dunkelberger of Gettysburg; Joseph Shaw of St. Olaf; and Martin Maehor of Concordia-Seward, Nebraska. Thereafter, LECNA commissioned preparation of the history of Lutheran Higher Education in North America. Richard Solberg, chief education executive for the Lutheran Church in America, was selected as the author, and I chaired the editorial committee. The book was published in 1986 and introduced to the public at the annual conference of LECNA. In attendance were the presidents of the three major Lutheran church bodies: the American Lutheran Church, the Lutheran Church in America, and the Lutheran Church Missouri Synod. I was grateful to have been a player in all of this and looked forward to the ways it might continue to nurture me, Concordia, and other Lutheran colleges.

Back at Concordia, the dialogue between mission and faith took the form of a summer workshop in the early eighties on "Christian Faith and the Liberal Arts." This workshop would be revived in the late eighties under the leadership of campus pastor Phil Holtan and faculty member Roger Spilde. A mix of new and veteran faculty was invited to participate in this workshop that included presentations on the Lutheran tradition and other religious traditions engaged in higher education ventures. The program was well received, even among some who thought it might be some sort of interrogation event.

As the leader of the faculty, I sought to contribute to a deeper understanding of the Lutheran tradition. This commitment was shared by many, and I especially valued the contributions of Tom Christenson (Philosophy), Ernie Simmons (Religion), Carl Bailey (Physics), Walther Prausnitz (English), Roger Spilde (Economics), and Gregg Muilenburg (Philosophy). *Blueprints III* and IV embodied the priorities, care, and depth of attention that was devoted to these matters. As times changed, this initiative took new forms, as is articulated in more detail in the chapter that follows.

My involvement in church relations in our region and my role on the national Lutheran scene led to a related assignment in 1985. The American Lutheran Church, the Lutheran Church in America, and the Lutheran Church in Mission had each voted their intention to form a new Lutheran church, which would eventually become the Evangelical Lutheran Church in America (ELCA) in 1988. The desire for a merged Lutheran church led to the creation of a commission tasked to develop the plan for that new church. While I had not favored a merger because I thought it was a distraction from mission and that it would lead to a weaker relationship between the church and its colleges, I bowed to the will of the majority and sought to do my best to support the process.

I was elected to the Commission for a New Lutheran Church and its steering committee. For three years there was a busy schedule of meetings and consultations. In addition, I was frequently on the road in the region to explain the commission's work and to gather feedback. I found this to be good and important work. I discovered that I knew little of church politics at that level, so it was a learning experience. I carried most of the commission work related to education in the new church. It was difficult to find a way to both respect the diversity of traditions relating to church identity and create a new structure with a unifying integrity. In the ALC, the colleges had a strong relationship with each other and with the church. On the other hand, in the LCA, the colleges were much less unified, with varying approaches. The result of the merger was to permit great diversity along with the accompanying struggle for common identity. That disappointed me because I had hoped for more unity with respect to mission and relationship to the Lutheran church and its traditions, but I accepted that there really was no alternative.

One component of the new ELCA structure that I appreciated was the Council of College and University Presidents. I was honored to serve as its first chair and would, in subsequent years, be involved in several initiatives related to faith and learning in our colleges. A particularly effective rallying point was the Lutheran idea of Vocation.

The terms of the merger meant that each college could more or less go its own way with respect to its relationship with the church. In the case of Concordia, the initiatives in church relations adopted in the seventies flourished and were expanded. The CORD program was funded in part by a grant and assisted Concordia in creating local committees across the corporate territory to assist in identifying potential students and provide feedback on our educational program. This led to further strengthening of the bonds. In addition, Don Rice, director of Church Relations, was constantly on the move visiting pastors and attending meetings. Twice a year we would venture out to a particular geographic area where on a Sunday, Don, three or four other faculty and staff members, and I would fill the pulpits of area churches. In addition, we sponsored listening sessions for area pastors to pass along news from Concordia and gain their feedback. In 1984, the college again hosted the national convention of the American Lutheran Church. This was yet another opportunity to tell the Concordia story and make new friends.

STUDENT LIFE

The golden age of the eighties also touched student life at Concordia, although many initiatives started with successful student life work long before that. The positive expansion of student life in the eighties also provided a solid foundation for years to come. The campus was energized by the diverse interests and activities of students. From athletics and the arts to social events and volunteer services, the campus reflected the preferences of students. Staff leadership had a good deal to do with this. Three examples of excellent staff leadership come to mind: first, the outdoor recreational program. Under the leadership of Paul Erickson, a former Cobber who joined the staff in the late seventies, Concordia became a leader in the outdoor education movement. The initiative began with the "Great Northwoods Bike Tour" in 1977 when nearly a hundred students spent their fall break biking across northern Minnesota. The program continued without interruption for another thirteen years. In addition, there were recreation seminars to Europe, an epic "Ski across Greenland" expedition that set a global record; a subsequent "Ski across Lapland" journey that included many Cobbers; the creation of a society, Ah Ke, that focused on outdoor recreation activities; and the introduction of a program in outdoor leadership. While the pace of these initiatives slackened when Paul Erickson left the college, some of his legacy remained.

A second example of student initiative and effective staff leadership came in volunteer services. Prior to the eighties, there were volunteer activities, but they were decentralized and involved everything from tutoring in the schools to visiting people in hospitals and nursing homes. In the eighties, however, student leaders, with staff assistance, began to bring more structure to these activities. By the end of the decade, student leaders formed SOS, or Sources of Service, with the staff support of Barbara Eiden Molinaro. SOS would expand volunteer opportunities for students in the community. By the early nineties, this serving/learning movement on college campuses gained state and regional status with coordinated resources and services. Concordia was both a provider and a recipient of these services and was often recognized as a leader in serving/learning.

The organized commitment to serving others in the broader Fargo-Moorhead community and beyond turned out to be a great success, a commitment that continues to be reflected in both academic and student life to this day. Beginning in 2017, for example, all students at Concordia are required to complete PEAKs (Pivotal Experiences in Applied Knowledge), a graduation requirement that has roots from the eighties and nineties to what was then called "service learning," that is, a blending of academic learning goals with service. The various approaches to service at Concordia, whether volunteering, service learning, or now PEAK, tap into the strong interest Concordia students have long held in making a difference in the here and now, consistent with the mission of the college.

The third example of student and staff magic in the golden era of the eighties was in the creation of CARES, Chemical Awareness and Responsibility, a program designed to provide education, resources, and support for students. With the counsel of Barbara Eiden Molinaro and campus pastor Carl Lee, this program provided a range of assistance to the community throughout the eighties. There were presentations and panels on various subjects from alcohol use to the rudiments of a healthy diet. The CARES student leaders provided material for a regular column in *The Concordian.*

In addition to these major and long-term areas of emphasis, leadership development remained a core activity. As noted in an earlier chapter, Morrie Lanning initiated a summer internship program for student leaders in the late sixties, and a version of the program remains in place. In the eighties, as mayor of Moorhead, Morrie Lanning was involved in a regional development entity known as the West Central Initiative Fund. Among its goals was the development of leaders for communities throughout west central Minnesota. Morrie was a major architect of that effort, and this led to the creation of a Leadership Center at Concordia, funded by the Initiative Fund. A $93,000 grant funded this initiative. The center's goal was to serve as a resource center for leaders from throughout the region. The Leadership Center had a good run but did not turn out to be sustainable. There have been varying student leadership development emphases through the years. In the nineties, leadership development opportunities were expanded to include many leaders in student organizations. In the 2000s, leadership growth opportunities would be extended to any interested student.

Another characteristic of student life in the eighties was a consistent interest in national and global issues. There were lively columns in *The Concordian* articulating diverse political views. For example, in 1986-87 Jeff Johnson, later to be active in Minnesota politics, wrote a tongue-in-cheek column reflecting a conservative point of view while Eric Torgerson parried with a liberal perspective. There were columns and essays about a range of issues from South African Apartheid, American policy in Nicaragua, homosexuality in the church, the status of women, and nuclear disarmament. Student political views were reflected in student polls during the elections of 1980 and 1984. In 1980, students favored Reagan over Carter by forty-one percent to thirty-five percent. In 1984, they favored Reagan by a two-to-one margin over Mondale. Over the years, Concordia students have expressed a range of political views, but in the eighties, they tended to lean to the conservative perspective.

This strong interest in public matters was facilitated by the parade of public luminaries who visited the Concordia campus in those years. There were such prominent media figures as Robert MacNeil, Paul Harvey, Ed Bradley, Edwin Newman, Charles Kuralt, William Buckley, and Hendrick Smith. In addition, the campus hosted Vice Presidents Mondale and Bush in the eighties, along with local and regional state and national representatives. Guests in the arts and education were impressive as well. Pulitzer Prize winner Gwendolyn Brooks, actresses Patricia Neal and Liv Ulmann, Ambassadors Ebba Eban and Jeanne Kirkpatrick, educator Jonathan Kozol, novelist Louis L'Amour, and humorist Garrison Keillor were among other public figures who engaged the campus community. In addition, Concordia sponsored the annual Faith, Reason, and World Affairs Arts Symposium, a two and a half-day symposium that addressed such matters as the Constitution, food and fiber, homelessness in America, and the biomedical revolution. In short, the eighties at Concordia were a stimulating time and place to live and learn.

Reflecting the national and global conversations, there were opportunities for continuing conversation and action. For example, related to women's issues, the Committee on the Status of Women and The Women's Center on campus played an active role in advancing the discussion. One of the outcomes was a campus policy on sexual harassment. In addition, there were special lectures and programs that enriched the conversation. In the eighties, South African Apartheid came to the fore, which sparked conversation and action across the country and on the Concordia campus. A committee was formed to address these matters, and there were regular articles about the topic in *The Concordian*. This eventually led to an action by the Board of Regents in Concordia endowment funds were no longer to be invested in corporations that supported the Apartheid regime.

Expanding on national topics of conversation, beginning in the eighties, Concordia formulated an affirmative action plan designed to increase the number of women and people of color on the faculty and staff. At both the campus and departmental levels, goals and strategies were identified to help achieve this aspiration. There also was an annual assessment of progress that was the focus of discussion by the Committee on the Status of Women and the President's Council. The director of personnel and the academic dean were responsible for developing the goals and monitoring performance. This did a good deal to raise consciousness across the campus and led to excellent results in the hiring of women but disappointing results in the hiring of persons of color. Although the goal remained, Concordia's location and other factors continued to be a challenge.

The issue of homosexuality also engendered campus-wide conversation, including a number of columns and news stories in *The Concordian*. In the earlier eighties, the American Lutheran Church had a policy that prohibited the ordination of practicing homosexuals, but this position came under assault later in the decade. In this broader context, however, one of the actions Concordia took was to provide a safe space for discussion of related issues. We also invited persons of opposing views to speak at a campus convocation and invited area pastors to join the discussions. That event was a civil and constructive conversation and, again, we believed the college was the appropriate venue for such conversation. Concordia also hosted a series of in-house, on campus conversations about human relations issues, including homosexuality. I recall at one of these events, a Cobber graduate, now a physician who had contracted AIDS, was speaking. Following his presentation at the morning chapel, this individual and I had a chat in my office since I knew his family and our son Erik, then in medical school, had done a clinical under his supervision. That evening, our campus guest spoke to a full house at the Centrum, and, during the question-and-answer period, I commended him for his witness and for his mentoring of my son. Based on feedback in the following days, my action was a sort of revelation to some students, who assumed that I was a status quo Lutheran.

In the eighties, there was equal consideration of more local issues such as intervisitation, refrigerators in dorm rooms, the teaching of Religion 100, the appropriate way to interpret the Bible, and the provision of birth control information and devices by the campus health center. These conversations were healthy, campuswide dialogues, and newspaper editor Dirk Meuleners took the initiative in assuring everyone that freedom of the press was alive and well at Concordia. Meuleners stood out among *The Concordian* editors in a number of ways. First, he was a transfer student and became editor in his first (junior) year due to the resignation of the sitting editor. Meuleners had wide-ranging interests and an openness to diverse points of view. He didn't duck issues like homosexuality, the campus mall project, curriculum changes, or intervisitation, but, at the same time, he boasted about the strengths of the college. *The Concordian* under Meuleners and other editors over the years has served as a central means of engaging the campus community in timely but sometimes difficult topics of conversation. As with most college student newspapers, *The Concordian*, too, has had its ups and downs, but has remained an important voice on campus.

Intervisitation was the issue that kept on living until well into the 2000s when, effectively, all restrictions were lifted, a decision that was decades in the making. In 1980-81, student body president Mark Orvick led an effort to extend hours of visitation. The move was not successful, whereupon Orvick told students that they needed to convince their parents before they could anticipate much change. In 1986, there was another concerted effort to make changes, including a demonstration in Lorentzsen Hall and a public forum. While *The Concordian* gave extensive coverage to the issue, the editor wrote a fairly balanced analysis of the pros and cons. Student proponents were well-organized and conducted a survey of students, faculty/staff, and parents. The students and faculty/staff favored the change, but, by a two-to-one margin, parents opposed it.

Students also sought permission to have refrigerators in their dorm rooms. This was a trend among colleges in those years, and we took a serious look at the issue. Reservations about the issue, especially with resident life leaders, had to do with the enforcement of Concordia's ban on alcohol possession or consumption on campus. We wanted to be sure that staff legally would be able to enter rooms and inspect refrigerators. Students were willing to work with staff on this issue and found a satisfactory resolution to that issue. Once in place, the policy worked effectively.

While this chapter is titled "The Golden Years" and highlights many positive aspects permeating the Concordia community, there were times when that perspective was not shared by some. In the spring of 1982, a group of seniors published a protest piece called "The Extra Mile." The article was written on the premise that "discord...is papered over to create a false appearance of contentment and acceptance, the famed 'community' atmosphere." Writers belittled campus efforts to address women's and minority issues, implied that *The Concordian* was, in effect, being censored, and characterized Wednesday night communion services as a sort of "spiritual pep fest." One writer was critical of the college and the faculty for lack of scholarly work and expressed concern that new tenure policies might protect the less than competent. Another essay pilloried the Music Department for giving undue attention to the concert choir. While these were serious critiques, it was not apparent that these views were widely shared. I was offended, however, that these students, who had broad access to community deliberations, had not presented their views in forums where these concerns might have been fully aired. Instead, the students published their views as they literally were going out the door, so, as a result, not much became of their sharp critique. In retrospect, I was a bit thin-skinned, a condition I would exhibit from time to time over the years. This sometimes led to constructive results and other times exacerbated situations better left undisturbed.

Students were not always issue-oriented or seemingly dissatisfied with the institution as that spring critique from the early eighties. Indeed, skits and pranks and parties were staples of campus life in the eighties and beyond. On Halloween in 1991, for example, a group of students "forked" the yard in front of the president's residence; that is, they stuck thousands of plastic forks into the grass, row upon row. It was a humorous and innocent prank that made us all laugh. Another Halloween eve, student leaders Jeff Johnson and Kent Knutson came to our home. Jeff had on a bald skull cap and sported a mustache—a perfect match for my visage, while Kent—robust and with proper gait, was a perfect match for Morrie Lanning. A photo of this pair found its way into the pages of the yearly spoof newspaper, *The Discordian*. On another occasion, this same annual publication reported that the popular musician Prince would be coming to campus to visit me, and it would be "his royal badness meeting with his royal baldness." Another annual campus event was called "The Dove Boat," a takeoff on *The Love Boat*, a popular TV series in the early eighties. I was, of course, the captain of the Dove Boat and was invited to the launch ceremonies. These and other fond memories were part of that golden decade of the eighties.

By the mid-eighties, the traditional societies were waning in their membership and role in campus life. Only five of the original nine societies were still active, although two new ones appeared on the scene—Ah Ke, devoted to outdoor recreation, and Alpha Psi Omega, devoted to service activities. Neither would endure. Students found other ways to engage with each other, however, often through campus-sponsored opportunities. Campus ministry sponsored an annual Lenten ingathering for various mission projects from Habitat for Humanity to Operation Bootstrap. In addition, there was an annual dance marathon that raised funds for other worthy causes of interest to students. As noted earlier, these years were the heydays in campus ministry, with strong participation in worship and a variety of related groups and events.

Again, as I had for many years, I felt connected to the student body in good times but also in difficult times. I delighted in my frequent, direct interactions with students. In our home on the northeast corner of campus, Mardy and I often hosted the student government leaders, the student committees for orientation, homecoming, and family weekend, and the seniors on the athletic teams. In addition, we attended every worship event, game, concert, play, and lecture that we could fit in our schedules. It was a privilege to live in community with Concordia students, and we were delighted in it. Along with the joys there were the sorrows. In the eighties, two students took their lives and two others died from disease. These events are sobering for a community whose members are in the prime of life. Campus pastors Carl Lee, Ernie Mancini, and Phil Holtan were very effective in responding to these tragic events, and they became teaching moments for our community.

BRICKS, BUCKS, and BTU'S

While there was only one major construction project in the eighties, the Olin Building, there were several medium and small projects, including the acquisition of the Cobber Club, an off-campus exercise/fitness club on south 8th Street; a twelve-plex across 8th Street and several residences adjacent to the campus; the renovation of Brown, Fjelstad, Bishop Whipple, and Grose Halls; significant improvements to Memorial Auditorium; and the construction of Bogstad East, the Welcome Center, the Centennial Mall, the Mugaas Maintenance Building, and the Berg Steam Plant. In addition, several facilities were added to the Concordia Language Villages campus near Bemidji. By my estimate, the college completed about fifteen million dollars in acquisition and construction activities in the eighties. The funding for these projects came from grants, gifts, debt reserve funds, rental income from dormitories (the bonds for which were self-amortizing), astute budget management, and year-end balances related to a growing enrollment. In the fall of 1989, Concordia had approximately fifteen million of long-term debt (including a recent issue of five million) and approximately eight million in debt reserves. In short, the institution was in a very strong financial position.

The financial disciplines that financial leaders had put in place in the seventies enabled the college to build substantial operating reserves that both helped cash flow and provided a resource for rainy days. Because of unpredicted growth in enrollment and gift ($1.6M in 1980 and $2.4M in 1990) and endowment income ($132,000 in 1980 and $1.1M in 1990), the college ended each year in the eighties with a positive fund balance, sometimes more than a million dollars. These funds were designated for non-recurring expenses. Indeed, these year-end balances were a significant resource in funding projects like those noted in the preceding paragraph.

Financial leaders also made effective use of public bonding opportunities through the Minnesota Higher Education Finance Authority. We would often bond new projects and, simultaneously, create sinking funds to service bond payments. There were also opportunities to refinance federal housing bonds that worked to Concordia's advantage. In addition, as some of our housing bonds were paid off, we retained the funding line in the budget and devoted the funds to new endeavors. Our financial approach was a well-coordinated, well-disciplined strategy and reflected the effective leadership of Concordia's board and the staff and the superb financial discipline of all the budget managers.

Another example of fiscal intelligence relates to the college's pursuit of damages related to the asbestos that had been used in many of Concordia's construction projects in the fifties and sixties. We joined a class action lawsuit seeking thirty million dollars in damages to be divided among 3,000 colleges and universities. A local attorney, in an informal conversation, suggested to Loren Anderson that Concordia might do much better by filing separately. Following that advice, we withdrew from the class action lawsuit, and Clyde Allen and Ansel Haakenson, who had accumulated substantial documentation for our claim, pursued the matter with Pemberton Law from Fergus Falls providing representation. As a result, Concordia secured a two-million-dollar settlement that has been a source of funds for subsequent asbestos removal projects.

The motivation for the purchase of the Cobber Club was the increasing student interest in fitness and recreation. The field house was inadequate for these purposes, and Concordia was some years away from building the Olson Forum. The Cobber Club was built as a private club in south Moorhead, only blocks from campus, and became available at a reasonable price. After purchasing the facility, Concordia made some minor renovations and created a shuttle service to ferry students and staff to and from the facility. This purchase and coordination provided an excellent stop-gap measure. With the completion of the Olson Forum in the mid-nineties, student demand for use of the Cobber Club waned, so the college first leased and then sold the facility to a private operator.

Of considerable importance in this period was the emphasis on energy conservation. High energy costs created interest on the part of students, faculty, and staff, and a committee was formed in 1976 to give oversight to college conservation efforts. With the leadership of Ansel Haakenson, director of buildings and grounds and a licensed engineer, the task force monitored campus energy use, identified potential improvements, and recommended such common-sense practices as turning down the heat at night and turning out the lights when space was not in use. Ansel also cited the outdated heating systems in Brown and Fjelstad Halls, which were replaced in subsequent renovations.

The accomplishments in this period were considerable. In a 1978 article in *The Concordian*, Ansel Haakenson reported on massive insulation projects completed in Old Main, Brown Hall, Academy Hall, Grose Hall, and Fjelstad Hall and new temperature control systems in Bishop Whipple and Academy Halls. In 1981, the National Association of College and University Business Officers (NACUBO) recognized Concordia as one of twenty-nine winners in a national competition. The award was given in recognition of a project to reduce steam generation that garnered annual savings of $39,000. In total, forty-four energy conservation projects were completed between 1976 and 1981. A comparative analysis of private colleges in Minnesota in 1978 found that Concordia's BTU consumption was below the average, despite having more degree days of cold temperatures than any other school in the comparison. These efforts would continue in subsequent decades. In the late eighties, a comparative study of Minnesota higher education indicated that Concordia's energy costs were below the average.

PUBLIC AGENDAS

The economy in the late seventies and early eighties was characterized by slow growth and galloping inflation. Consequently, at both state and federal levels income lagged; therefore, expenses were under increasing pressure, including financial aid funds for Concordia students. Under the leadership of James Hausmann and Student Association officers, students responded to the threat of aid cuts with massive letter-writing campaigns and conversations with many elected officials who visited the campus. In addition, working through state and national associations, students and leaders from Concordia engaged in systematic lobbying activity. I spent time visiting state legislators each year and made biannual trips to Washington, D.C. to confer with national officeholders. At the state level, Roger Moe, DFL Leader of the Senate, and Calvin Larson, a ranking Republican senator, were accessible and effective advocates for student aid. Senator Moe became a visiting lecturer in Concordia's Political Science Department, where he shared his experience with our students. Senator Larson was a member of the Board of Regents, where he provided excellent information and encouraged his colleagues to reach out to their legislators. Even in the context of challenging times for Concordia and higher education, there were also opportunities for learning and growth.

I recall an occasion in the late seventies when I worked with Cobber alumnus and Republican Senatorial Campaign fundraiser Paul Arneson. He arranged a dinner event with U.S. Senators from North Dakota and Minnesota. Senators David Durenberger, Rudy Boschwitz, and Mark Andrews and their spouses attended the event. This made a strong impression on the executive director of the National Association of Independent Colleges and Universities, the private college lobbying group in D.C. Subsequently, in the winter of 1982, I was one of five college presidents invited to brief Senate Majority Leader Howard Baker on financial aid matters.

My predecessor, President Joseph Knutson, was a visible and popular Republican spokesperson. On more than one occasion, he was encouraged to run for public office. Fortunately for the college, however, he always declined to do so. I could identify with Knutson's politics since I had grown up in a Republican family. My political views, however, were more nuanced than his. Except for my attendance at one political caucus in the sixties, I did not engage in organized political activity. This was a conscious decision on my part because I worked with a wide range of people and political perspectives in my interactions on behalf of Concordia, and I saw myself as a centrist. Over time, in presidential elections I crossed party lines, depending upon the issue and the candidates, and I made financial contributions to Republican Senator Boschwitz, Democratic State Senators Roger Moe and Keith Langseth, Republican State Senator Cal Larson, and Republican State Representative Morris Lanning. I was, and remain, among a vanishing number of centrists, who believe that compromise is a legitimate and necessary outcome of the political process. While most of the people I worked with on the Concordia board and in my fundraising contacts were from the conservative spectrum, we could almost always find common ground on basic issues. Indeed, discussing political matters was a normal part of most conversations. That became less true as society in general became increasingly polarized in the 2000s.

Most faculty members lean toward liberal and Democratic positions on public issues. That was true on the Concordia campus as well and was reflected in the lecturers invited to campus and the speakers who participated in the annual fall symposium. I believe that campuses should model the free exchange of diverse points of view, but that is rarely the reality. During my years in the presidency, we achieved some balance through the selection of speakers for commencement and C400 programs. Indeed, I kept a sharp eye on these matters.

LEADERSHIP: IT'S ABOUT PEOPLE

The Concordia Board of Regents' leadership strength was shown in many ways through the eighties. Norman Lorentzsen chaired the board through most of the decade. His experience as a senior executive of the Burlington Northern Railroad gave him the ability to always focus on the big picture. Norm kept the board focused on the large issues rather than getting distracted by the details. His fiscal conservatism coincided with my own values, yet he was not averse to risk in borrowing money or embarking on new projects when prudent to do so. Over the years, Norm was accompanied by very able colleagues on the board, including Norman Jones, Beverly Clayburg, Harry Forse, Bob Englestad, Cal Larson, and Ray Siegle. The Board of Regents was attentive to its role in oversight and strategic planning. I can hardly recall a meeting that was not anchored in some aspect of long-range plans. There was a consistent working harmony between board members and the senior administrative staff. Students, faculty, and staff members frequently participated in committee meetings and always in the annual board retreat. This kept the lines of communication open and enriched the content of the conversation.

One of the richest board experiences was the annual retreat in the fall, held at either the Fair Hills Resort or the Language Villages near Bemidji. Former board members were invited to the opening day and evening of the retreat. This gave current and former board members a chance to get to know each other, share an update on the college, and think together about future plans. Some of my presidential colleagues told of the anxiety they would experience in anticipation of board meetings. I always looked forward to the board retreats as gatherings of colleagues in common cause.

On campus, we began the decade of the eighties with the administrative leadership team of Helland, Gring, Anderson, Lanning, and Hausmann. We ended the decade with Allen, Homann, Anderson, Lanning, and Hausmann. In short, we had remarkable continuity, and that gave us great strength.

Unfortunately, Don Helland died suddenly in 1982. He had led us to major breakthroughs in financial planning, budget management, and campus beautification. While Don's demeanor occasionally ruffled feathers, everyone saluted the results. I still recall his monthly one-page, handwritten budget reports. Although these weren't the most sophisticated approach to budget reports, his reports offered constructive discipline for all of us. For most of two decades, the college maintained a lean administrative staff and spent less on administration than the norm for Concordia's size and type of institution. We worked at that, and success would not have been possible without highly qualified staff. By the late 1990s and especially into the 2000s, however, the administrative staff grew substantially, in part because of increased oversight requirements by state and federal agencies and in part because of internal pressures for new services, including technology.

Although Concordia had been fortunate to have had a lot of continuity among administrative leadership over the years, turnover is also a natural occurrence. Upon Don Helland's unexpected passing, after a careful search, Clyde Allen was selected to succeed Don as Concordia's new chief financial officer. Clyde had served as commissioner of finance for the state of Minnesota during the governorship of Al Quie. Clyde also brought both financial acumen and gifts for communication, planning, and building relationships. Clyde served the college with great effect for two decades. His wife, Esther, formerly executive assistant to Governor Quie, became my assistant. She had a gift for managing details and for building community. Esther's impact extended into the Fargo-Moorhead community through her work as a volunteer and member of many boards. Loren Anderson would leave the college for three years of service with the ELCA, returning in time to help frame and then lead Concordia's Centennial Campaign. After an incredible run as academic dean, David Gring left to become president of Roanoke College in 1989, and Robert Homann was selected to replace him. Homann had served as associate dean in the seventies and was well-respected by the faculty.

Although there was occasional turnover in key personnel in the eighties, there were consistencies in the work of the President's Council that unified the working relationships. For example, the President's Council met each Monday morning following chapel. In addition, we held mid-year and year-end planning and assessment sessions, usually offsite. The Council's work was framed by an annual plan in which, following extensive discussion, each administrative division would identify its primary initiatives for the coming year, from which we would identify four to six institution-wide initiatives. This annual plan was shaped by the *Blueprints* and the exigencies of our changing enterprise and environment. The weekly meetings focused on progress toward Concordia's goals, issues that emerged over the year that required collective wisdom, budget performance, the financial plan for the coming year, and on program changes and adjustments.

What I appreciated most about the group was that people shared responsibility for institutional matters. People were not territorial in approaching our common agenda. As I review the eighties, I note that we devoted a great deal of time to capital planning; there were plans and amended plans. I also recall the dynamics of budget management related to emerging needs for computer hardware and software and to evolving needs related to campus electrical and mechanical systems. Administrative leaders spent a good deal of time dealing with the expanding reporting requirements related to personnel and financial aid. In addition, as noted earlier, there were periodic discussions related to student life, affirmative action, and public policy. What impressed me was the willingness of my colleagues to dig in, to take responsibility for problem-solving on matters essentially unrelated to their division. There was good chemistry among us and shared leadership. We operated by consensus, and, while it was clear that I had the final word, very rarely was the case that I uttered any word other than a statement of our consensus.

An indication of the strength of the leadership team is what happened when I was out of town. For example, on two or three occasions, I accompanied musical groups on tours in Europe. At most, I may have called in one time during a two-week absence. In turn, I rarely received a call from campus. If there was the need to act regarding some unanticipated matter during my absence, I would designate a member of the leadership team to convene and expedite the matter. I was only to be called if there was a crisis or lack of agreement. There never was.

As the eighties drew to a close, the leadership team spent more time on budget matters. While Concordia was maintaining strong enrollments and raising tuition by a percentage or two over inflation, the institution was hard pressed to meet all its needs. As previously noted, there was increasing pressure to expand staff to meet regulatory requirements and increasingly competitive enrollment and fundraising marketplaces. Technology was demanding, financial aid expenditures were growing, and we wanted to maintain the strength of the college's compensation program. In addition, we wanted to have room to make improvements in the quality of program offerings. We engaged in exercises designed to capture budget dollars to meet the highest priorities, and, overall, we made good choices, but it wasn't easy.

We also had extensive discussions about enrollment. On the one hand, enrollment numbers were our life blood; on the other, those numbers put pressure on facilities and people. Throughout the eighties, we scrambled to provide sufficient faculty, staff, and space to serve Concordia students. By the late eighties, we were in serious conversations about enrollment: What is the ideal enrollment for Concordia? On the one hand, we could already see the demographic shifts predicted to occur in the nineties and beyond, especially in our region. On the other hand, we enjoyed the blessings that growth had provided. Considerable time was spent discussing this matter in the Long-Range Planning Committee, the President's Council, and in campus-wide forums. Out of those discussions came a consensus among the Council that the ideal size for Concordia might be in the 2,500-2,750 range. Not everyone agreed, particularly not faculty in departments that had been able to expand because of enrollment growth. We did not ever take any steps to implement this goal, trusting, I suppose, that our experience in the market would somehow see us through.

In this section titled "Leadership: It's about People," I think of a significant leadership change that occurred in the Music Department when Paul J. Christiansen retired after fifty years of service. As both a conductor and composer, Paul J. was a national figure in choral music and had, more than any other person, brought regional and national recognition to the college. Under his leadership, the college had assembled a first-rate music faculty that each year produced outstanding graduates who would spread the fame of the college to hundreds of schools and colleges. After considering candidates from across the country, Rene Clausen was selected as Concordia's new conductor in the spring of 1986. Clausen was a young, energetic, and highly respected composer and conductor. I recall my interview with Rene when we discussed the prospect of succeeding an iconic figure like Christiansen. I noted that I had exactly that experience in following Joseph Knutson. During my early years as president, a reporter once asked me what it was like to try to fill the shoes of Knutson, to which I responded, "I have my own shoes." I shared this story with Rene, and I heard him repeat it on more than one occasion. Our confidence was well placed in this appointment, and it's worth noting that the choral program did not skip a beat in the transition. Clausen brought his own distinctions to the position and built a reputation for excellence both on and off the campus. He became one of the most respected and sought after choral composers of his time.

This may seem an addendum at this point in the story, but as you read on, I trust you will agree that it is not. As I reflect on key people and leadership, I want to comment on the support I received from individuals during these critical years. Norman Lorentzsen was an important source of counsel and personal encouragement. I recall Norm's frequent and hand-written notes all through the years. From the faculty, I think of Walther Prausnitz. Every few months, he would send a note of appreciation, usually highlighting some recent event. He was a great source of wisdom and encouragement all through the years. James Hofrenning was another faithful source of encouragement, with especially good insights on matters of mission and faculty politics in the Religion Department. I also think of Paul Hanson, who had been our pastor at Trinity in the sixties and seventies. I could usually expect one of his personally typed messages about every three or four months. Paul was a wonderful supporter and a source of good information on church politics, but it was the deep personal regard that meant the most to me. Sidney Rand was the president of St. Olaf when I became president. Perhaps because he was a Cobber, Sid took a personal interest in me. At presidential conclaves, he would seek me out and offer a word or two of encouragement or thanks. As the years moved by, he frequently sent handwritten notes regarding some college event or activity. Sid and I stayed in touch all through the years following his retirement. Our final visit occurred just weeks before his death. As you can imagine, this list could go on, but people such as those I have mentioned, both insiders and outsiders, were very important in my life and career. I would be remiss not to include Mardy as those significant to my life and career. Without question, Mardy was and is my greatest source of inspiration and support.

HEARTH AND HOME

The eighties were great years not just for the college, but for our family as well. Both Louise and Erik were good students with many friends. They were involved in a very strong youth program at Trinity Lutheran Church in Moorhead. Both were involved in music and theater in high school, and Erik was a member of the cross-country team. Erik was an outdoorsman and active in Boy Scouts, where he reached the rank of Eagle. Louise graduated at the top of her high school class at Moorhead High School and enrolled at Luther College. Erik graduated among the top ten in his class and followed his sister to Luther three years later.

People may have wondered about our children's college choices. While we were not heavy-handed about it, we encouraged and supported both Louise and Erik in their decisions. We knew from observation and experience that going to college where your dad is president can be complicated. There will invariably be campus criticism of a president, and children are put in an awkward position with their peers. Also, inevitably, some will believe that the president's children are favored by the faculty. So, we affirmed the choices that our children made. Luther was much like Concordia, and our children received great education there. Both were involved in music activities and elected to Phi Beta Kappa. Following graduation, Louise went to law school and Erik to medical school, both at the University of Minnesota.

Our children were and continue to be a great delight to us. When the children were living at home, Sunday night around our house was always family night when we shared pizza and popcorn, visited about the coming week, and watched a favorite Sunday night show. In the winter, we took skiing trips to Montana, and in the summer, we enjoyed great times at our cabin on Bad Medicine Lake. In addition, our extended families gathered for frequent reunions, and we enjoyed numerous friendships.

Mardy "kept on, keeping on" with her part-time teaching assignment at Fargo South High School and her involvement in several community activities, including the Mayor's Advisory Council, the Fargo-Moorhead Junior League, and the Senior Choir at Trinity Lutheran. Mardy took on an added responsibility at Fargo South when she chaired one of the committees responsible for preparing the decennial North Central accreditation report. In her role as the first lady of the college, she helped host numerous events at our house and attended a wide range of college concerts, plays, and games. Mardy and I tried to hold one weekend each month for ourselves. That didn't work out perfectly—sometimes we couldn't find that weekend at all, and other times, it turned out to be a one-day weekend, but the effort to keep time for ourselves remained a priority.

Overall, we were quite successful in preserving some personal time, and there was always catch-up time in the summers.

As Cobbers ourselves, Mardy and I have maintained close ties with our college friends. Until recently, Mardy gathered each summer with a group of six college friends. Similarly, we met annually with a group of five of my college friends and spouses. In addition, we maintained a close relationship with two couples from our college days—Ed and Ann Ellenson and Bev and Jerry Bjelde—with whom we traveled and met regularly. In all these associations, we exemplified Concordia, which means "hearts together."

SMELLING THE ROSES

The eighties were golden years for the college and also for Mardy and me. The college experienced record enrollments, and multiple fund-raising goals were surpassed. Concordia received the largest gift in its history from a nationally recognized foundation, and the college was nationally recognized as a "best buy in higher education" by providing high quality education at an affordable price. In addition, Concordia was recognized by the Carnegie Foundation as a national liberal arts college. The college's financial profile was stronger than at any time in its history, compensation levels were very competitive, and faculty and staff morale were strong. On a personal note, I was twice re-elected as president of Concordia during the eighties following, in each case, an assessment process. I also served in leadership roles among Lutheran colleges and Minnesota private colleges, and I was named to the list of "one hundred most effective college presidents" by the Exxon Foundation. Most heartwarming was being awarded to the Order of St. Olaf by King Olav V. The award was presented by the Norwegian ambassador at a ceremony held in Memorial Auditorium at the homecoming banquet, with my mother in attendance. In addition, to recognize Mardy's strategic role in the life of the college, she was feted on "Mardy Dovre Day" in 1985. This celebration of Mardy's contributions to the college included a morning limousine ride to her school (she had the day off), a special presentation at morning chapel, a luncheon in her honor, a helicopter ride, the surprise visits of our children and her sisters, an evening banquet, and a subsequent weekend trip to Winnipeg. Happily, she took me along.

The Board of Regents granted me a sabbatical leave in the summer of 1987, time we used for a study opportunity in Europe, reading, and relaxation. This was a nice pause in the action before we began serious preparation for the observance of the college's centennial. In short, the eighties had been a golden decade not only for Concordia, but also for the Dovres.

7. Watershed Decade: 1990-1999

I think of the nineties as a watershed decade in the sense that the nineties were both a time of fulfilled aspirations and, toward the end, a time of incipient change. This narrative is shaped by both integrative and paradoxical themes: the integrative themes were continuity, celebration, and community; the paradoxical themes were abundance and scarcity, identity and diversity, and stability and change. The ongoing stories of student and academic life held their own combinations of surprise and continuity.

CONTINUITY: BLUEPRINTS FOR THE NINETIES

Concordia launched the new decade the same way we had in the sixties, seventies, and eighties, with the preparation of a blueprint to guide the development of the college over the coming decade. The process to create *Blueprint* IV was an energizing and joyful project occurring at a time of strong enrollment, healthy budgets, a strong economy, and supportive public policies. Coming on the heels of the golden decade, the document authors wrote: "This era has witnessed the maturing of several elements of the college: the near completion of the physical plant, the growth of endowment, the quality and scholarly energy of the faculty, and the breadth and depth of the program." Continuing, they added:

> Concordia addresses the future through this current *Blueprint* from a position of strength. We are mature enough to claim our strengths, admit our faults, and welcome and encourage change. Our plans and actions during the next decade must flow from what has been built over the past one hundred years—a college clear about its mission, confident of its character, and effective in its Vocation. Soli Deo Gloria.

Blueprint IV was developed around four themes: first, a reaffirmation of mission, program, and community; second, the intention to live out actively all areas of mission and program; third, a call to global awareness and commitment; and, finally, recognition of growing diversity in the culture and an institutional commitment to diversity in our program and community. With respect to curricular matters, Concordia made a commitment to continuity and fine tuning with selective additions in women's studies, ethnic studies, and multicultural studies together with a strengthening of the language requirement and consideration of a math requirement. We recognized that the experience of community was under stress from both the multiplication of the institution's agendas and the growth of an individualism that tended to atomize the campus. This notion was expressed in, among other things, the suggestion that faculty governance ought to be simplified and streamlined to make governance less cumbersome and an intentional study about the ways in which community could be facilitated and strengthened through new strategies.

In terms of external relations, there was the continuing theme of building quality and access. Indeed, this was the rallying cry for much of the college's Advancement agenda. We were also getting used to life in the still new Evangelical Lutheran Church in America (ELCA), where we sensed that the individual colleges would be largely responsible for the relationship with the church. This led to suggestions that Concordia continue to build upon the strength of our past and current relationships with congregations in our corporate territory.

The accompanying *Financial Blueprint* to help guide financial decisions in the nineties took account of emerging demographic and economic trends in our region. The document reaffirmed the practice of conservative budgeting and the maintenance of strong operating reserves. The document suggested enrollment in the range of 2,750 to 2,950, reflecting anticipated shifts in the demographics of the region. We set future goals of funding current operations with seventy percent from tuition, ten percent from endowment, and twenty percent from gifts and other income sources, including auxiliary operations. Events would prove these goals to be unrealistic. The commitment to grow the endowment, however, was sustained with an excellent impact on the operating budget. The endowment grew from $4.6 million in 1981 to sixty-five million in 1997, evidence that our long-range planning had been successful. Dating back to the sixties, attention was paid to estate planning with Concordia's constituents, so when these gifts matured, the college gratefully benefitted. More time was spent in subsequent decades to help explain the importance of endowment to constituents, so endowments were a significant element of capital campaigns in the eighties. I was pleased to see all that had been accomplished through strategic planning and conservative budgeting, representing the hard work and deep commitment of many dedicated financial leaders.

As had been the case with previous *Blueprints*, *Blueprint* IV and the *Financial Blueprint* documents were prepared with broad input from the community over a two-year period of study, drafting, review, and eventual approval by the Board of Regents. In retrospect, however, those instrumental to the process missed some changes in the environment that would have a significant impact as noted in subsequent sections of this chapter. Among those changes were the leveling out of enrollment in the second half of the decade; the financial pressures from student aid, new technologies, and new regulations; a change in faculty culture that diminished the appetite for and the rate of change; the incredible growth in student engagement in public service in the local community and beyond; and the continuing evolution in student and public values.

CELEBRATION

The celebration of the college's centennial in 1991-92 was easily the highlight of my years at Concordia. The momentous event was a celebration of the college's heritage, founders, achievement, service, and, above all else, Concordia's mission. In good Concordia tradition, the college had begun planning for the celebration about five years in advance. First, a Centennial Planning Commission under the leadership of Carl Bailey was appointed, and, second, history professor Carroll Engelhardt was commissioned to prepare a history of the college. Last, but not least, funds were allocated to finance the celebration.

Dating back to the forties, campus leaders had envisioned construction of an appropriate architectural symbol of the college—a campanile. The idea was revived in connection with the construction of the Knutson Center, but the funds were not then available. The Centennial Planning Commission and other stakeholders revisited the idea in anticipation of the centennial. Concordia's long-term campus architect Ed Sovik and associates assisted with a comprehensive physical plan for the central campus area that was to include the creation of a mall with esthetic integrity, added green space, fresh plantings, relocation of parking, and the campanile at the apex. Earlier I described something about the politics of this project. What some might have seen as "Dovre's folly" became the central and beloved symbol of Concordia's centennial celebration and the college's continuing identity as a place of Christian mission.

The centennial celebration commenced with the annual Cobber corn feed on August 28, 1991. For the first time, the event was scheduled to include students, neighbors, friends, faculty, and staff. The grand celebration would continue throughout the year with various events and highlights. The college featured distinguished alumni in several events over the course of the year. A first-class interpretive exhibit about the history of the college was installed in Moorhead's Heritage Hjemkomst Interpretive Center under the direction of artist David Hetland, with the strategic assistance of Sharon Hoverson (Library) and Duane Mickelson (Art). The annual fall symposium addressed the future of the church with a troop of distinguished scholars and theologians led by Martin Marty. There were art exhibits featuring distinguished alumni, a commissioned orchestral work by J. Robert Hanson, and a historical pageant created by James and Helen Cermak (Communication and Theatre Arts).

In addition, a special feature of the centennial celebration was the presentation of centennial medallions to ten people, including two couples from the region who exemplified the values of the college. Selected by the Centennial Planning Commission, the group included teachers, farmers, artists, pastors, a doctor, and a banker. Their selection reflected well the mission and rootedness of the college in the region. The weekend of October 31 marked the date of Concordia's founding, so the college hosted a birthday party with a supersized cake, a reception recognizing the role of the Fargo-Moorhead community in nurturing the college, a convocation featuring reflection around the mission of the school, the pageant referred to above, special recognition of families involved in the founding of Concordia, a grand banquet featuring many of the centennial medallion honorees, and a Sunday worship service featuring the bishop of the ELCA, Herbert Chilstrom.

The centennial was an incredible year that reflected the values, accomplishments, excellence, and mission of the college. Homecoming was extraordinary with over-the-top attendance, great pageantry, and a festive mood. The central event of homecoming in those years was always the Sunday morning service that drew upwards of two thousand people. The centennial worship was even larger in 1991 and featured, as usual, exceptional music by the concert choir and Concordia band. The title of my homily that day was "In the Face of the West Wind," a theme recognizing the challenges that the founders overcame and expressing confidence in the ability of current and future generations to do the same, with the help of God. My closing remarks were shaped by a reference to a familiar passage from Hebrews:

> We each name a cloud of witnesses in our hearts today as did the writer of Hebrews 2,000 years ago. The names will be different, but the place of these people in our lives is the same—founders in the faith, saints for all seasons, sent forth to be God's people. Since we are surrounded by so great a cloud of witnesses, let us run with perseverance the race that is set before us. Let us turn our face to the West Wind.

The success of the celebration was attributable to exceptional planning, excellent staff work, a widely shared sense of responsibility and excitement, and a constituency that genuinely revered the college. Lowell Larson was the executive director of the celebration, and he brought to his work both his prodigious energy and his high standards; hence, the centennial event also exemplified the college's commitment to excellence. As will be noted subsequently, the celebration included a major fundraising campaign that exceeded the goal and provided several special events and occasions for celebration and rededication.

One of the memorable events of 1991 occurred just after the college concluded the centennial homecoming celebration. The Minnesota Twins were in the World Series, and on the Sunday night of homecoming weekend, the Twins were playing in the seventh and deciding game against the Atlanta Braves. Mardy and I watched the game, and behind the incredible pitching of Jack Morris, the Twins won in the tenth inning. The president's residence is on the corner of 8th Street and 7th Avenue, and within minutes of the game's conclusion, that intersection began filling with students from the adjoining Bogstad apartments as well as other neighborhood apartments. The scene became loud and somewhat raucous, with students running to the center of the intersection when the stoplights turned red on 8th Street. A few students began rocking cars as unsuspecting drivers entered the intersection, and the police soon arrived. I decided that I would try to be of assistance, so I dressed, complete with my Cobber cap, of course, and proceeded to enter the scene to the accompaniment of a student chant, "Here comes the Dove!" A police officer came to ask if I could be of assistance. I chatted with several students I knew, most of whom were in "good spirits," and suggested we move the party to the newly dedicated campanile. The party quickly dispersed, and the next day the chief of police came by my office to express appreciation. Through the years, scores of Cobbers have approached me and claimed their role in this joyful event.

Another event worth noting from that auspicious centennial year in 1991-92 had roots in the late eighties. On a fall afternoon in 1989, I received a call from Garrison Keillor, the well-known host of NPR's *A Prairie Home Companion*. Keillor's career began in Minnesota, and his nationally broadcast radio show was named after the Prairie Home Cemetery on 8th Street, located across from the Concordia campus. He asked me if the college would be interested in hosting *A Prairie Home* festival for hymn singing and folk dancing the coming March. According to Keillor, its purpose would be to combat the depressing effect of a long winter by engaging in hearty song and joyful dance. We agreed and joined with Garrison and his staff in planning the festival that would begin on Friday evening and conclude on Saturday evening. The festival included many of Garrison's featured musicians and entertainers and some local musicians and groups, including the Concordia choir. Throughout the day, there were a variety of workshops and performances. Hundreds of people from across the region gathered for the festival, which would be repeated in 1991 and 1992. The last two festivals included his live Saturday night broadcast of *A Prairie Home Companion*. On one of those occasions, he asked me to sing a duet with him. Sitting in the front row of Memorial Auditorium, Keillor and I rehearsed for about five minutes before the show commenced. Garrison and I sang about two lines, and he said we were ready to go. I wasn't so sure, but I had confidence in him. It was a blast! And Garrison was right—the singing, dancing, and storytelling did indeed shorten the dreary effects of the long winter season. As was his custom, after three successful festivals at Concordia, Keillor's road show moved on to new venues.

Other celebrations in the nineties included the two occasions on which Concordia College hosted the Nobel Peace Prize Forum. The Peace Prize Forums were sponsored by Norwegian heritage colleges Augsburg, Augustana, Concordia, Luther, and St. Olaf in coordination with the

Norwegian Peace Prize Institute of Norway. The Forums rotated among the five campuses and included faculty and students from all the schools plus members of the public in the host community. The overarching theme of the Forums was "Striving for Peace," and each Forum featured a Peace Prize Laureate as well as other prominent scholars, diplomats, and peace advocates. These were high quality events with a full day and a half of programming. The Nobel Peace Prize Forums provided a splendid opportunity for students and faculty from the five schools to celebrate our shared heritage and aspirations.

The 1993 Forum focused on the United Nations and featured Peace Prize recipient, the United Nations Children Fund. Speakers included former Vice President Walter Mondale; Paul Wee of the Lutheran World Federation; Edwin Perkins, the United Nations High Commissioner for Refugees; and Harold Stassen, former governor of Minnesota and a signatory of the United Nations Charter. The 1998 Forum featured laureate Jose Ramos-Horta, a dissident reformer from East Timor; Nien Cheng, a Chinese human rights advocate; and former Vice President Mondale.

Mardy and I enjoyed hosting these distinguished guests on the Concordia campus and colleagues from other schools. Unfortunately, however, there was always a bit of tension between the schools and the director of the Nobel Peace Institute, Geir Lundestad. Lundestad was used to Norway, where Institute programs were always front-page events attended by national leaders. He was looking for something of the same in these Midwestern locales, but that was not likely to happen, even on those occasions when Augsburg hosted the events in the population and media center of the Twin Cities. Nonetheless, the Forums were great events for the college, and Concordia faculty and students alike invested heavily in the occasions. Sadly, by 2011 the Nobel Peace Prize Forum was modified and transformed into an Augsburg-Twin Cities event. The transition to Augsburg was occasioned by the declining interest on a couple of the participating campuses and the hope that Augsburg might provide the kind of venue that would attract broader public participation and consistently strong media coverage. The event later transitioned to the Human Rights Forum in 2019.

The most intensively orchestrated celebrative event of the nineties at Concordia was the visit of Norway's King Harold V and Queen Sonia in 1995. The king and queen were wonderful guests, and their visit brought thousands of people to the Concordia campus. The afternoon visit included a public convocation at which the king was awarded an honorary degree, a press conference, a procession down the campus mall, and a reception in the Centrum. My assistant, Esther Allen, coordinated the event along with a hardworking committee. With matters of protocol, security, and politics in play, the event was a complicated undertaking. We later learned that the Concordia convocation was the best attended event on the king and queen's American tour.

We had previously hosted then Crown Princess Sonia of Norway during a visit to the campus in the late seventies, and I had met the king in Oslo while he was crown prince. In addition, on one of the Concordia choir tours, the royals hosted the choir at a reception in their home outside of Oslo. They had also regularly attended concerts by the choir during its tours in Norway, so they were significantly familiar with the college and with Mardy and me. Once again, we found the royal couple to be gracious, easy company, and interested in the life of the college.

Hosting Norwegian royalty on campus was a monumental undertaking, down to the last detail. In planning the king and queen's campus itinerary, for example, we had to allow time for a smoke break on our non-smoking campus, but the accommodation was managed just fine. I also recall that at the reception for approximately two hundred people, we formed two lines; Mardy introduced guests to the king in one line, and I did the same for the queen in the other. One gentleman remarked to the king that "he was lucky" to have a wife like Sonia, to which the king agreed. The queen asked each guest a question about where they lived or their connection to the college or Norway. Some guests were a bit flustered, but Queen Sonia put them at ease. At the end of that busy day, the planning committee convened for a celebrative gathering at Esther Allen's home, and a group of distinguished guests gathered at the Fargo Country Club for dinner. Mardy and I attended both events. King Harold V and Queen Sonia's visit and all the accompanying festivities been one of the college's great days. The day had been great for me on a personal basis as well because one of my sisters and my brother and their spouses were able to attend the festivities. I was grateful for the opportunity to share the occasion with my family. Interactions with Norwegian royalty on several occasions on behalf of the college over the years has been an honor for Concordia and memorable for Mardy and me.

COMMUNITY

In addition to integrative themes of continuity and celebration, the third integrative theme in the nineties was community. The college placed a strong value on offering a rich and nurturing campus environment. The friendliness of the campus is what students and alumni often commented on first when describing their Concordia experience. *Blueprint* IV not only affirmed the continuing importance of community but also recognized that things were changing, and the experience of community was not what it had been when the college was smaller and more homogeneous. In its macro expression, community had grown weaker—attendance at athletic events, concerts, lectures, chapel, and faculty meetings had declined. On the other hand, in its micro expression—that is, at the department or building or residence hall levels—community was perhaps stronger than it had been. For example, in the sixties and seventies, dozens of faculty and staff would gather for morning coffee at the Red Room, a small gathering space just off the cafeteria. By the nineties, however, only a dozen or so would gather for this morning ritual because most were gathering in coffee klatches in their department or building.

Recognizing the importance of community but also noting the changes that were occurring, a Commission on Community was formed in 1993 to study these matters and make appropriate recommendations to the college community. Dean of Students Morris Lanning chaired the commission, and, in its early work, the work of the commission was aided by the recently published study by the Carnegie Commission titled "Campus Life: In Search of Community." The Commission conducted a campus survey that affirmed both the importance and the positive experience of community. Ninety percent of the faculty, ninety-five percent of the administrative staff, and eighty-seven percent of the students agreed on the importance of community, and eighty-nine percent of the faculty, eighty-three percent of the staff, and fifty-two percent of the students said they were personally committed to the community life of the college. Concordia's Commission on Community identified eight core values of community that included academic, religious, and social elements among the eight values. The Commission acknowledged the various changes in the experience of community and identified some of the underlying reasons, such as more diversity among students, faculty, and staff; a more complex community;

conflicting priorities for time and attention; changing religious practices (people did not worship as frequently); and tension between the academic and the co-curricular. Some of the best work of the Commission was seen in its attention to the philosophical and theological principles of community. Campus pastor Phil Holtan picked up on the challenge of maintaining religious identity amid increasing diversity. Historian Carroll Engelhardt provided a perceptive historical analysis of the evolution of community over the college's history.

The recommendations of the Commission on Community were often elusive. There were calls to attend to the tension between academic expectation and extracurricular activities. There was strong emphasis on Concordia becoming more welcoming and inclusive even as the college became more diverse. There was the recognition that with the increasing diversity, more differences of opinion were likely to emerge, and the college should prepare to accept and process those differences in a constructive way. To deal with the stresses and time demands of faculty governance, the Commission recommended that the faculty make a comprehensive review of its governance. In doing so, the faculty developed a new constitution, which, ironically, created a more complex and time-consuming governance structure than the replaced one. This change in governance also may have reflected both the significant turnover in faculty and staff related to retirements and growth that resulted in a lack of familiarity and trust.

In summary, amidst all the changes in culture, size, and expectations, community, there remained a strong underlying value. The stresses that occasioned appointment of the Commission did not disappear, but the Concordia community's understanding of and ability to respond to those changes was enhanced. Formal study and deliberation aside, the most intimate and strategic expressions of a sense of community at Concordia occurred in the interactions between students and their advisors and teachers, between colleague faculty and staff dealing with their common work, among the small group work of committees and planning groups, and within the fellowship of teammates, choir-mates, and actors in common cause. My observation was that these expressions of community were very healthy and, with respect to the student experience, tended to grow deeper and richer as traditions of authority in earlier ages diminished.

IDENTITY AND CULTURAL DIVERSITY

As noted, diversity was a focus in the work of those instrumental in the process of preparing *Blueprint* IV. The diversity theme applied to matters of gender, sexuality, race, and ethnicity. Document authors and contributors envisioned that the college would be serving a more diverse constituency and that Concordia graduates would be living out their vocations in a more diverse society and world. With that vision in mind, key decision makers and planners urged the college community to examine Concordia's programs and outward markers and distinctions of community to ensure that the institution was prepared to both attract and serve a more diverse population. Several follow-up projects were initiated in the years following the publication of *Blueprint* IV. My assistants, Esther Allen in the early nineties and Tracey Moorhead in the late nineties, played significant roles in organizing and implementing many special events under the auspices of the Human Relations Committee, which consisted of students, faculty, and staff, to help move those goals forward. Reverend Walter McDuffy, director of Intercultural Affairs, was another reliable partner and leader.

There is a personal story related to this topic of diversity that comes to mind. In the late eighties and particularly during the preparation of *Blueprint* IV, I became interested in the diversity movement. I found conversation with faculty colleagues to be helpful. I also read widely on the topic and attended conferences related to the topic of diversity. I was particularly intrigued by how an institution like Concordia could balance concerns for its own identity with the desire for and the reality of a more diverse community. At the turn of the decade, the Board of Regents encouraged me to take a sabbatical leave, which I did in the fall of 1992. With the assistance of board member Paul Peterson, a faculty member at Harvard's Kennedy School of Government, I was appointed as a visiting scholar at the Graduate School of Education. Mardy and I spent two months in Cambridge, where I had access to a wide range of human and library resources. The focus of my reading and listening was on diversity. My time as visiting scholar at Harvard's Graduate School of Education was an invaluable experience and equipped me to bring leadership to Concordia's diversity agenda.

Although diversity was a broad umbrella topic at the time, gender was a major emphasis in Concordia's diversity agenda in the nineties. A significant beginning had been made in the eighties with the creation of a women's studies program and a women's center. The Women's Studies program grew in quality and participation. In the nineties, the college continued programs to strengthen the role of women in leadership at the college. Among other efforts, the college sponsored the participation of women faculty and staff at leadership development activities in the community, the region, and nationally. Concordia sponsored a number of participants in the Bryn Mawr University program for women in higher education. Under the theme "Wholeness through Diversity," Concordia hosted several consciousness-raising events and activities, including campus presentations by Mary Francis Berry, former assistant secretary of education in the Carter administration; Earl Lewis, a University of Michigan historian (and a Cobber); and Bonnie Wallace, a leader in Augsburg College's Indian Center. Later programs in the series focused on gender issues. The observance of Women's History Week became an annual element in the Concordia calendar.

There was broadly shared leadership on the gender agenda, beginning in the seventies, continuing in the eighties, but substantially expanding in the nineties. The percentage of women on the faculty grew as did the percentages of women in faculty and administrative leadership roles. Likewise, women expanded their leadership in student government and campus life. This was perhaps the highlight of the college's diversity agenda in the last quarter of the decade, while progress in other areas was challenging and often subject to factors outside of our control.

With increased focus on diversity, the Native American program came in for special consideration. The college received a $269,000 grant from the McKnight Foundation that enabled Concordia to augment our Native American staff, host visiting scholars, and provide graduate fellowships for potential future faculty. The 1992 annual fall symposium theme "Gathering of Spirit: Gifts of Native Americans" also reflected the college's Native American diversity focus. The symposium featured several respected scholars and Native American resource people. In addition, an annual Native American Week featured notable artists, scholars, and public figures as well as the annual Tri-College Powwow, co-sponsored with North Dakota State University and Minnesota State University at Moorhead. Warner Huss, a Native American and longtime member of Concordia's Admissions staff, provided excellent leadership to this initiative. The results of the college's special emphasis were a modest uptick in enrollment, a broader campus awareness of Native American history and contemporary issues, and outreach to Native American communities. Despite the college's best efforts, however, we were not able to build a substantial enrollment of Native American students, a reality of the 2000s as well.

As described earlier, the college made concerted efforts to attract and retain African American students as well. The enrollment of African American students, however, continued to be a challenge as it had been since the early seventies when African American students began to take increasing advantage of educational opportunities closer to home. As noted in earlier chapters, despite enhanced recruiting efforts, Fargo-Moorhead was a difficult sell due to the lack of diversity. The same factor made the recruitment of minority faculty difficult, most of whom had multiple employment opportunities elsewhere because higher education across the country was also emphasizing increased diversity.

While challenges remained in recruiting and retraining diverse students and faculty in the nineties, Concordia's efforts to equip students for global diversity were quite successful. Global awareness had been an underlying priority dating back to the seventies, and the college continued to build on previous success. For example, the May Seminar program celebrated twenty-five years of service in the nineties and continued to prosper. Concordia had very successful study abroad programs in Spanish, German, and French, and developed new study abroad programs in Norway, Tanzania, and India. In the late nineties, the college and the Massai girls' school in Arusha, Tanzania, initiated a program that would bring two graduates of the Massai school to Concordia each year, resulting in a potential total of eight women. The school had been nurtured by former Cobber missionary David Simonson. The goal was to prepare the graduates to assume leadership roles in Tanzania upon completion of their studies at Concordia. Even decades later, Concordia continues to have a special relationship with the Massai girls' school and surrounding community in Tanzania.

Concordia's substantial grant from the Knight Foundation enabled forty-eight of our faculty members to study abroad and, upon their return, to help internationalize the curriculum and learning experience of their students. On the domestic side to reflect increasing first-hand experiences with diversity, the Chicago Seminar continued to provide an opportunity for students to experience the diversity of an urban community. In addition, there were numerous opportunities for student service projects in the

South and Southwest, many of them under the direction of campus pastor Philip Holtan, often organized through Habitat for Humanity or Concordia's Justice Journeys program, which were spring trip opportunities for the purposes of "encountering, engaging, learning, and accompanying as an issue of justice..." in diverse settings, both nationally and sometimes internationally. In various measures of learning, these off-campus and international study opportunities received very high marks from Concordia students and faculty/staff leaders.

These movements toward ethnic, racial, and cultural diversity generated great interest, activity, and support in the nineties. One positive consequence was the addition of a multicultural requirement to the Core Curriculum. Another was the creativity of Concordia faculty in developing new curricula, offering additional global study opportunities, and emphasizing exchange programs. Taken together with the college's extensive opportunities for internships and work study opportunities, these programs made Concordia College a national leader in experiential learning.

This period of the nineties brought increased awareness of and conversations about diversity. The most difficult conversations about diversity were related to sexual identity and homosexuality. The culture of the early eighties was generally hostile to homosexuals, and they remained a largely hidden population. Nationwide in the eighties, activists on behalf of the rights and dignity of homosexuals increased in number and effect. Churches were one of the places of cultural contention around these issues. National and local church leaders stressed that faith communities should "hate the sin" but "love the sinner." Activists in the Evangelical Lutheran Church in America, however, would not sit still for such a view. Some gay and lesbian Lutheran pastors on the West Coast publicly declared their status and sought to retain their calls, thus setting off a long and contentious debate that extended into the 2000s when the ELCA authorized the ordination of homosexual persons, an action that would create significant chaos in many Midwestern congregations.

Back to the Concordia campus story: We recognized and valued the reality that we had several students, faculty, and staff who were homosexual. Given the church policy at the time, we took the position that we would welcome education and conversation but not advocacy for a homosexual lifestyle. At the same time, we encouraged and supported campus counseling staff led by Pastor Carl Lee to provide support for gays and lesbians in the Concordia community. Because we recognized the lack of understanding and hospitality, the college initiated a comprehensive and extended series of events and activities designed to address the related issues. The theme of the first series of events was "Wholeness through Diversity." In 1992, the campus hosted a convocation featuring a Lutheran theologian, Donald Juell, who opposed any change in the ELCA's policies, and Karen Bloomquist, who was more open to change. Pastors in the community were invited to attend the convocation and a luncheon question and answer session following the event. The convocation was followed by dozens of small group conversations around the campus that included faculty, staff, and students.

The fall symposium in 1993 included a session on "Growing Up Different: Gays and Lesbians." Two students shared their experience as gay and lesbian. That same fall, the ELCA published a draft social statement on homosexuality. Among other points, the draft statement viewed homosexuality not as a matter of choice but as a part of one's identity, and the draft statement called for the ELCA to move toward the blessing of same sex unions. The draft report created a furor and, again, Concordia's response was to sponsor discussions groups on campus and another convocation featuring church leaders who held opposing views. In my mind, we were both providing an opportunity for the campus community to gain understanding and serving as a sort of laboratory for the church in discerning its future course. I believe this approach was good work that made a difference and was consistent with the ELCA's deep roots in seeking meaning through inquiry and relationship building, where questions and doubts are welcome.

Concordia's more activist-minded students were not satisfied with conversation and education, however, and wanted more action. First, a Tri-College group called The Ten Percent Society sought recognition on the Concordia campus. Because the group advocated on behalf of a gay lifestyle, a position then at odds with the ELCA policy, we did not formally recognize the society. Subsequently, Dean Lanning worked with a group of interested Concordia students in forming FLAG, acronym for Friends of Lesbians and Gays, a group committed to providing education and support.

More than twenty-five years after these events, it is perhaps hard to fully understand the conflicting opinions of the nineties. Both the church and society are in such a different place today on these issues, but in the late eighties and the nineties, these were complex and sensitive matters. As a college of the ELCA, we wanted to address the issues in depth and with the seriousness they deserved and in a manner that respected the tradition then in place in the church and the Concordia community. I think we walked that tight rope successfully and in a way that people of various opinions respected.

INSTITUTIONAL IDENTITY AND DIVERSITY

The generational changes in the faculty had many dimensions and multiple consequences. From the 1950s through the early 1980s, the mission and religious identity of Concordia were taken for granted and embodied in the faculty and staff. That is, most of the faculty and staff had been formed in the Lutheran church and the Lutheran liberal arts traditions. These traditions were kept alive primarily in the life and witness of the faculty and staff and articulated with grace and clarity by Dean Bailey, President Knutson, and me. We did not spend a lot of time in theological reflection or in exploring the relationship between faith and our respective academic endeavors because those were natural expressions of who we were.

Whereas in the fifties and sixties, most of the new faculty and staff came through the so-called Lutheran pipeline. By the late seventies and accelerating in the eighties, most of the college's faculty came from other places, which meant, in effect, that the Concordia story and Lutheran tradition were not a part of their formation. Add to that the fact that by the sixties, the academy was largely shaped by the scientific paradigm, which often had the effect of marginalizing the humanities, including religion.

Concordia welcomed this growing diversity, on the one hand, because we believed diversity made us stronger and more hospitable. At the time, however, the bylaws of the college indicated that, generally, members of the faculty were to be Lutheran and in all cases Christian. We had interpreted that bylaw as a guideline and not a rule, so Catholics, Baptists, Presbyterians, Methodists, and Jews were among the more recent hires along with a significant number of Lutherans. Again, while Concordia welcomed this diversity, we did not want to give up the institution's distinctive ethos and logos as a college of the Lutheran church. With this in mind, Concordia sponsored a workshop for interested faculty on the Lutheran college and the liberal arts in the mid-seventies and again in the early eighties. Two of faculty members from the Philosophy Department,

Tom Christenson and Gregg Muilenburg, were deeply interested in this program and were lively contributors to its success. These workshops were highly rated but involved only a small number of faculty members. In addition, Concordia joined sister Lutheran colleges in conversation about the meaning and implications of identity as Lutheran colleges, conversations that I helped form and in which I frequently participated.

In the mid-eighties, I began to notice that an increasing number of candidates for faculty positions lacked both experience with and credible interest in the mission dimension of Concordia's enterprise. I called this to the attention of the dean and the department chairs. I suggested that we initiate a sort of affirmative action strategy to add to our recruitment pools larger numbers of candidates who were Lutheran and persons of other traditions who gave evidence of something more than a passing interest in our mission identity. By the early nineties, I was not satisfied with our progress and raised the issue again for campus discussion. This was a contentious matter that people had been dancing around, but it was clear to me that my duty as president was first and foremost to safeguard the mission of the college, so some stress and strain in the community around this issue was inevitable. Coincidentally, and following up on some of the recommendations of *Blueprint* IV, Concordia was in the process of creating four commissions: one related to quality, another to community, a third to academic integrity, and the fourth to faith and learning. *Blueprint* IV had called for more concrete study of ways in which Concordia's mission could be embodied in the life of the college, and we took this as a mandate to study faith and learning at Concordia College by creating a commission by the same name.

A first-rate group of faculty and one student were appointed to the Commission on Faith and Learning at Concordia College, which was co-chaired by Professor Ernest Simmons (Religion) and me. While it may have seemed risky to take on that assignment, I did so as a way of sending a message about the importance I assigned to the subject. Commission members included faculty from a variety of disciplines and religious traditions as well as both long term and recently appointed members. The commission conducted a significant study and developed a schedule for community dialogue. The commission invited nationally recognized spokespersons from various religious traditions to visit campus and share with us how faith and learning intersected in their academic traditions. We also initiated a series of dinner conversations at which representative faculty members explained how they related faith to learning in their disciplines. During the same time period, I invited the faculty to an open meeting at which I responded to their questions and concerns. This was a tense but necessary meeting. Providing the opportunity established the fact that I was willing to take on tough questions on this subject, and there were several of them.

While in the beginning of this period of more deeply exploring Lutheran identity and diversity my role was to identify the issue, but my role in the succeeding year and a half was to insure open, hospitable, and high-quality conversation about the issue that was at the core of our institutional being. In that year and a half of conversation, the commission effort gained credibility, and the faculty claimed their work by approving recommendations to establish a permanent Center for Faith and Learning. The purpose of the center would be to provide a resource to the faculty in addressing issues related to faith and learning at Concordia through a mentorship program, research grants, faculty study opportunities on campus and abroad, and public lectures on an array of topics.

Faculty response to the program of the Center for Faith and Learning was consistent and positive. Nearly every faculty member engaged with the center in one or more of its activities. The work of the Commission on Faith and Learning and the center have lifted up the Lutheran intellectual and academic traditions. The Lutheran understanding of Vocation came to define the way we understand our callings as members of the faculty and staff and one of the goals of the educational experience at Concordia. The work of the Center for Faith and Learning was directed by the highly able and credible Ernie Simmons, and I was gratified by the fact that, at my retirement, the center was named in my honor. The good and important work of the Dovre Center for Faith and Learning continues today, I'm pleased to note.

Coming into the national collegiate scene almost simultaneously with the work of the Commission on Faith and Learning was an initiative of the Lilly Foundation designed to stimulate campus reflection on the identity of religious colleges and its implications. Grants were made to scores of church-related colleges in the 1990s and early 2000s, including Concordia. The grant program had the effect of making faith and learning the subject of campus-wide conversation, one that included students as well as the faculty and staff, through a variety of workshops and study opportunities. The product of these two ventures—the Commission on Faith and Learning and the Lilly grant—was substantial. For Concordia, our self-understanding as individuals and as a college came to be grounded in the Lutheran understanding of Vocation, that we are called to serve our neighbor in the world.

Someone asked me if Concordia's focus on Lutheran identity and Vocation was at cross purposes with the college's desire for ethnic diversity. From an intellectual point of view, that is doubtful since the Lutheran theological tradition emphasizes freedom, dialogue, and hospitality. The work of the Dovre Center and the Vocation theme both illustrated the ecumenical and interfaith traditions of the Lutheran church. These initiatives were very important in achieving the integration of the identity and diversity themes; Lutherans, after all, have a tradition of addressing paradoxical issues in a reconciling way.

It was propitious that a comprehensive review of the curriculum was initiated in 1998, and the reconsideration of the institution's identity and mission would contribute to that process in significant ways. The most visible impact was manifest in the brand of the new Core Curriculum, "Being Responsibly Engaged in the World," the acronym for which was BREW. This brand encapsulated Concordia's mission and facilitated fresh conversations in almost every dimension of campus life, both in and out of the classroom experience.

The result of these two interrelated projects, that is, the commission's work and the curriculum review, was a renaissance of mission. It was sometimes a challenging, stressful process, but also a life giving one. It is my belief that such renewing events are essential to the ongoing vitality and faithfulness of colleges like Concordia.

LEADERSHIP, MANAGEMENT, AND OVERSIGHT

I also believe that leaders are expected to set the tone, anticipate change, articulate the mission, stimulate imagination, and inspire service. People want to know what their leader thinks, what he or she values, and how the person sees the present and the future. Further, sometimes unconsciously, people look to leaders for inspiration, assurance, and strength. Aware of these expectations, I sought to consistently address these expectations for leadership to the best of my ability. I also recognized, however, that leadership is not a solo operation, which explains the need for a variety of gifts and competencies on the leadership team and for a broad sharing of responsibility.

As noted earlier, I preferred working from a carefully considered strategic plan. Informed by the college's long-range plan and our ongoing administrative needs, the President's Council would set annual goals for the administration and each division. Each division's staff was involved in setting their goals, which provided grass roots ownership of the product. The resulting plan gave us a road map that shaped weekly meetings as a group and my weekly meetings with individual members.

Following the example of my mentor Joseph Knutson, I believed in the delegation of responsibility for execution of our plan. Mine was a "no surprises" approach to management. Twice a year, the President's Council met in retreat to review our work and make necessary mid-course corrections. I rarely became involved in the details of management within a division; the exceptions were when an unexpected event occurred or there was a need for problem-solving.

Let me comment about each member of the 1990s leadership team. As noted in earlier chapters, I became acquainted with Loren Anderson when he was a student in the early sixties. I recruited Loren to our staff in the early seventies, and, except for a few years working with the American Lutheran Church, he served the college until accepting the presidency of Pacific Lutheran University in 1992. Loren's primary responsibilities were in Advancement and long-range planning. His influence on the college's progress was inestimable, as seen by the success of Concordia's capital campaigns and strategic plans. Loren possessed a combination of emotional intelligence and strategic capacity. His skills of observation enabled him to read people and situations accurately, and his analytical skills were closely matched by his communication skills. Undergirding all of this was his passion for Concordia's mission. Loren and I enjoyed a deep mutual trust and shared vision and values. Loren had an outstanding run as president of Pacific Lutheran University and emerged as a national spokesperson for private higher education.

Clyde Allen, another member of the leadership team, was a Yale graduate who appreciated the inherent and practical values of the liberal arts. We worked together efficiently and almost intuitively on account of shared trust, common values, and agreement on financial principles. Clyde's political skills, developed as a lobbyist and then as a member of Minnesota

Governor Al Quie's cabinet, served him well in the collegiate environment of the college. Clyde had strong ties to the faculty and did an excellent job of explaining the budget and securing support and cooperation. He also led the community in the preparation of *Financial Blueprints* for the eighties and nineties.

Bob Homann came to the deanship with already deep experience from his earlier service as associate dean and his key role in faculty governance. Bob was a major player in the curriculum reform activities in the seventies and eighties and was a champion for faculty development projects. He enjoyed the trust of his colleagues and fit into his role as dean with ease and effectiveness. Bob led the college in a series of faculty and curriculum innovations related to governance, global studies, and technology. Bob was a scientist by training but with the outlook of a humanist, an academic with a sense of humor that would lighten tense moments.

Linda Brown succeeded Loren Anderson in a move that may have surprised outsiders, given her previous position as accountant and comptroller. While in that position, Linda developed a strong working relationship with the faculty in budget planning and with the Advancement Office in structuring and administering sometimes complicated charitable trust and gift annuity agreements. She had an excellent way with both colleagues and constituents, which earned friendship and trust. Linda presided over several successful fund-raising initiatives. For many years, Linda and I enjoyed working together in developing and implementing fundraising plans.

Morris Lanning, vice president for Student Affairs and dean of students, I often referred to as our "Rock of Gibraltar" during the sometimes-unpredictable waves of student sentiment and action. Morrie brought an unusual combination of steadiness and imagination to his work, and the latter often caught people unaware. His imagination, and that of his capable staff, was evident in the creation of the student leadership and service-learning programs, both of which were pace-setting programs in the community of private colleges. He was a very effective voice for student interests and needs, the architect of both Concordia's student rights document and the extensive involvement of students in various governance functions. In addition to being an effective leader, Morrie was a natural ham, surprising the community in skits and performances. Morrie was also active in Moorhead city government in the eighties and nineties, serving as alderman and then as mayor. His effectiveness brought respect and appreciation to the college, and he was a significant role model for our students.

Jim Hausmann, another strong leader in the nineties, presided over monumental changes in financial aid policy and admissions marketing. The college's record enrollments were no accident; rather, strong enrollment numbers reflected careful selection of staff, a carefully honed and shepherded recruiting strategy, and a very successful marketing program. None of us will forget The Concordia Equation under Jim's leadership, which was a masterful way of telling the Concordia story to prospective students. Financial aid became increasingly complex and important in the eighties and nineties with fluctuations in federal and state support, the advent of merit-based aid, and heightened competition for students. Jim guided the college through this transition in an almost seamless way. State financial aid was of great importance to the college, and Jim was effective in building and maintaining relationships with key political and legislative leaders. In fact, Jim became a role model among the private colleges of Minnesota.

Esther Allen and Tracey Moorhead provided staff support for the planning activities of the cabinet and the college's Long-Range Planning Committee. They oversaw the development of agendas and supporting materials for meetings of the Board of Regents. They were efficient and diplomatic in all those roles. In addition, they both played strategic roles in addressing the needs of the campus community. For example, Esther and Tracey did formative work on initiatives related to diversity, women's issues, and human sexuality. Esther was the staff coordinator for the highly successful royal visit of King Harold V and Queen Sonia, and Tracey filled a similar role in the annual National Book Award event on campus. Perhaps equally important was the informal feedback and counsel they provided to me. I would try out ideas with them, and they would provide valuable feedback on various campus issues. Assistants to presidents are sometimes thought of as people who are seen but not heard, but these two remarkable women were both seen and heard because they were competent and respected.

Elizabeth Danielson joined the leadership team as academic dean in the late nineties upon Bob Homann's return to the faculty. She brought clarity and competence to difficult issues at a time of increasing anxiety and tension related to the new experience of scarcity and the changing culture of the faculty. Elizabeth's training as a psychologist and her previous leadership experience in different venues were especially helpful as administrative leadership sought to reframe our academic strategy. She played a strategic role in the reformulation of the Core Curriculum, a task initiated and largely completed during her four-year term of leadership. Elizabeth also played a key role in framing campus reflections on Vocation, a project funded by a significant grant from the Lilly Endowment.

One of the hallmarks of this leadership team was the high level of accountability we practiced through the annual planning cycle, regular budget reviews, occasional program reviews, and periodic professional assessments. I believe an important factor in the administrative leadership team's success is that we enjoyed and respected one another. Our annual Christmas and summer social gatherings were festive and fun filled. In addition, at our regular weekly meetings, we could always count on Bob Homann or Esther Allen to keep us from taking ourselves too seriously.

When discussing the administrative leadership cadre, it is essential to recognize the second level people who carried out substantial responsibilities. Let me start with John Pierce, David Benson, Ernie Mancini, Rosalie Lier, and Donald Rice, all from the Development team. John Pierce formed strong bonds with more constituents than anyone in the college's history. David Benson did groundbreaking work in estate planning. Ernie Mancini became the face and the cheerleader for our alumni, and Rosalie Lier was a creative foundation officer who opened doors for the college at the Bush, McKnight, and Kresge Foundations as well as secured substantial personal gifts from Stanley and Dorothy Kresge. Don Rice pioneered best practices in church relations. Each of these talented, committed staff brought unique gifts to bear in their respective work on behalf of Concordia.

Strong, capable personnel were notable in other aspects of the day-to-day running of the college as well. In Business Affairs, for example, Ansel Haakenson gave outstanding leadership in the oversight and maintenance of Concordia's physical plant. His engineering background saved the college substantial money, and Ansel picked exceptionally able staff. Jane Grant Shambaugh was an excellent manager of the college's auxiliary services and built our catering service into an important source of service and revenue. Mark Lillehaugen, the comptroller, was always spot-on with the numbers. I recall the consistent excellence of Donald Dale's service as Concordia registrar; he understood that his primary mission was to serve the needs of students. Verlyn Anderson, director of our library services, was always on top of needs and opportunities. The Academic Affairs office drew strength from a succession of outstanding associate deans in the nineties, including faculty members Jim Forde, Marilyn Guy, and Polly Fassinger.

Strong leadership was evident at the Concordia Language Village as well. Beginning in the eighties, Christine Schultz became the executive director of the Concordia Language Villages. She would lead this program for over three decades with deep commitment and great effectiveness. Under Christine's leadership, the program grew to at least fifteen languages, and new Language Village sites were developed for Finnish, Swedish, Russian, and Spanish. In the 2000s, the Villages were providing cultural immersion programs for the U.S. Department of Defense. Christine combined academic expertise with success in fund raising to make the CLV a truly national brand.

There were additional administrative leaders who played key roles in supporting Concordia students. Phil Hanson was a steady and reliable placement director who shifted gears when business emerged as the leading major for Concordia students. Jim Meier managed student housing in a low-key manner, but with attention to all the details of maintenance and discipline. The student health service was ably served by physicians Alf Borge and Mary Ellen Obert, and always at the center providing continuity and stability was Kathy Benson, campus nurse and a campus icon. Barbara Eiden Molinero was an innovator in student services, especially regarding volunteer services. She was succeeded by the equally skillful Chelle Lyons Hanson, who led the campus in the widely recognized SOS (Sources of Service) program with its roots in experiential learning. Walter McDuffy had a long run as director of Intercultural Affairs. Walt's background as an Army chaplain gave him an ideal combination of order and grace. Lee Johnson brought management and strategic skills to the Admissions function, and Dale Thornton managed our complex financial aid enterprise with fairness and skill. In his later years on the staff, Dale worked with the Native American communities, for which he had a special passion.

While this list is incomplete, it is sufficient to conclude that the quality level of our administrative staff was high, and their skills and passion for their work ran deep. Beyond the high level of confidence I had in our staff, there was an equally high level of trust. People could be counted upon; they were loyal to their leaders and to one another. The people with whom I worked were simply extraordinary!

A key element in the effectiveness of administrative staff leadership was an institutional commitment to staff development. In the eighties, we initiated a staff development program. Individuals could apply for financial support and leave to pursue programs that would enhance their professional effectiveness and personal growth. Several staff members earned graduate degrees through this Concordia's staff development program; others attended regional and national events. This program enabled individuals to upgrade their skills and stay in touch with a wider professional world, which, in turn, benefited Concordia.

In addition to a close, effective President's Council and a capable, creative administrative staff, Concordia had a strong Board of Regents. The board's role is to give oversight to the college's work on behalf of its moral and legal stakeholders. The character and dedication of the Board of Regent members was always impressive, but it's fair to say that in the last half of the eighties and in the nineties, the board moved to a higher level of accountability and oversight. The leadership of board chairs Norman Lorentzsen, Norm Jones, Cal Larson, David Birkeland, Earl Stein, and Ron Offutt was outstanding. Board members sought to improve their governance capacities by participating in the annual conferences of the Association of Governing Boards, an organization that provides expertise and counsel to academic governing boards. In addition, board members took time to visit the campus and participate in the life of the college through the Regents in Residence program. To ensure that they were getting adequate input in decision-making, the board regularly invited students, faculty, and staff to attend committee meetings and the annual fall board retreat. These years were, in many respects, a coming-of-age time for the Concordia board, acting with a remarkable combination of passion and professionalism.

ABUNDANCE AND SCARCITY

The contrasting themes of abundance and scarcity provide one window into the experience of the college in the nineties. To begin with, there was the abundance of the Centennial Campaign, initiated in the late eighties and completed in the early nineties. The goal of the campaign was $46.5 million of which twenty-five million was designated for endowment, $13.2 million for the operating budget, and $8.3 million for facilities. The themes of quality and access were prominent in the campaign. Co-chairs for the campaign were newcomer Ron Offutt, class of 1964, and veteran campaign leaders Norm Jones, class of 1954, Loanne Thrane, class of 1955, and Norman Lorentzsen, class of 1941. They were an all-star cast, and the campaign was sparked by Earl and Dorothy Olson's five-million-dollar lead gift. Earl was the founder and CEO of Jennie-O Foods, a turkey production and processing operation in Willmar, Minnesota. The Olsons were parents of five Cobbers. The campaign raised over $58.5 million, exceeding the campaign goal by more than ten million dollars. This result reflected the strength of the economy, the growing capacities of Concordia's constituency, the strength of our fundraising staff, and the enthusiasm of the Cobber support base.

I have many fond memories from this campaign. As the campaign leadership team planned for the project, it was clear that we needed a substantial lead gift. I visited with the Olsons early and often in their Willmar home to talk about the necessity of a lead gift to the success of the overall campaign. The standard giving pyramid indicated that if Concordia were to raise nearly fifty million, we needed a lead gift of five million. I was candid with the Olsons on the point that they were essentially our only prospect for such a gift. They had recently sold Jennie-O to the Hormel Company and were able to make such a gift, which they did with humility and joy. Later, the Olson Forum was named to honor their generosity to Concordia. There were regular meetings of the campaign committees with people sharing their experiences, both the disappointments and the successes. I recall scores of area campaign meetings in places like Devil's Lake and Dickinson, North Dakota; Bozeman and Sidney, Montana; and Willmar and Rochester, Minnesota. As with previous campaigns, I enjoyed my role with fund raising because I strongly believed in the mission of the college and was eager to share the Concordia story.

Campaign proceeds contributed in a significant way to the growth of Concordia's endowment from $10.3 million in 1989 to sixty-five million by 1997. Some of those endowment funds were designated for financial aid and others for faculty development. We did such an excellent job of emphasizing the importance of endowment that we had difficulty making our goal for facility improvements (not a bad problem). The campaign funded the Centennial Mall and Campanile, renovations in Memorial Auditorium, new facilities at the French Language Village near Bemidji, the renovation of Bishop Whipple Hall, and, in part, the Olson Forum. Funding for the Forum was completed in a subsequent special project appeal.

The college, staff, campaign volunteers, and I found our fundraising stride in this campaign. Concordia had moved to a larger stage with success, securing eight gifts of one million dollars or more and 102 gifts exceeding $100,000. Board members provided leadership by providing over eight million dollars in pledges, and the faculty and staff pledged over three million. It had been good and great work, real abundance. There would be more successful fundraising efforts to follow with C400 projects in support of technology, several program grants, and leadership commitments for the forthcoming Spanish Language Village.

As the nineties ended, Concordia launched another campaign, The Twenty-First Century Fund: Sustaining the Mission. The goal was sixty million dollars, and, again, there was a focus on endowment, including the establishment of two endowed chairs in honor of Walther G. Prausnitz (English) and Olin Storvick (Classics), recognizing the contributions of these fine scholar-teachers, just as we had done in the Centennial Campaign when we established a chair honoring Paul J. Christiansen. Capital elements in the Twenty-First Century Fund campaign included the renovation and expansion of Hvidsten Hall and construction of the Spanish Village on the Bemidji campus. The response to this campaign was again abundant, with over fifty-nine million of commitments toward the sixty-million-dollar goal by the time of my retirement in the spring of 1999. Another reflection of the success of these campaigns was the record-setting cash gifts totaling nine million in 1990 and $11.6 million in 1998-99. These successes in fundraising reflected several factors including confidence in the college, a generally robust economy, a mature and effective Development staff, the expanded role of key volunteers, growth in the financial capacity of our constituents, and enthusiasm for Concordia and its future.

Financial and program abundance went hand in hand with our success in earning significant grants from the Council for the Advancement of Higher Education (CAPHE) for service learning, the Knight Foundation for internationalizing the curriculum and the faculty, the Hughes Foundation for research in the biological sciences. In addition, Concordia received grants from the McKnight Foundation for initiatives related to Native American programs and enrollment, the Taegle Foundation for technology, Lutheran Brotherhood for the endowment of campus ministry, and the Max Cade Foundation for international education. Also, there was national recognition from the Templeton College ratings of colleges of character as well as favorable rankings from the Carnegie Commission and U.S. *News and World Report*. On the program front, Concordia's accreditation was reviewed every decade, and this occurred again in the early nineties. Dean Robert Homann and his team did an excellent job of preparing materials for the visit. The visiting team was impressed by the progress the college had made on the academic side since the last site visit and by the quality of support and administrative services. Noted in the final accreditation report, "In every respect, Concordia is a strong institution. Longstanding, excellent leadership, commitment to faculty, loyalty of students and alumni all contribute to the solidity of Concordia in its educational mission." High praise indeed to recognize the hard work and deep commitment of so many.

Program assessment had become a major expectation in higher education, and the accreditation team also gave Concordia high marks for its innovative and comprehensive approach. I should note that this high mark was attributable to a program initially set in place in the seventies when we set up a research process designed to ensure the quality of instruction in the Core Curriculum. This program, described in an earlier chapter, was improved and expanded through the eighties and into the nineties under the leadership of Walther Prausnitz, director of Liberal Arts Studies. One cannot overestimate the significance of his leadership in developing and administering our assessment program, which largely explains its adoption and support by the faculty and staff. While the final report noted many strengths of the institution, the accreditation team noted Concordia's lack of racial diversity as an area in need of improvement, an observation already recognized, one with which we agreed. Following the visiting team's report, however, the college was approved for reaccreditation without reservation.

Because of growth in enrollment (from 2,607 in 1980 to 2,970 in 1995), endowment income (from $186 thousand in 1980 to $2.7 million in 1995), and gifts for current operations (from $1.5 million in 1980 to $3.9 million in 1995) Concordia operated with a strong budget (from $11.5 million in 1980 to $38.4 million in 1995). Significant surpluses were plowed back into reserves and non-recurring expenditures for facilities, programs, and operating and debt retirement reserves. Faculty salaries stood at or above the eightieth percentile (AAUP ratings for Concordia's category of colleges) for most faculty ranks. Consistent with historic practice, Concordia's administrative costs were below the average for peer institutions. For example, in 1996 administrative costs were 11.7% vs the ELCA average of 13.9%; Concordia's student to staff ratio was 30:1 vs 19.7:1.

In the face of all this abundance, you might ask, how could there have been any scarcity? It was a subtle development. While the college's enrollment was at record levels, there was no longer the surge of unanticipated income that comes with unexpectedly high enrollments. The campus was at its capacity; we didn't have room for more students in the nineties, but this new steady state enrollment impacted the income growth that Concordia had been experiencing. In addition, we saw the demographic projections for our region and knew that Concordia's ability to maintain an enrollment in the desired range of 2,750 to 2,950 would be a challenge. Add to that the sizable investment in technology that the college had taken on and the double-digit annual growth in financial aid that was more or less forced upon us by the shortfalls in federal and state aid programs, resulting in the subtle bend toward times of scarcity. By the mid-nineties, it became apparent that the funding formula that had worked so well for Concordia in the eighties and nineties was under growing stress. Consequently, by the late nineties, increases in compensation were less robust. We were forced to reallocate to innovate, and we were looking for new ways to increase our income. In economic terms, in the late nineties, we experienced income inelasticity alongside expense elasticity. This economic experience would be with us for at least two decades.

COLLEGE BUDGETING 101

One way to understand the consequences of economic change on the college is to identify the key variables in college financing, with a focus on the current operating expenses and not including capital costs (e.g. new buildings and major upkeep.) The financial model for Concordia current operating budget was, and is, not very complicated. The budget model consists of only a few elements:

Income	Expenses
Tuition and fees	Academic program
Auxiliary enterprises (food service, housing, CLV)	Student services
Annual gifts	Administration
Endowment	Maintenance
	Financial aid
	Capital (repair, replacement)

When any of the income elements declines, it must be offset by increasing income from one of the other elements and/or curbing expenses. In the face of the flat and then declining growth in tuition income in the late nineties and 2000s, the preferred options were adding new academic programs and admissions initiatives that brought in additional tuition income, increasing annual gift income, and growing the endowment income. Obviously, curbing expenses would have to fill in the income gaps. That meant that growing our endowment would be a priority and that it would be used primarily to fund existing programs rather than new ones. Similarly, the focus in developing new programs would be on those that could add to net revenue (i.e. after expenses). Along with these budgeting strategies, it would be essential that new capital projects be funded outside the operating budget by designated gifts, lest they add drag to that budget. Thus, read our strategic challenges and options for coming decades.

STABILITY AND CHANGE (1)

One of the laws of human nature is that we naturally prefer to be in a state of equilibrium or stability, where things are in balance and under control. Disequilibrium often leads to resistance due to a lack of information, fear, or simply contentment with the status quo. I think all of these were in play in the late nineties as we sought to deal with the growing scarcity noted above.

Concordia's experience with growing scarcity was shared by other colleges similar to us, that is, schools with good reputations but small endowments. Like those peer institutions, Concordia was experiencing expanding expenses for new technology but without new income streams to fund the expenses. There was growing public pressure to maintain stable tuition rates and an expanding need for financial aid while public support for state and federal student aid was declining. As previously noted, the financial model that had worked so well for the college in the eighties and early nineties was falling short by the mid-nineties.

In my fall 1995 report on the state of the college, I noted that the early nineties were years of abundance with growing enrollments, strong fundraising, growth in endowment income, and strong publicly funded aid programs. I went on to note that these trends were bending. While the number of 15-19 year-olds in Minnesota was predicted to grow thirteen percent by 2010, the growth among Caucasians would be only four percent, and the high school completion and college attendance rates among students of color were forecast to be low. I also noted that with increased costs, Concordia was seeing a shift among middle class families from private to public schools. In addition, publicly funded financial aid was declining. In 1993 state and federal aid provided forty-six percent of all grant assistance, but by 1995 that percentage had slipped to thirty-nine percent, with institutions making up much of the difference. National columnist Jane Bryant Quinn opined that growth in tuition costs would slow dramatically. I concluded this analysis by saying, "The Concordia story is repeated with similar scripts in institutions of every kind across the land making resource concerns the number one vital issue in higher education today. Restructuring, reformation, and redistribution are orders of the day across the academy." In my 1996 report, I noted:

> Both *Blueprint* IV and the *Financial Blueprint* IV have been pretty much on target with four significant exceptions: the unexpected softening of publicly-funded financial aid, the increasing resistance of the public to high annual increases in tuition, the cost and pace of technological change and, finally, the growing instability of student enrollment—particularly in the public sector.

Administrative and board leaders observed how Concordia's competitor institutions were anticipating and responding to these emerging pressures through reallocation, more aggressive recruitment of traditional students, and the creation of new, largely nontraditional programs that would create new streams of income. In response to the emerging challenges on many fronts, Concordia engaged the faculty and staff in conversations about implementing a reallocation strategy called Project Focus. One working group focused on administrative services while the other focused on academic programs. The college's student-to-faculty ratio had slipped from our target of 15:1 to 13.6:1, so we began looking for savings in that area. Consequently, Concordia closed the German Institute in the mid-nineties due to low enrollment, and this resulted in some savings. We also sought to consolidate some administrative services and expand the income potential of the college's catering services. Since tuition was two to three thousand dollars less than the average for private colleges in Minnesota, we believed that there was room for Concordia to make larger than average increases in tuition, which we did, partially justified by using some percentage of the increase as support for our expanding technology program. After the nineties, the tuition differential between Concordia and other Minnesota private colleges expanded greatly, to our detriment. We also initiated C400 fundraising activities in support of expanded financial aid and technology. The results of these actions were helpful but transitory. Financial aid and technology budget pressures were relentless.

The reports from our budget focus groups also lifted the possibility of generating additional income by developing new programs in response to the emerging needs of Concordia's constituents. Administrative leadership, including the board, observed that many peer institutions were moving in this direction with real success. The most successful of these schools was St. Thomas, beginning in the late seventies, but other schools (Augsburg, Hamline, Bethel, St. Catherine's, St. Mary's, St. Scholastica, Concordia-St. Paul) were following their lead in the late eighties and nineties. This led us to think about opportunities to provide programs that might serve Concordia constituents. After some preliminary work in the spring and summer of 1997, a task force on New Programs for New Clienteles was established by the Faculty Senate. The task force initiated a research effort to identify the educational needs of Concordia's immediate constituents, those in the Fargo-Moorhead area. The survey indicated strong interest in a degree completion program. There was also some interest in graduate programs in business and education. Many discussions across campus ensued, including Faculty Senate. The Faculty Senate did not warm up to these ideas, however, despite establishing a Council on Graduate Studies and approving a framework to vet and process proposed new programs. Some students feared that new programs would compromise the existing undergraduate experience. More significantly, there was not adequate support within the faculty to move in this direction.

As a leader, I pondered this brief and unsuccessful initiative to advance degree completion programs. Why was the effort unsuccessful? There are many explanations: contentment with the status quo, an insufficient sense of urgency with respect to new economic realities, lack of sufficient information about new programs, fear of change, the lack of a sufficient number of faculty advocates, and a diminution in my ability to persuade, although I do not believe that Moses's mouthpiece Aaron would have been able to persuade the faculty to pursue the initiative. In addition, the conventional faculty governance model was perhaps not appropriate for this initiative. Because most of the college's faculty was schooled in traditional pedagogies, it was a challenge to understand how on-line, off-campus models with less facetime instruction could produce the quality outcomes Concordia honored. I was an academic, so my natural inclination was to turn to the faculty for leadership and counsel on any academic matter, and Concordia's strong faculty governance was a rich part of institutional decision-making. What I learned subsequently was that most nontraditional initiatives in other institutions were the result of board mandates or board commissioned initiatives, and that the governance for those programs was unique. Typically, a new program rubric was created, such as a Center for Adult Studies or a School of Special Studies, with its own governance system. Three of Concordia's most successful nontraditional programs—the Concordia Language Villages, the Communiversity, and Charis—were not subject to faculty oversight, and these programs were nimble and innovative. Presidential colleagues from schools with successful nontraditional academic programs testified to the need for flexibility and rapid response to changing academic needs, all of which pointed toward a different faculty governance model.

While new programs would not have been any magic bullet, they would have strengthened and diversified Concordia's income stream and broadened our constituent base. Consequently, the college was left with a financial model that was no longer able to support the budget health to which we had grown accustomed. Unfortunately, this problem persisted well into the 2000s. I see this as a missed opportunity that handicapped the college in the years that followed.

STABILITY AND CHANGE (2)

In the fall of 1998, following discussion with several key faculty leaders, Dean Danielson and I proposed that the Faculty Senate initiate a comprehensive review of the curriculum. In my state of the college remarks, I explained the rationale:

> A second way in which we can leverage our strength is through a comprehensive reexamination of our curriculum. It is thirty years since we initiated the last such comprehensive examination of the curriculum and I believe it is time to do it again for many reasons. In the first place, for most of you our present curriculum design is a received tradition rather than an owned one. Even if we don't change the curriculum by a comma, the reexamination will enable the ninety percent of you who have come since 1970 to claim it for yourselves.
>
> And a second reason to reconsider the curriculum is because the world we would influence has changed and we ought to test whether or not our curriculum design is appropriate to this newer world. We have lately been pushing and striving to make everything fit into our curriculum. Indeed, I think we have added more weight than it can bear. That is, I think, why the alternatives offered to us by the Core Committee last year failed to raise a consensus—we just weren't sure where, or how, to put everything.
>
> And then there are the new pedagogies and the changing majors and the hard disciplines of curriculum management, all pointing to the necessity for a comprehensive reassessment of the curriculum.

An Agenda for Concordia's Academic Life had been completed in the early eighties. This document set out the college's academic goals, established a modest change in the requirements for graduation, and articulated some important refinements in the Core Curriculum. The effort at the time was not, nor was it intended to be, a comprehensive review and reformulation of the curriculum such as the Curriculum Commission, known as Curcom, had been in the late sixties. Curcom led to restructuring the unit of academic study, the content and requirements of every major, the requirements for graduation, and the purpose and content of the Core Curriculum. What Dean Danielson and I proposed was another comprehensive curriculum review to respond to emerging challenges and to prepare for the new millennium.

The faculty and the Faculty Senate deliberated about the proposed study over several weeks before deciding on a structure and process for the study. Much about the plan was good. The undertaking would attend to fundamental matters of mission, trends in liberal arts curricula, new pedagogies, the emerging awakening to the idea of Vocation, and much more. Funds were set aside to support the work. Outside consultants were engaged and two discussion opportunities known as Future's Forums were convened that focused on demographic shifts, learning styles, pedagogies, and models of liberal arts education.

The curriculum review process moved slowly, and consensus was a challenge. I think there were at least two important factors explaining the slow progress. First, there had been a dramatic change in the composition of the faculty by the late nineties; fifty percent were new since 1989, seventy-three percent since 1984, and eighty-eight percent since 1972. In other words, over seventy percent of the faculty had not been part of a major curriculum discussion. The temperament of the newly formed faculty reflected their formative experience as students in the seventies and eighties, a time when there was less trust of leaders, more critical analysis, more focus on one's academic discipline, fewer liberal arts college graduates, less participation in academic community, and fewer shared commitments. I believe these characteristics made it much harder to accomplish the necessary work of a deep, comprehensive curriculum review. Although Concordia had some strong faculty leaders at the time, they lacked the experience to lead a full curriculum review. As a result, the curriculum review work of the late nineties dragged on, and the emerging proposal was complex.

Mark Krejci, professor of psychology, emerged from the process as a key architect of curriculum reform. Through his skill, diplomacy, and respected relationship with his colleagues, Mark was finally able to fashion the necessary consensus around key issues. The resulting product was improved clarity around curricular goals, a Core Curriculum that reflected those goals, and a curriculum that opened doors to new content. One of the unfortunate consequences of the new Core Curriculum, however, was that completion of the new Core became more difficult for students in some pre-professional programs.

From this reform process in the late nineties, informed by the work of the

Dovre Center and the Lilly funded work on Vocation, the engaging theme of the Core Curriculum, "Being Responsibly Engaged in the World," emerged along with its catchy acronym BREW. BREW became more than a brand for the new Core Curriculum. The theme became a defining reality in the academic experience of Concordia students and is the most significant legacy of this curriculum reform endeavor.

AND THE BEAT GOES ON

While the topics I have treated above represent the decade defining trends and developments in the late nineties, a good deal of campus life revolved around recurring themes and activities. Students continued to rally around service projects and SOS (Sources of Service), and service-learning programs grew in significance and reputation under the leadership of Chelle Lyons Hanson. Consistent with Concordia's mission statement, the campus community was steeped in service, which was never more evident than in the time of crisis. In 1997, the Fargo-Moorhead community experienced the flood of a century. In response, the three schools of higher education (MSUM, NDSU, and Concordia) joined others in the Fargo-Moorhead area by providing thousands of volunteers. The three colleges and universities took turns cancelling classes to meet the need for sandbag services. I, along with many others from the Concordia community, took many shifts to both fill and place sandbags throughout the community, while Mardy and others assisted in providing food for the volunteers. Also in response, the college provided classroom space for Oak Grove Lutheran School students, whose facilities had been flooded out. The flood, while a crisis on the ground, was in so many ways one of Concordia's finest hours to live out our mission in real time. I venture to say that those who were involved in the flood volunteer effort that spring remember the event as a time of true Cobber spirit.

I can't leave memories of the 1997 flood without noting there were glimpses of humor as well. Prior to the flood, the Fargo-Moorhead region had experienced record-breaking snow fall, well over one hundred inches. This had forced the closing of school on more than one occasion on account of the inability of faculty and staff members to access the campus. I recall one morning when I looked out the west window of our house to see how the day was shaping up. The answer was not well, lots of new snow in windswept drifts. Across from our house was Park Region dormitory, and in the window of one of the rooms was a large sign with the simple message: "Please." We ended up cancelling classes for the day, and when I returned home that evening, there was another message in the window: "Thank you."

The campus ministry aspect of campus life in the nineties was changing as well, prompted in part by two significant changes. The first was the retirement of Reverend Art Grimstad in 1990 after some thirty years as director of the Christian Outreach Program and the Monday night Bible studies. His gifts for ministry were evangelism and Bible study, and his impact was very significant, as noted in an earlier chapter. Art Grimstad was succeeded by a series of two or three persons over the next decade, but the size and vitality of the outreach and Bible study programs waned, perhaps reflecting changes in both leadership and the preferences of a new generation of students. The second significant change was the retirement of Concordia's first full-time campus pastor, Reverend Carl Lee, in the mid-nineties. His ministry gifts were primarily pastoral. Carl was accessible to students in need at all hours of the day and night. He had great skill and credibility in his role as director of counseling. Carl also had great influence across campus due to his sensitivity and wisdom. Carl Lee was succeeded by Reverend Gretchen Person. Her primary responsibilities were student counseling and worship. Fortunately, the third member of the ministry team, Reverend Phil Holtan, stayed in place and provided continuity. Phil's gifts for ministry lay in worship and social ministry outreach. Under his leadership and energy, hundreds of students were involved in Habitat for Humanity, Justice Journeys, and a variety of other forms of applied service ministry.

As noted earlier, student and faculty attendance at college cultural and athletic events continued to decline in the eighties. Similarly, the decline of student participation in worship activities that had begun in the eighties continued apace in the nineties. While leadership commissioned special studies and attempted innovations in worship, we were unable to reverse the trend, an experience common in religious colleges across the country, including MIAC sister institutions in the region. I believe this trend reflected, to some extent, families' changing worship practices, the triumph of individualism, and the growing complexity and secularity of campus life. On the other hand, social ministry initiatives at Concordia thrived in the nineties and produced graduates who hopefully would carry those practices into their post-college lives.

Not surprisingly, in the nineties students continued to press for greater personal freedom, principally in underclass residence halls. There were several proposals followed by detailed and respectful conversations, followed by some tinkering of the rules for inter-dorm visitation. The underlying framework for Concordia's differentiated rules was that underclass students benefited from some structure, and upper-class students could handle more freedom. Underclass students were required to live in campus residence halls with some explicit rules and expectations, while upper-class students had the full range of living options with some rules or none at all. I believe this was a sound policy framework, and for most of my years, parents were quick to support the framework, and students, while not necessarily liking the policy, didn't make much fuss about it. By the mid-nineties, however, it became apparent to me that the culture of Concordia families was changing as society was becoming more secular. In response, Concordia added mid-week evening visitation in the nineties, and all such rules would disappear in the 2000s. In retrospect, I think we should have changed Concordia's policy framework sooner, not because it wasn't defensible, but because the policies had lost sufficient cultural sanction.

All through the nineties, I continued to enjoy my interaction with students. Students knew they mattered. They had a voice in the important work of the college, from hiring faculty to building the budget, setting tuition, approving curriculum changes, and disciplining their peers, with student representation on the student conduct and responsibility board. The inclusion of student voices in this wide range of matters on campus was a remarkable arrangement, and I think explains why we were able to deal with occasional differences of opinion with mutual respect and affection. I cultivated my relationship with student leaders assiduously. I continued to make occasional visits to the offices of student government and the student newspaper, and student leaders made frequent and welcome visits to my office. Mardy and I also entertained students at our home many times over a year.

Mardy and I didn't just entertain students at our home. There also were regular receptions and dinners events for regents, Alumni Board members, faculty and staff members, and special campus guests, all welcome in our home. Of especially valuable assistance to us in these matters was the campus dining service. Under the direction of Jane Grant Shambaugh, Concordia's dining services became a best practice leader in the industry. This enterprise was distinguished for good quality and excellent service. They were so transparent and welcoming of student input that student complaints about the food almost disappeared. Bill Fradet was the catering manager in the nineties and was especially helpful in serving us and our guests. Like many on campus, it was clear that Bill saw his work as a calling and not a job.

The physical realities of the college continued to evolve in the nineties: the construction of the Finnish Language Village, the Olson Forum, the Mugaas Physical Plant building, the Berg Steam Plant, and the Olson Skyway. Projects also included the renovation of Hvidsten, Bishop Whipple, and Park Region Halls; and the acquisition of the Professional Center (now home of the Advancement Office) and "A Place in the Woods," which is the CLV Russian Village on Turtle River Lake outside Bemidji. Concordia's physical plant department, under the able leadership of Ansel Haakenson, was efficient and excellent in caring for the grounds and all campus facilities.

The Olson Skyway project followed the decision in the early nineties by the Minnesota Department of Transportation to widen 8th Street, since the street was the major north-south traffic corridor in Moorhead. The traffic count had grown over the years and would accelerate with the widening of the street. There had been one serious accident involving a student making the street crossing from the East Complex, plus several smaller incidents. Concordia was very concerned about the safety of our students going forward, so we began exploring the possibility of building an overpass. Designated leaders studied various designs and cost estimates. The discussion in the leadership group was vigorous. One of the members said that if we'd taken a vote, it would probably have been six opposed and two (Dovre and Lanning) in support of building an overpass. There was the possibility that it would be a "Dovre Folly" project, but the Board of Regents shared my concern about long-term moral liability for the safety of Concordia students, so plans for the overpass began to emerge. The project struck a responsive chord with Earl and Dorothy Olson, generous lead donors in the past, so they agreed to fund the $2.7 million dollar structure. And much like an earlier "Dovre Folly," the campanile, once the skyway was completed, the finished project had a thousand friends.

In the nineties, Concordia co-curriculars in athletics, the arts, and forensics continued to remain strong. Athletic teams remained competitive in the MIAC with numerous playoff appearances, and Concordia musical groups enhanced their reputations for excellence. In addition, the theater program provided opportunities for hundreds of students, and the forensic team sustained its national reputation. Mardy and I rarely missed a concert or play, and we attended as many athletic events as we could manage. I tried to find time to join Concordia's touring musical ensembles from time to time, including the band's tour in the Nordic countries and the choir's tour of the Baltic nations and Norway. Spending time with the touring ensembles and attending concerts and productions on campus highlighted the gifts of Concordia faculty and students that inspired not only the Concordia community, but also other communities well beyond our campus.

HOME AND COMMUNITY

The Dovre family grew in the nineties with the births of grandson Luke and granddaughters Anna and Erika. They brought delight to all of our lives and increased the number of road trips to Eau Claire, Wisconsin, where Erik practiced ob/gyn medicine and his spouse Ellen practiced physical therapy, and to Roseville, Minnesota, where daughter Louise was in the state court system and her spouse John was a practicing attorney. Occasionally, our children would bequeath their children to us when they went on holiday or a business trip. Mardy was especially effective in the role of child sitter, while I was more or less along for the ride. The grandchildren were introduced to our lake cabin on Bad Medicine almost at birth, and so came to regard the place as the family home. We were often together for holidays like Easter, Thanksgiving, and Christmas. We made it a practice not to talk shop in much detail at our family events. Even though Erik and Louise attended Luther College, they had grown up as Cobbers, so Concordia was in their bones by virtue of their life experience, many friendships, and a deep appreciation for its mission and history.

Beyond the importance of our family, Mardy and I also treasured our friendships with people near and far. Mardy and I enjoyed international trips with dear friends Bev and Gerald Bjelde and Ed and Ann Ellenson. We gathered with Moorhead friends for occasional receptions, parties, and dinner events. We made friendships with other college presidents along the way, notably Bob and Sally Vogel, who served at Wartburg College, and David and Susan Gring, who served at Roanoke College. Loren and Mary Anderson were next-door neighbors at Bad Medicine Lake, and our friendship stretched over fifty years.

Both Mardy and I were involved in the life of the broader community in various ways through the years. For example, locally in the seventies and eighties, I served on the boards of the Moorhead Chamber of Commerce, the Fargo-Moorhead Symphony, and the United Way. I was a member of the Fargo Kiwanis Club and later the Moorhead Rotary Club. In addition, I was involved with the Heritage Hjemkomst Center and various church activities. In the realm of private enterprise, I was a member of the board of the Fargo U.S. Bank. On the statewide level, I served on the advisory committee for the School of Health Sciences at the University of Minnesota, the Regent Candidate Advisory Committee for the University of Minnesota, and the Judicial Selection Committee. On the national level, I served as board member and vice chair of the Council of Independent Colleges and board member of the National Council of Independent Colleges and Universities; the former focused on program issues and the latter on political matters. With respect to Lutheran higher education on the national level, I was active in the Lutheran Educational Conference of North America and served on various committees of the ELCA's Division of Colleges and Schools. All these varied activities kept me in touch with important constituencies and gave the college a voice on issues of vital importance. I thoroughly enjoyed my participation in these local, state, and national conversations and found the work useful to my role as president at Concordia.

When it came to involvement in the local community, Mardy was the champion in our family. I have already mentioned some of her service activities in previous chapters. In the early nineties, Mardy gave up her part-time teaching position in the Fargo school system to give more time to her involvement in the life of the college and the community. She became a member of the Mayor's Citizens Advisory Council, which led to her appointment as the founding chair of the Moorhead Healthy Community Initiative, a successful effort to build assets among children in the community. She served on the board of the Fargo-Moorhead Symphony. She was elected to the board of the local Hospice in the 1990s, serving a term as its chair and co-chairing their endowment campaign. Mardy was one of the founding members of what became The Women's Fund, a program affiliated with the Fargo-Moorhead Area Foundation. These activities led Mardy to be named to the committee that competed successfully for Fargo-Moorhead's designation as an All-American City. On the more personal side, Mardy enjoyed her decades long membership in a lively book club and a local chapter of PEO.

Mardy and I lived through a period when the role of women was shifting, and the conception of the college presidency was changing. In my case, leadership of the college was not a solo activity. I could not have done this work without the incredible partnership of Mardy. She was "all in" in the life of the college and, as noted above, the community. While I tend toward introversion, Mardy is an extrovert and simply masterful at making people feel valued and at ease. Her positive spirit would light up a room, just as it constantly lit up my life and the life of our family.

TRANSITION

When I accepted election to a fourth term as president of Concordia College in 1992, Mardy and I anticipated that, barring the unforeseen, this would be our last term of service. We kept this thought to ourselves, not even sharing this likely decision with our family. As the term wound down, Mardy and I reconfirmed the thought. I would be sixty-four and a half years-old in June of 1999. I had given the leadership assignments my best over thirty-two years and enjoyed the work and its many rewards. This span of time had been a great run for Concordia: record enrollments, a stronger faculty, significant quality improvements in the curriculum, dynamic student leadership and service programs, competitive compensation, expansion and improvement of campus facilities, record-breaking fundraising, incredible growth in the endowment, regional and national recognition, a strong and expanded constituency, and the list goes on. These signs of abundance reflected the great strengths of Concordia's Board of Regents, leadership team, faculty and staff, and countless volunteers who supported the work and mission of the college.

It is important that a leader recognizes when it is time to step away, and I believe that I did. I recognized in myself a certain weariness with the routine and detail. The faculty was moving more slowly on strategic work, perhaps in part because they were weary of me. "The times they were a changing," as the Bob Dylan song suggests, and those changing times for the college included important strategic work to accomplish as it prepared to roll out a new plan for the first decade of the twenty-first century. For all these reasons, I believed that new leadership would be helpful, someone with fresh eyes, experience, and energy. Mardy and I were eager for a schedule that was less structured, the freedom to choose our course and pursue long anticipated interests, and to spend lots more time with family and friends.

I announced my decision to retire at the opening faculty workshop in the fall of 1998. In the months that followed, there were various occasions of recognition and appreciation on campus and throughout the region. Mardy and I were blessed by all these events. Of special meaning to me was the tribute presented at the faculty retirement banquet in spring 1999 by Cynthia Carver, chair of the Speech Communication and Theatre Arts Department, my academic home of origin. Also, at the honors convocation that spring, I received an incredible selection of books, as each academic department presented two or three volumes representative of the scholarship in their respective disciplines. It was also in my final year that the Board of Regents named the Center for Faith and Learning in my honor.

Our family and friends all gathered for the Founders' Day banquet that spring, where we were honored in tributes from my mentor Allwin Monson, my former student and leadership partner Loren Anderson and his wife Mary Ann, and board chair Ron Offutt. Our children Louise and Erik shared some reminiscences to the delight of all. The Concordia choir, in which Mardy had sung as a student, presented a program of favorite anthems. The final academic year had been rich with tributes and wonderful, humbling recognitions for my time of service. In later years, I was equally honored when honorary degrees were conferred by Wartburg, Luther, Concordia, Capital, and St. Olaf. The Luther Institute extended the Wittenberg Award in 2002 to me, and in 2012, Concordia named the Campanile in my honor. My cup runneth over!

Fortunately, back in that spring of 1999, however, my plans for the immediate future came together when Paul Peterson, a Cobber alum, Board of Regents member, and Harvard professor, invited me to join him at the Kennedy School of Government as a Scholar-in-Residence. My time as president of Concordia had been an incredible run, and we were delighted to welcome our successors, Tom and Barbara Thomsen, to the college in June of 1999. Our season of service to the college had brought us gladness and fulfillment. At the end of the day, the college motto "Soli Deo Gloria," to God alone be the glory, rang in our hearts and memories.

8. The Next Chapter: 1999-

Our post-presidency began with a leisurely, no-deadline summer at the cabin, followed by a trip to Alaska via ship from Vancouver and train in Alaska. This trip commenced as the school year was getting underway at Concordia in the fall of 1999, making the trip a welcome break from an uninterrupted tradition dating back to my student years in 1952.

As noted in the last chapter, as I completed my service at Concordia and now following our fall trip to Alaska, I had one opportunity on the schedule, the invitation from Paul E. Peterson to join his group at the Program on Educational Policy and Governance at Harvard's Kennedy School of Government, so Mardy and I were off to Cambridge for the next several months. I had some writing projects in mind, but beyond that, no firm plans except an openness to emerging possibilities. In good Lutheran fashion, while I had retired from my career, I had not retired from my Vocation.

Because Paul Peterson knew of my interest in the evolution of religious colleges from sectarian to secular, he invited me to construct a research project of my own design. As a visiting scholar, I had access to the treasures of the Harvard library as well as several seminars and public programs. I spent my early weeks reading the relevant literature, the middle weeks reaching out to scholars, and the last weeks planning a national conference for the fall of 2000. I discovered that my Harvard affiliation opened many doors, giving me access to all of the most renowned scholars of the day, including James Tunstead Burtchaell, author of a major work detailing the secularization of religious colleges (*The Dying of the Light: The Disengagement of Colleges and Universities from their Christian Churches*), George M. Marsden, author of a book detailing the secularization of the academy in general (*The Soul of the American University: From Protestant Establishment to Established Nonbelief*), and the Lutheran Mark Schwehn, author of *Exiles from Eden: Religion and the Academic Vocation in America*. All agreed to assist in developing a conference, "The Future of Religious College," and Marsden and Schwehn agreed to present papers. Other distinguished scholars who agreed to be part of the conference included church historian Mark Noll of Wheaton College; theologian Robert Benne of Roanoke College; historian Jon Carpenter of Calvin College; philosopher Michael Beaty of Baylor University; David M. O'Connell, president of The

Catholic University of America; and Monika K. Hellwig, Executive Director of the Association of Catholic Colleges and Universities. All were respected scholars and teachers spanning a range of traditions and practices.

The conference was held in the Kennedy School and included twenty presenters and an additional eighty participants. Eerdmans Publishing contacted me to arrange publication of the papers in the volume *The Future of Religious Colleges*, which was published in 2002. This led to invitations to present and participate in a variety of venues in the following years, and the project was a capstone experience in my long-time engagement with issues related to faith and learning.

In the conclusion of the volume, I expressed optimism that a renaissance was taking place in many church colleges stimulated by the scholars noted above, the encouragement and support of the Lilly Endowment, and stirrings on many campuses across the country. In the fifteen years that passed following the conference, the renaissance continues, but not without the significant challenges of the secular hegemony that continues to dominate higher education, the declining significance of religious particularities in the society, and uneven leadership from college boards and presidents. As *New York Times* columnist David Brooks has observed, there has been a growing tendency to avoid theological and moral analysis in our society. People either do not want to risk offending others in an increasingly diverse society, or they are committed to the point of view that everyone is entitled to her or his own opinion. We are inclined to avoid debate or any particular religious affirmation. I believe that this is especially true of the academy, including Lutheran academies. In short, it is a challenge to both affirm the identity of religious colleges and show respect for difference. To the extent these institutions find the voice and conviction to do so, we may see further renaissance in religious colleges and universities.

With respect to Lutheran colleges, which I know best, I have seen a decline in Lutheran identity. The explanations are many: the declining numbers of Lutheran students, faculty, staff, and governing board members; the growing diversity of faculty and staff with respect to mission; the necessity of appealing to an increasingly heterogeneous and secular population of students and donors; the decline in the capacity and influence of the sponsoring church body; and the loss of Lutheran consciousness among college leaders, in particular, the presidents of the institutions. As noted in my preceding comments, I saw encouraging evidence of renaissance in the 1990s and early 2000s, but as I look at the landscape in the second decade, I am not as optimistic.

The hopeful word is that among religiously affiliated colleges, Lutheran schools may be best equipped to maintain, even reclaim, their religious identity. Lutherans have a built-in inclination to dialogue and dialectic with faith partners; ecumenism is in the DNA. Historically and continuing today, Lutherans have been willing to test all traditions in the interest of the truth that sets one free. Further, Lutherans have been a culture-affirming church, willing to engage the secular culture to which they are called in service. There is the energizing theology of Vocation that emphasizes the wholeness of life in faith. To be credible, both the dialogue and the emphasis on Vocation need to be grounded in an informed understanding of Lutheran theology and tradition. I believe this is the key to Lutheran identity in the future. Claiming and cultivating this tradition will be, primarily, the work of leaders and teachers, but will also require many committed stakeholders, strategic faculty and staff development activities, and a holistic curriculum that features core religious issues and understandings. Schools pursuing this path will be unapologetic about their religious identity; indeed, they will see it as a source of strength and distinction.

NEXT GENERATION LEADERS

In the last years of my time at Concordia, many Lutheran college presidents expressed concern about the size and quality of applicant pools for leadership positions in our respective institutions. We were concerned that many candidates lacked knowledge and interest in the mission and religious tradition of Lutheran schools. In fact, the Council of College Presidents of the Evangelical Lutheran Church in America commissioned a group of Lutheran college presidents to come up with a plan to address this challenge. I was asked to stay with this project after leaving Concordia and was pleased to do so. The commission developed a proposal, and the Lutheran Brotherhood Foundation (subsequently Thrivent Financial for Lutherans) funded the undertaking, eventually named the Thrivent Fellows Program in recognition of Thrivent support. I was asked to lead the project, but because I was by then serving as interim president of Capital University, I sought a partner and found one in Steven Titus, then on the staff at

Gustavus Adolphus College. Steve had both a law degree and a Ph.D. in leadership studies from the University of Virginia, so I was confident in his expertise and leadership.

Our first class of Thrivent Fellows convened in the summer of 2002 on the campus of Gustavus Adolphus College in St. Peter, Minnesota. The program had three components: the theology of Vocation, leadership theory and practice, and best leadership practices in Lutheran higher education. The program began with a ten-day seminar experience in a retreat-like setting, a three-day conference held in connection with the annual meeting of Lutheran college presidents, and a three-day closing seminar held in late spring. Steve and I would co-lead the program through the Thrivent Fellows class of 2015.

The Thrivent Fellows program was a great success. Scores of leaders came through the program and now occupy senior leadership positions in most Lutheran colleges. The program was sponsored by colleges and universities of the ELCA and the Lutheran Church Missouri Synod. Thrivent Financial continued as a financial sponsor after the start-up years but at a considerably reduced level. In 2015, Tom Cedel and my former student, colleague, and friend Loren Anderson assumed leadership of the program. MaryAnn Anderson was a member of that team and made major contributions to many of the Fellows as a leadership coach.

LUTHERAN ACADEMY OF SCHOLARS

Among my other interests during this period was the Lutheran Academy of Scholars, created under the auspices of the ELCA in the nineties. This came out of another study group of which I was a member. The Lutheran Academy of Scholars initially flourished with financial support from the Lilly Endowment. In my study of religious colleges, I noted that scholars from the reformed tradition were much more active in addressing matters of faith and learning than were scholars from the main line traditions, partly a matter of inattention and partly a matter of theological and confessional practice. That is, the reformed tradition had an interest in converting academic disciplines into Christian disciplines, while colleges in the mainline saw a separation between religious and secular matters. But I knew that inherent in the Lutheran tradition was an interest in the relationship between faith and learning, a relationship that was dialectical in nature. Lutherans were not interested in making history or chemistry into Christian history or Christian chemistry, but they did have an interest in seeing how Christian views might shape historical understanding or scientific understanding and practice, for example. They also had an interest in seeing how the Christian faith might be enriched by what could be learned from history or science. This was largely a latent interest on the part of Lutherans, and I thought it was time for faculty at Lutheran colleges to engage these matters with all the considerable resources at their disposal. The Lutheran Academy of Scholars took on this immodest agenda, and the project thrived for at least a ten-year period under the sagacious leadership of Ronald Thieman of the Harvard Divinity School. Several dozen faculty members participated in the program from across the country and produced many high-quality scholarly papers and books. Sadly, funding was in short supply by 2013, and the program went into hibernation. My hope is that someone might find a way to resurrect it.

INTERIM I

In 2000, I began a new, unexpected career in interim and project leadership. Each experience over the next few years was unique, and all were energizing. Lutheran higher education had been my life; I was intrigued by both the why (Lutheran tradition) and the how (leadership and strategy) of it. As it turned out, I would have several opportunities to experience in new venues my fundamental calling in Lutheran education.

In September of 2000, I was on my way to Waldorf College for a board workshop when I received a call from David Tiede, president of Luther Seminary. He told me that their dean of students had resigned to accept a new position, and he invited me to serve as interim dean. I respected David, had an appreciation for the seminary, and a lively interest in the work of preparing women and men for parish ministry, so I readily accepted the position. Mardy and I agreed that she would remain in Moorhead since she was busy with her own commitments. So, for the next several months, I found myself enjoying a new challenge at Luther Seminary. The seminary provided housing for me on campus, where I enjoyed the atmosphere, theological conversation, church gossip, and the chance to work with a different kind of student. Luther was in the midst of adopting a new strategic plan, about which I was very impressed. The seminary was revising its mission in stating that the seminary was preparing leaders for Christian communities. The paradigm was shifting from a pastoral focus to a leadership focus, and was changing from preparing only pastors to preparing students for a variety of church leadership roles.

President Tiede and his leadership team extended hospitality to me in many ways, including participation in meetings of their leadership team and board of directors. By April, a new dean had been appointed, and I returned to Moorhead. Shortly thereafter, I was invited to serve on the Luther Seminary board of directors, which I did for ten years, including time as board chair. My time on the board was good work with a lively, well-qualified board and seminary leaders. They understood effective governance as a calling that was inherent in their Vocations.

INTERIM II

Within months of completing the interim work at Luther in 2000, I received a phone call from a board member at Capital University in Columbus, Ohio. They had just asked their president to resign and were looking for interim leadership while they searched for a new president. The previous, long-term president was Joe Blackmore, whom I had come to enjoy and respect during the years we were colleague ELCA college presidents. Joe had suggested that the search committee contact me, so I went to Capital for a visit in May.

Let me say a word or two about interim leaders. The goal of an interim president is to do everything possible to set a good table for the next president. An interim president should not undertake long-range projects that cannot be completed in his/her tenure or that would tie the hands of the successor. The agenda should focus on the most urgent institutional priorities. I was relieved to discover that Cap's challenges were not related to finances or enrollment, but rather to morale and confidence. They were looking for some steadiness, predictability, and a re-engagement with their tradition, and I believed these priorities aligned with my strengths.

Capital was a university in the full sense of the term. There was a music conservatory and schools of law, business, nursing, and arts and sciences.

The enrollment was about evenly divided between traditional liberal arts undergraduates and nontraditional undergraduate and graduate students. For a school with about 3,900 students, Capital was a fairly complicated place from the standpoint of academic administration. I discovered that the deans carried significant influence in comparison with the provost, who was supposed to be the chief academic officer. This was largely due to the authority deans had in the curriculum, budgeting, and appointment processes. Revamping all of this was not a project for an interim president, although I did pass along some ideas to the next president.

I arrived in late May, and it was quickly apparent that the university was hungry for effective leadership and very willing to respond to that leadership in a constructive way. The provost was leaving for a new appointment, and, after consulting with several senior faculty members, I appointed one of them, Cheryl Ney, to the position of interim provost; Vern Tuesdale, vice president for Resource Management; Shae McGrew, vice president for Advancement; and J. Victor Hahn, university counsel provided great leadership for the university, and we worked together very effectively. In addition, the board chair was Robert Weiler, a Columbus businessman and graduate of the law school. He was a gem to work with, and we met each week at Cup O' Joe coffee shop to discuss the affairs of both the world and Capital University. I reached out to faculty, staff, friends, and alumni of the university, all of whom I found to be welcoming and supportive. I initiated steps to make the planning and budgeting process as transparent and participative as possible. People had ample opportunities for input on key decisions and expressed their gratitude.

During my time at Capital in Columbus, I took a special interest in the Lutheran constituency and contacted several area pastors, occasionally preaching in their churches and visiting about Capital University's mission and heritage. At the opening convocation of the new academic year, I spoke about Capital's mission and its relevance to contemporary society. The response was a standing ovation. People told me that they had not heard these matters discussed in a while. I found that Capital was ambivalent with respect to its religious identity. While there was a program designed to engage faculty in conversations about faith and learning, it had a low profile on the campus. This was not due to the lack of competent leadership, for that person was Tom Christenson, widely respected on the campus and in Lutheran academic circles. At a meeting of the Board of Regents, I addressed this issue as follows:

> Does Capital want to be clear, forthright, and well-informed about its religious identity or does it wish to minimize this dimension of its existence? The Lutheran tradition is distinctive and certainly not parochial in any sense. Taken at its best, Lutheran identity can shape, inform, and invigorate the university. Properly understood, being Lutheran adds value to Capital University just as being Catholic adds value to Notre Dame, being Dutch Reformed adds value to Calvin College, being Baptist adds value to Baylor University, and being Lutheran adds value to Valparaiso University. And so it can be for Capital University.
>
> But this result requires a commitment to the tradition, a studied effort to educate constituents both internal and external, and a cultivation of the pedagogies characteristic of a Lutheran academic community. And to dismiss a popular canard from the beginning, being Lutheran and being ecumenical are not mutually exclusive. In fact, given the Lutheran tradition, quite the opposite is true.

Subsequently, although a Lutheran was appointed president, he was not equipped to advance this conversation. His successor, in turn, did not nourish the conversation, so the religious identity of the university continued to erode, a sad and unnecessary development in a state with so many Lutherans. Capital University is a classic illustration of what can happen to a religious college that fails to be attentive and explicit about its religious mission. The responsibility for this erosion is borne by several principals, beginning with boards of regents, presidents and deans, and those responsible for the selection of faculty and administrative personnel.

Upon the arrival of President Ted Fredrickson in spring of 2001, my time at Capital University had ended. Once again, I had been fortunate to have been immersed in my passion for Lutheran tradition and effective leadership. We made many good friends while at Capital University, and I believe the leadership team and I had done everything possible to, in fact, set a good table for the incoming president. Although I left in early April 2001, I was invited to give the commencement address later that spring, when I was also awarded an honorary degree. Another good run.

ELCA SOCIAL STATEMENT ON EDUCATION

Following the eventful year as interim president, I returned to Moorhead and to some of my ongoing extracurricular activities and ventured into some new ones. In 2001, I agreed to co-chair a task force created by the ELCA, tasked with preparing a social statement on education. Preparation of such a statement seemed timely considering educational reform efforts at the PreK-12 level, the advent of character education, and the introduction of voucher programs in several states. It was also the case that tight finances in the church led to declining staff and support for church ventures in campus ministry and higher education. The task force's responsibility was to revisit the church's mission in education, address emerging concerns, and make appropriate recommendations to the church. I recognized the importance of the work that lay ahead of our task force, and I felt eager to contribute what I could to the task force and the eventual social statement on education for the ELCA.

The work of our eighteen-member task force commenced in 2002 and was completed in 2006. We met twice a year. Early on, the task force's work focused on collecting data and opinions and revisiting the theological and historical roots of the Lutheran venture in education. Members of the task force held hearings at various locations and received helpful input from educators.

Some of our best work centered on the mission of the church in education, its theological and confessional underpinnings. Our work went smoothly, and task force members were very conscientious. The final report encouraged the ELCA to be engaged in education at every level in both the public and church related sectors. The report also encouraged members of the church to attend to tax and funding issues, and we provided frameworks for the analysis of various initiatives, including vouchers and charter schools. The final report was presented at the 2007 national assembly of the ELCA, where the report was received and approved with nearly unanimous support.

The disappointing sequel to our work was that, as stated earlier, the church's financial resources were declining, resulting in restructuring at the national and synodical levels. Staff reductions limited the church's capacity to follow through on some recommendations in the report. I believe the strongest elements of the task force's work were the restatement of the church's commitment to education and the encouragement of members and professionals to embody that commitment. As I reflect, I appreciated the opportunity to share my experience and insights on this church-wide project and to engage with Lutheran stakeholders across the church. I hoped that the product of this work would be a resource to the church and its several educational ventures well into the future.

Since the task force work was spread over a span of time, I also did a modest amount of consulting during these years, principally in Lutheran colleges. For several years, I was a mentor/coach to a college president who was a product of the Thrivent Fellows Program. I also did some consulting in theological seminaries as a member of the In Trust Mentor program. I did not put a shingle out in search of such opportunities; rather, I responded to invitations when I was able to do so and in places where I had an affinity.

GOVERNANCE ACTIVITIES

I was involved in various governance-related activities in the late nineties and the first decade of the 2000s. I continued to serve on the Minnesota Humanities Commission, the Minnesota Judicial Selection Committee, and the Regent Candidate Selection Committee, which I chaired for a term. As previously noted, I served on the board of Luther Seminary and as its chair. Locally, I was a member and chair of the Heritage Hjemkomst Interpretive Center board of directors. I also served as a member of the board and executive committee of the Luther Institute for a term. In 2009, I was invited to join the board of the Oak Grove Lutheran Schools and the board of Lutheran Social Services of Minnesota in 2011. I enjoyed the scope of these governance activities ranging from public to private and from religious to secular. Each organization served a mission that was important to me, and my board colleagues were people of enthusiasm and capacity.

Over this period of years, I noticed how critical board governance was to the effectiveness and fidelity of the entities they served. Given the dynamics of society and the economy, most service organizations face increasing pressure, thus, the role of governing boards has become more demanding. Sometimes financial survival was the centering issue, and other times it was leadership or, occasionally, mission. There are excellent resources to assist governing boards in understanding their role and assessing their effectiveness. In this regard, organizations like In Trust, in relationship to theological education, and the Association of Governing Boards, in relation to higher education, provide excellent resources.

ACADEMIC VENTURES

In 2002, I was invited by the Lilly Endowment to do a critical review of the various studies of religious higher education that they had sponsored in the eighties and nineties. This was, to say the least, an ambitious endeavor. The experience enriched my understanding of the secularization of higher education and the relative successes of various efforts to sustain Christian identity. In this project, I had the opportunity to read the work of some postmodern scholars who were dismissive of religious truth claims in contrast with traditional scholars who defended them. I was especially impressed by younger scholars who were bridging the gap between traditional and innovative approaches to reliable knowledge. Other Lilly sponsored studies focused on pedagogical strategies to strengthen the faith and learning dialogue in classrooms. I believed that this combination of scholarly and pedagogical activities would continue to nourish a renaissance in the religious identity and practices of religious colleges, for which I was an unabashed cheerleader and still am. Lilly would continue to provide significant resources to the renaissance into the 2000s. The Foundation threw a wide net by funding ventures in scores of schools. In retrospect, I have wondered if the project might have been more successful if the Foundation had assisted fewer schools, using tighter criteria and more sophisticated accountability, and with a longer duration of support.

Three other projects proved both challenging and interesting in those years. Augsburg Fortress invited me to prepare a manuscript of homilies that I had preached during my years as president. This volume, *A Holy Restlessness*, was published in 2009. In addition, the second project entailed that I spend fall semester of 2005 at Harvard's Kennedy School of Government as a visiting scholar. This was familiar turf and Cobber Paul Peterson was again my mentor. The focus of my research was the character education movement developed in several K-12 schools in the preceding decade. I visited several of those schools and reviewed pertinent literature. It was interesting to see the creative ways teachers and schools were cultivating values-based commitments and practices in such a variety of educational settings. The result was "From Aristotle to Angelou," an essay that appeared in the Spring 2007 issue of *Education Next.*

The third project was in 2009-2010 when I edited a selection of papers and speeches I had presented over the years on Lutheran higher education. *The Cross and the Academy* was sponsored by Concordia's Dovre Center for Faith and Learning and was published by Lutheran University Press. In a sense, from the perspective of Lutheran higher education, this was my legacy document. In assembling the contents that spanned nearly forty years, I discussed both the evolution of my thinking and the continuity in my basic convictions.

INTERIM III

In the spring of 2003, Mardy and I and two other couples celebrated our forty-fifth wedding anniversaries by making a trip to Italy. We had a glorious time, finding enjoyment in new sites, memorable food, good wine, and great friendships. That same spring, conversations at Concordia led to the resignation of President Tom Thomsen after four years of service, and a search was initiated for an interim leader. When invited to do so, I suggested several interim leadership possibilities. While my name had been mentioned as a possibility, assuming the interim role of president didn't seem like a good idea to Mardy and me, and I expressed that view in a letter to search committee chair Roger Gilbertson and board chair Ron Offutt. In early June, some faculty and staff reached out to me, asking me to reconsider my earlier decision. After some deep conversation, Mardy and I agreed to reconsider. Shortly thereafter, I met with a group of faculty members who were advising the search committee. I asked them if it would be a good idea for me to come back under the new circumstances. They were unqualified in their encouragement. I also met with representative groups of students and administrative leaders. Based on all these conversations, the search committee brought my name to the Board of Regents, where the board clergy members cited the church rule that pastors never return to former congregations. It was apparently a vigorous discussion about which I was unaware. In any case, I was elected and began my service as interim president with full heart and energy. Incidentally, I think that what the clergy board members missed in drawing their analogy were the great differences between a parish and a college campus, where the president is not the pastor to the community, and there are several layers of staff and faculty. Regardless, I felt full support from the board and campus community when my interim presidency commenced in 2003.

I spent the early days of my interim sizing up the leadership needs of the college. As I had already learned, an interim president can accomplish only so much in a brief period of service, so what were the priorities for Concordia? I identified three priorities: first, move the student center project forward; second, fix the budget; and third, rebuild faculty confidence in the college. The construction of a new campus center had been a dream for years, and credit goes to former President Tom Thomsen for initiating the planning effort. The bad news was that the initial plan, while impressive, was well beyond the college's fundraising capacity. In addition, the fundraising effort was stalled by changes in leadership. The co-chairs of the capital campaign felt that the effort should be suspended, but I disagreed.

Key leaders proceeded to revise the plan and bring it within Concordia's budget, so we revived the fund-raising campaign, "The Campaign for Concordia College: Moving to the Next Level". We also reset the campaign goal at eighty million, and I rehired the chief Advancement officer, Linda Brown. The result of these changes was a reenergized fundraising effort that secured nearly forty-eight million in gifts and pledges by April 2004. The campaign goal was exceeded during the subsequent presidency of Pamela Jolicoeur, and a beautiful and functional student center was completed, a win for the college's campus community and stakeholders.

The second challenge that I recognized as interim president was related to the budget. We knew there were some issues but not the details, so we did a comprehensive analysis. This analysis yielded important information:

- We discovered that 36.3 employees were added between the 1998-99 and 2003-04 budget years while FTE enrollment declined from 2,762 to 2,617 and head count enrollment declined from 2,979 to 2,774.
- Due to a recession in the stock market, the value of our endowment had declined from $70.4 million in 1998-1999 to $58.6 million by 2002-03. We were drawing seven percent annually from our endowment compared to the industry average of five percent.
- Year-end balances had declined from $1.4 million in 1998-99 to $3154 in

2002-03.

- Gift income had gone from $10.7 million in 1998-99 to $6.7 million in 2002-03.
- Compensation for faculty had declined when measured against our benchmarks. (Full professor salaries had been at the 76th percentile in the American Association of University Professors ratings in 1998-1999, but were at the 68th percentile by 2002-2003.)
- In comparison to requests and previous practice, we were significantly underfunding technology, equipment, and major projects, and there were essentially no year-end balances to take up the slack.
- Funding for recent program initiatives had been provided by the Bush and Lilly foundations; that funding was being phased out and the college would need to take responsibility for ongoing expenses.

We brought the analysis to the attention of the Board of Regents in September 2003, and they charged us with preparation of a plan to achieve approximately $1.2 million in savings and/or new resources. The goal was to achieve sustainable savings and a sustainable budget.

After briefing the college's Budget Planning Committee, which had an advisory oversight role in the process, the CFO and the dean held a series of briefings for the faculty, department and division chairs, staff, and student leaders. Key leaders set out a schedule for completing the work in anticipation of the December meeting of the Board of Regents. A variety of suggestions were solicited, and many ideas were vetted because we knew that achieving $1.2 million in savings would be a difficult challenge since any budget decisions would impact people's lives, yet must be balanced with what was best for the college. By mid-November, we reported back to the community with a set of recommendations that included phasing out seven faculty and 10.5 administrative positions, proposing a variety of specific budget cuts, and suggesting selected strategies for increasing revenue. The proposed plans provided nearly $900,000 in savings, and new revenue sources would add $300,000 for the $1.2 million in funds available to fund priority needs in the 2004-2005 budget. These recommendations, along with a proposed 6.4% increase in tuition and fees, were approved by the board at its December meeting. The budget plan called for a five percent increase in compensation and significant increases in funds available for equipment, technology, and major projects. This amounted to a budget reset, but as would become clearer in the following years, without significant new tuition sources, these changes were not sustainable; consequently, budget adjustments would be an almost perennial problem.

The budget was not the only challenge during my interim presidency. In the years following my previous time at the helm at Concordia, the Church Relations program had receded in importance. During my presidency, I had always enjoyed contact with area constituents and believed outreach on behalf of Concordia was important. The contacts with congregations and synods in the college's corporate area had grown less frequent, which was noticed by these constituents. In response, my assistant Marti Hoffman and I put together a mini outreach campaign. We arranged for a team of faculty and staff to appear in nearly twenty congregations during the second semester. As a result of this effort, it was estimated that we reached 20,000 constituents in the four target areas: Grand Forks, Jamestown, St. Cloud, and Billings. This provided a sort of mutual affirmation on the part of the college and its constituent congregations. I regarded this as significant in terms of mission and strategic in terms of enrollment, for while the demographics indicated that Concordia could not expect the number of students from the region that we had experienced in the past, the region would continue to be the college's primary source of students. While we needed to continue expanding Concordia's enrollment outreach beyond our region, and were doing so with some success, we simply could not afford to abandon our more immediate home ground. I regret that this strategy was again diminished in the years that followed.

On the campus, the year of my interim presidency was highlighted by a series of presentations on the impact of the Reformation on education. This began with an emphasis at the opening workshop, where I shared some of what I had learned in my recent years of research on church related to higher education. This address, included as Appendix B, received a very positive response from the assembled faculty. The annual Faith, Reason, and World Affairs fall symposium would also examine related issues. There were additional follow-up conversations among the faculty featuring Rollie Martinson, who was a Cobber alum, distinguished theologian at Luther Seminary, and member of our Board of Regents, among others. The resulting series was excellent and well supported.

The dean of the college at the time (vice president for Academic Affairs) was Sabine O'Hara, a German-trained economist with great energy and flair. I credit her for renewing discussion among the faculty about curriculum reform, an effort that had ground to a halt a couple of years earlier. Sabine had a winsome way of challenging the faculty and leading them to consideration of new ideas and high academic standards. By the spring of her second year at Concordia, she had been appointed to the presidency of Roanoke College, so she never really had the time to make a long-term impact. Since that resignation came late in the year and we needed the new president to participate in selecting a new dean, after consulting with the faculty executive committee, I appointed Mark Krejci (Psychology) to the interim position. Following a national search, he was appointed to the permanent position. Mark's experience, knowledge of the faculty, and high trust level would enable him to lead a successful effort to revise the Core Curriculum and undertake several other initiatives.

My time as interim president wasn't without its campus challenges as well. One of the emerging topics of great interest to the campus community in those years before and after my interim was the status of gay, lesbian, and transgender persons. There was a campus committee that focused on matters of inclusion and equality. During my interim, the status of LGBT persons was the subject of several columns in *The Concordian* with some lively dialogue. Somewhat related to this was the principal controversy of the year when a faculty member spoke in chapel during Women's History Week. She used some vulgar language in her talk that upset several people, including some of the families who were visiting campus on one of the days we were interviewing prospective students for scholarships. This led Admissions Vice President Lindsay Rhodenbaugh to issue a statement of concern to his staff and the removal of the faculty member from the panel of faculty interviewers. There was, of course, uproar in some faculty circles and a petition asking Rhodenbaugh to apologize. Once again, there were columns and letters to the editor in *The Concordian* pleading the case for open discussion and freedom of expression.

I decided to let the dust clear before speaking publicly to the issue. As time passed, some respected members of the community, including Per Anderson (Religion) and campus pastor Phil Holtan, weighed in. They said that the issue wasn't freedom but appropriateness, particularly where a religious ceremony was concerned. I thought they made good sense. I had conversations with the individuals at the center of the conflict, and that contributed to easing the stress. At the closing meeting of the Faculty Senate that spring, I made a statement both defending freedom of inquiry and expression, very much a Lutheran staple, and encouraging respectful and appropriate speech, a Concordia tradition.

By springtime, Dr. Pamela Joliceour, provost at California Lutheran University, had visited the campus and was appointed as the new president of Concordia College. I had known Pam for some time, and we had served together on a couple of committees. She had an excellent academic background and well-grounded convictions about the mission of the college. Pam and I had some time together during the transition. She brought a combination of empathy, humility, and academic rigor to the campus that was most timely. In a very short time, the Concordia community embraced her and would follow her lead in a variety of areas, including the creation of the Offutt School of Business. Her short tenure would unite and inspire the campus, which is why her untimely death would lead to deep mourning.

INTERIM IV

At about 7 a.m. on the morning of June 8, 2010, I received a call from Tracey Moorhead, executive assistant to President Pamela Jolicoeur. She informed me that Pam had suffered a brain aneurism, had been transferred to palliative care, and that her death was imminent. She asked me to join her and board chair Ron Offutt at Ron's office as soon as I could get there. Shortly after I arrived, campus pastor Tim Megorden joined us and then Provost Mark Krejci. Together, we were preparing ourselves for Pam's death and for how to share this news with the community.

Following this conversation, Tracey and I went to say our farewells to Pam. Shortly thereafter, we received word of her passing. This was a shock to the whole community, but especially the campus community, where Pam's spirit and intellect had led to what the apostle once termed "a season of refreshing." The following morning, June 9, the campus community gathered for prayer, remembrance, and simply holding one another—we were truly "hearts together," the very meaning of the word "Concordia." I joined Pam's husband Mike Doyle, Tim Megorden, Tracey, and Ron in making plans for the memorial service that would be held on June 14. The service at Trinity Lutheran Church was well attended. Reverend Mark Hanson, bishop of the ELCA, brought a greeting from the church. I spoke on behalf of the college, and Steve Wold, senior pastor at Trinity and a member of the Board of Regents, delivered the homily. My remarks included these words:

> ...it is a challenge to think of anything important that Pam did not do exceedingly well. On her watch, we saw the student academic profile improve; a new Core Curriculum established; completion of a major fund campaign; reconstruction of the Knutson Campus Center; the restructuring of the leadership team; the expansion of an already distinguished international studies program; planning a new school of business; and the list goes on. Indeed, the sense of our momentum was palpable. And beyond the campus, Pam's voice and wisdom were sought and valued in national and international conversations. I told Pam's mother Kitty yesterday that I thought that Pam had given Concordia the best years of her life. Kitty agreed and said, 'and they were also the happiest years of her life.'

Following the service, attendees walked south on 7th Street from Trinity to the Knutson Center for a reception. It was a moving experience for all of us, still reeling from Pam's untimely death and the inevitable question, what next? Days later, Ron Offutt asked me if I would be willing to serve as interim president while a search was conducted for a new leader. My first response was, "But Ron, I am seventy-five years old," to which he responded, "So?" Well, at the least, I suggested, he needed to vet this idea with the leadership team, to which he replied that he already had. So, without much ado, on June 30, 2010, my appointment was announced. I think that on this, my third election to the presidency, the vote was unanimous from the beginning. In accepting the appointment, I said:

> Today is a day of necessity occasioned by an earlier day of grief. Cobbers everywhere will miss the bright engaging and life-giving leadership of Pamela Jolicoeur for years to come. We will find balm for our grief in the promises of our faith, in our memories of this distinguished leader, in the fellowship of this community, and in our work.
>
> I undertake this assignment with two goals in mind: to lead the way and to stay out of the way. I will lead the way by articulating the mission, by telling the story of the College and by maintaining the momentum of Pam's vision. President Jolicoeur's vision was intended to take full advantage of the richness of this community in

confronting the realities of a new environment usually characterized by scarcity rather than abundance. In Pam's view, it was about abundance; about stewarding our resources; about shaping a future of service rather than permitting external forces to shape the college. In short, our calling is to embody Pam's legacy.

And I will stay out of the way: out of the way of a leadership cabinet of unusual strength; out of the way of a Board of Regents that has never been stronger or more involved; out of the way of faculty, staff, and student leaders who span the generations and out of the way of a constituency of alumni and friends who are, in increasing numbers, fully engaged in the mission of this college. Together, we will put flesh on the vision which Pam led us to embrace. And with the help of God, this work will be our own.

The strength and continuity of the Board of Regents is critical in a time of unexpected and, in our case, tragic transition. Concordia's board was up to the task. Ron Offutt was the outgoing chair, and David Solberg was the chair elect. Both were experienced board leaders, and their wisdom and counsel were a steadying influence throughout the year. Norman Jones was another strong, experienced member, whose board service dated from the seventies. His judgment was always rock solid. Randy Boushek was a relative newcomer to the board, but had quickly established himself as a leader and was chosen to chair the committee charged with finding a new president. John Quello was another experienced member with a keen eye for investment and finance; Mary Alice Bergan, board secretary, was a champion for the science renovation project; Lowell Almen, former secretary of the ELCA, always kept us straight on procedure and board protocol; and Joyce Tsongas provided wise counsel on an array of issues. Rollie Martinson was a respected theologian with keen sensitivities to board culture, and when board member The Honorable John (Jack) Tunheim spoke, everyone listened, which led to his succession as board chair upon David Solberg's retirement. In short, the Concordia Board of Regents was strong and rallied to the unexpected with wisdom and calm confidence.

On June 28, I met with the President's Cabinet, whose members were Tracey Moorhead, senior associate to the President; Linda Brown, chief financial officer; Mark Krejci, chief academic officer; Omar Correa, chief Enrollment officer; Christine Schulze, director of the Concordia Language Villages; Teresa Harland, interim Advancement officer; Bruce Viewig, chief information officer; Raymond Or, dean of students; and Tim Megorden, campus pastor. By mid-September, "interim" was removed from Teresa's title, James Hausmann had been appointed interim chief Enrollment officer upon the departure of Correa, and Vieweg added Student Affairs to his portfolio upon the departure of Or in December. This was a strong, capable leadership team used to accountability and collaboration.

The agenda for the year began to be shaped at that first meeting of the cabinet, as each member was invited to list their office's priorities for the coming year. At the top of the emerging list were these three priorities: assist the campus in recovering from the loss of Pam Jolicoeur, complete the fifty-million-dollar campaign for the new school of business, and complete a five-year financial plan and a budget reset for 2011-2012. There was another list of important, subsidiary issues, including continued planning for the anticipated renovation of the science facilities, recovering the financial health of the CLV, moving forward with campus sustainability initiatives, and reforming the congregational relations and campus ministry programs. I knew we had a busy, challenging time ahead.

Once again, my goals as interim president were to set a good table for the next president, avoid any long-term projects or commitments, and focus on the most urgent institutional priorities. The mourning of Pam's death was the most important priority, and the leadership team was very intentional about providing opportunities for the community to mourn. We remembered Pam in early meetings and on public occasions. A memorial chapel service in early September provided opportunity for returning students to express their grief and cherish memories of Pam. Some weeks later, an engraved stone near the entrance to the Knutson Center was unveiled. A scholarship was established in her honor and, subsequently, the boardroom/classroom in the Offutt School of Business was named in her honor. As the year unfolded, the whole campus seemed to rally in her honor out of gratitude for her service.

The fifty-million-dollar campaign for the Offutt School of Business was well underway, and by the September 23, public announcement of the naming, thirty-seven million had been committed, and by year's end, the goal had essentially been achieved. These funds were committed to the repurposing of the Grant Center, endowment of faculty positions and scholarships, and new program development. Offutt School of Business Dean Greg Cant was the perfect choice as the OSB's founding dean. Greg was enthusiastic and energetic, which helped him recruit promising additions to the faculty. He was also a natural fundraiser. I enjoyed my involvement in this initiative because I liked both program innovation and fundraising. Given the interest and generosity of donors, the undertaking of this campaign turned out to be the easiest and most successful fundraising experience in my career. By year's end, gift income for all purposes totaled over $19.7 million, the largest total in Concordia's history, fueled by a matured deferred gift and generous gifts to the Offutt School project.

Completing a five-year budget plan and restoring the health of the current budget was the most challenging of the three major agenda items. Declining enrollment, the lack of offsetting new revenues, and additions to the staff and faculty put Concordia in the same sort of bind the college had experienced in the 2000-2003 period. The results were our inability to sustain competitive compensation, to replace equipment and make needed repairs to the physical plant in a timely fashion, and to fund new initiatives. The cabinet got its arms around this challenge in the summer months and then shared our analysis with faculty, staff, and student leaders in September. The goal was to find savings of $1.3 million, which would be re-allocated to priority needs. Meetings were held with various internal constituents through September and October, and in November, the results were shared with the campus community. While seventeen full-time equivalent positions were eliminated from the faculty and staff, the general response of the community was positive, owing in no small measure to the transparency of the process that had been led by Mark Krejci and Linda Brown. The reallocation decisions followed through the budgeting process and included a significant improvement in compensation, the funding of new initiatives including the college's investment in technology, and the establishment of a coordinator position for Concordia's emerging sustainability initiative. This last initiative was designed to save energy, improve the environment, and encourage healthy lifestyles. The initiative enjoyed strong support from students, faculty, and staff.

One conflicting activity during the reallocation process was the prioritization exercise that had been initiated and largely completed the preceding year. The exercise was a very complicated process based on a public university model. It was time-consuming and required departments to make complex judgments about the importance of various programs and activities. Human nature being what it is, there was a lot of grumbling about what departments were expected to do. While we did not ignore the results of the exercise, neither did we keep the results in the forefront during the re-allocation process. One of the most controversial decisions we made was to drop the computer science major and shift to a management information science (MIS) concentration. While the computer science program was initiated with much enthusiasm and high hopes in the eighties, the program did not live up to expectations. Enrollment was low and enthusiasm was lacking. Two of the three faculty members in this program were transferred to the Offutt School of Business, where the new MIS program would be located. The good news is that, subsequently, the computer science major was reinstated with new leadership, renewed energy, and a solid interdisciplinary base.

Another challenge in the budget rebuilding process was dealing with the operating deficits in the Concordia Language Villages program. Historically, the CLV was expected to operate with a ten percent positive margin, and those funds were transferred at year's end to a capital reserve fund. In the early 2000s, this requirement was waived as the college sought to add new revenue-producing programs in the CLV. Included among the initiatives was rental of a conference center for language and cultural programs near Stillwater, Minnesota, which would provide better access to the Twin City market. The timing of these initiatives was inopportune. The Great Recession, beginning in 2007, would have a negative effect on Concordia's traditional Language Village enrollment, and, not surprisingly, the new initiatives faced head winds as well. The result was operating deficits of more than one million dollars. While a special board committee had been formed to encourage and oversee CLV activities, it was clear to all parties that budget leaders needed to restore the financial health of this strategic program. Board member Randy Boushek, Linda Brown, Christine Schulze, and I formed a working group to address these matters. Changes were initiated, which, over time, led to renewed fiscal well-being.

In the meantime, work was completed on a five-year budget plan. The prognosis was guarded. Given the demographics, public policy regarding financial aid, and the marketplace's dynamics, growth in net tuition income would be modest. While the college endowment was growing, it would not be sufficient to close the gap between our hopes and our current budget reality. Here is a statement from a record of conversations on the plan:

> These budget challenges will be with us for some time. Looking ahead, we must find new avenues of revenue, perhaps through net revenue programs in the Offutt School of Business, perhaps through

> overhead contributions from the CLV. Other areas might involve reducing expenses by increasing student/faculty ratios and utilizing online learning as part of the Concordia experience. Moving into additional graduate programs might be another possibility.

The new realities in higher education had begun to emerge in the mid-nineties, and outside of new marketing initiatives, Concordia had done little in response beyond reallocation strategies, which could only take the college so far. Tuition was providing ninety percent of operating income, but was under increasing pressure due to market resistance to tuition raises, the pressure of tuition aid discounts, and challenging demographics. At the same time, Concordia had added new staff in marketing, Advancement, technology, Admissions, and compliance. In addition, the college's student faculty ratio had strayed far from its 1980s standard of 15:1. Higher education observers rightly concluded that for colleges like Concordia, the old tuition-driven budget model was no longer working, and some breakthroughs would be required. Concordia's experience would illustrate this observation. Reallocations had been made in the late 1990s, in 2004, and again in 2011. It was predictable that, without enrollment growth or new net income-producing programs, there would be further shrinkage in the staff and resources to meet priority needs. Unfortunately, this prediction became reality within a few short years.

Planning for the science center's renovation was highlighted at the opening faculty meeting in fall 2010. In retrospect, that was unfortunate. First, our capital project for the year was planning for the renovation of the Grant Center and related fundraising; second, there were some key and unanswered questions about the science project such as what we could afford. In hindsight, I have pondered our misstep in giving the project such premature prominence on the community agenda, partly explained because the train was already out of the station. That is, the planning that had already been completed was expansive—faculty had been asked to dream, impressive facilities at other campus had been inspected, so, naturally, enthusiasm ran high and the faculty was expecting a full report. Shiny, attractive images were prepared and displayed, all of which further fueled unrealistic expectations.

In the fall, the estimated cost of the science project was $53.7 million, and subsequent estimates ranged from $63.6 million to $72.9 million. Incredible—and I use the word advisedly. In hindsight, I believed that we had been ill served by our architects, and we had permitted faculty expectations that were not achievable since there was not a ghost of a chance that we could raise $50-80 million dollars for the project. Uffda! This was reminiscent of the Student Center estimates I had encountered in 2003. As I handed this project off to incoming President Craft, I was candid about all of this, and my advice was that in view of the analysis above, a new start was needed. That's what happened under Craft's able leadership. The reset took considerable time and anguish, but the outcome was excellent, a functional facility that serves Concordia well and at an affordable cost.

Another strategic initiative for my interim year was sorting out and implementing some of Pam Jolicoeur's ideas for the future of Concordia's external programs related to church and community. Charis, an ecumenical center serving lay and clergy in the region, had been in decline for a few years and was closed. At about the same time, Church Relations director Bruce Anderson retired. Pamela Jolicoeur had been interested in forming some new structure that would integrate the college's church and community outreach with campus programs, including campus ministry and the Vocation program that had been initiated with the support of the Lilly Endowment ten years earlier.

Without a firm outline in mind, Pam had invited Billing's pastor and Concordia Regent Tom Schlotterbach to join the staff as Concordia's director of Church Relations and continuing education programs among our church constituents. She invited him to work with her and other stakeholders in forming a new enterprise suited to changing needs and circumstances in the regional church, the college, and in society. Since there was no clear blueprint, we began inventing one. A Forum on Faith and Life had been identified as one element of the new venture, which was to provide a venue for lay and clergy to address key issues in the intersection between faith and life. We thought of the Forum on Faith and Life as a new and more strategic version of the work we had done through Charis. Schlotterbach worked with faculty and church stakeholders in shaping the Forum, and in the spring of 2011, Jacqueline Bussie was appointed to serve as director. In addition, we appointed a person to fill a position overseeing our Vocation program, which was closely aligned with the Office of Campus Ministry. Tom was to provide oversight to this new and diverse enterprise, ensuring that the hoped for synergies would emerge and prosper. In addition, he was to tend the college's relationships to the congregations of the Concordia Corporation. Toward that end, Tom arranged for the college to be represented at various assemblies and conferences in the corporate territory, managed the annual meetings of the corporation, developed some new initiatives to ensure good communication with congregations, and he and others visited congregations for various preaching and educational ventures. In short, Schlotterbach's plate was heavy, and not all of the details were in place. With the arrival of President Craft, however, there would be a new vision and emphasis, which no doubt influenced Schlotterbach's decision to accept a newly created position at the St. John's Care Center in Billings, Montana.

While it seemed to me that the restructuring envisioned by Pam and almost fully implemented by Tom promised some good outcomes, the subsequent implementation of the plan led to a diminished relationship between the college and the ELCA congregations of our corporate area of northern Minnesota, Montana, and North Dakota. There were fewer visits to pastors and congregations, few remaining program service opportunities, less effective communication strategies—all of which meant that the college was much less visible and relevant. Subsequently, the role of the Concordia Corporation was diminished and participation declined. The number of clergy on the Board of Regents was reduced, and fewer board members were from the corporate territory. This seemed hazardous from both theological and practical perspectives. Historically, Concordia had served congregations by providing excellent educational opportunities to its members and strong leadership from graduates who returned to the region. In turn, the congregations provided students, support, and historical and theological grounding. The college is weakened by any diminishment in that relationship. This is not to suggest that a resetting and a reframing of these relationships was not in order; surely such a reset was due because of changes in church, college, and society in general. In fact, these were the reasons Jolicoeur was interested in revisiting and reforming the relationship between the college and the congregations. Unfortunately, however, the result was a diminished relationship accompanied by both practical and intangible consequences.

Some saw the shift away from the college's historic region of service and toward the Twin Cities as a necessary imperative due to changing demographics. That shift had been underway for thirty years, and, in response to it, the college had successfully expanded its enrollment and Advancement activities in that direction. It was not a matter of either the historic relationships or the formation of new ones; rather, it was a both/

and strategy. In the second decade of the twenty-first century, that strategy was significantly altered.

In other administrative areas, the work progressed well. Jim Hausmann rallied an admissions staff somewhat dispirited by the unexpected departure of Omar Correa. Admissions ended up producing a fall 2011 enrollment that was stronger than the preceding year, both in new students and total enrollment. The Office of Student Success was created a year before to improve student retention. Mike Reese, director, recruited a group of able students to lead this initiative, and they moved the retention percentage from seventy-nine percent in 2009 to eighty-four percent in 2010.

For me personally during my interim, it was a pleasure to reconnect with students. During my first week on the job, students Anna Haugo and Whitney Myhra took me out for an afternoon break at the Dairy Queen. Erik George was president of the Student Association, and we formed a strong working relationship. Bruno Sudo, a Chicago native, was a spark in the Student Success program, and we became acquainted as well. At least once each week, I ate lunch or dinner at the Anderson Dining Center, eating with different groups of students and initiating conversation about their backgrounds and their Concordia experience. Concerts, athletic events, and plays were also part of Mardy's and my weekly schedules as well as daily chapel, which, by then, was poorly attended in spite of good music, liturgy, and preaching under the leadership of Pastor Tim Megorden.

Changes in the wider culture reshaped student choices; the culture was more secular and religious practices were among the casualties. The focus on individualism led to lower attendance at all campus events, a trend that had begun in the eighties, as previously noted. The one group of activities that remained strong was in the service sector. Concordia students were motivated to "do good," fueled by the curricular focus on BREW—that is, "Being Responsibly Engaged in the World"—as well as the social sensitivity and consciousness of the millennial generation.

The Concordian continued to reflect student concerns and initiatives. There were several feature stories related to sexuality, gay and lesbian concerns, and sexual harassment. In addition, editorials and features reflected a growing awareness and commitment to the environment and sustainability. While Concordia initiatives in these matters did not set the pace among collegiate institutions of our kind, concerned students, faculty, and staff led to new initiatives and increased campus awareness.

As winter turned to spring of my interim year, the search for a new president moved to completion. Early in that search, it became obvious that William Craft would be a strong candidate. He had been mentored for a decade by a very effective president, Richard Torgerson, at Luther College. In addition, Bill was an articulate, optimistic, and energetic leader, whose intellectual sensibilities gave him an easy rapport with the faculty. I welcomed his selection as did the Concordia community. It did not take Bill long to get up to speed, and we enjoyed a strong relationship. As the year drew to a close, a writer for *The Concordian* asked me to reflect on the year. Here is what I said:

> The measure of the health of a community is how it responds to a crisis or tragedy, and, judged by that standard this community is a very healthy one. What could have been a year of uncertainty and anxiety became instead a year of movement and progress.

INTERIM V

My friend and Concordia "giant in the earth" Norman Lorentzsen had a strong interest in business ethics. His experience as an executive and CEO with Burlington Northern had impressed upon him the importance of strong ethical grounding and behavior in the business world. He saw the establishment of the Offutt School of Business as a singular opportunity for the college to distinguish itself with a focus on business ethics. Norman's resources followed his conviction in the establishment and funding of the Lorentzsen Center for Faith and Work in 2012. After a year to reset, President Craft and OSB Dean Greg Cant asked me to lead the formation and first year of programming for the Center, and I agreed to do so because of my respect for Norman, my enthusiasm for the OSB, and my conviction about the role of ethics in the preparation of business leaders.

The first-year tasks were to offer a series of public programs, refine the focus of the Center, develop some strategies for the integration of ethics into the curriculum, and assist in selecting a permanent leader for the Center. This was an assignment I relished because it aligned with my interests, experience, and strengths. I formed two working groups, one focused on public programs and the other focused on curricular strategies and goals. We launched a successful series of public programs that drew capacity audiences in OSB Barry Auditorium. The grand opening event featured Dr. David Miller, a professor at Princeton and a nationally recognized figure in business ethics. Among other program elements initiated that year was a monthly gathering of 8-12 emerging leaders. Subsequently, Center for Faith and Work programming leadership organized a summer faculty workshop titled "Capitalism and Christianity." In the spring of 2013, we invited Dr. Faith Ngunjiri to become program director, a position to which she brought her distinctive charisms. After completing my active work in establishing the Center, I continued to participate in some of its activities and stood in for Faith Ngunjiri during her child-care leaves from the college. This latest return to Concordia was good work, and I felt energized by my role and optimistic about the OSB's Center for Faith and Work. Appendix C includes further reflections on leadership.

CONTINUING VENTURES

Following my interim assignment with the Lorentzsen Center, I devoted time to writing these memoirs, but found other ways to channel my time and interests. Until 2015, I worked with the Thrivent Fellows program referred to earlier. I served as a Hospice volunteer beginning in 2010 out of a desire to do volunteer work at the retail level (e.g., service delivery) after years of volunteer work at the wholesale level (board governance). Every two weeks, I also meet with six fellow Concordia retirees—we call ourselves "the So So 7." After discussing the news of the day, we focus on an article or essay of contemporary significance. In addition, I continue as a member of the local Rotary Club. From time to time, I assisted with fundraising ventures for the ELCA, LSS of Minnesota, Trinity Lutheran Church, and Oak Grove School. I find these varied activities align with my values of service and community and connect me with many different people.

Mardy's schedule was oriented around PEO, her book club, and her bridge group, and she also served on the grant review committee of the FM Area Foundation. Mardy's primary role, however, as it has always been, is keeper of the family flame. She is our cheerleader, encourager, counselor, and sunshine on a rainy day. Great and good gifts. In 2008, Mardy and I celebrated our golden wedding anniversary. Our children and grandchildren hosted a reception event with family friends and a wonderful weekend of celebration and sightseeing on the North Shore of Lake Superior. As I write this now, Mardy and I have been life partners for more than sixty-six years—what a rich and full life we've been blessed with. Our immediate family has always grounded us and always will, and Concordia constitutes a second family for us, which we deeply value.

One of the great joys of retirement—that is, finally being fully retired—is having more freedom. We have taken full advantage of that freedom, enjoying time with our grandchildren, attending their school events, and celebrating their achievements. We spend an increasing amount of time at our cabin on Bad Medicine Lake, which, beginning with our years in the presidency, really has become our family hearth. We have also exercised our freedom with frequent travel abroad. In 2006, our extended family traveled to Norway, meeting family and enjoying the fantastic beauty. In 2008, Mardy and I were part of a tour that visited Israel, Jordan, and Egypt. In 2009, we traveled to Spain and Portugal; in 2012, we traveled to Greece and Turkey; in 2016, we were back to Norway again while our granddaughter Anna was a student at the University of Tromso; and, in 2017, we cruised the Rhine from Switzerland to Amsterdam. On several occasions, we traveled to Jamaica for a winter warm up. We have found much joy in experiencing the richness of this diverse world.

In closing this journey through my life, I extend gratitude to you, dear reader, for your perseverance; to my beloved Mardy for her boundless love, patience, and joy; and to the scores of friends, mentors, and colleagues who filled my cup with their competence, encouragement, and grace. No doubt, new ventures await, of which we cannot see the ending. Soli Deo Gloria.

Appendix A: Look to the Rock

Author's Note:

In an earlier era, inaugural addresses were thought of as a kind of credo statement of the incoming president's values and convictions, a sort of "here I stand" oration. And, oh yes, it was also acceptable to speak for longer than twenty minutes. This address met both of those criteria—it was a statement of my credo, and it was longer than twenty minutes. The assembly of 2,000 students, visiting academics, and friends was patient and attentive—or so it seemed to me. As I reflect on the address years later, I recognize that in the 1970s, we were much less aware of the importance of using inclusive language in written and spoken communication; that said, the content continues to affirm where I stood at the time and continue to stand today.

In the mid-1970s, the academy was still reeling from the social maelstrom of the 1960s. There had been many changes on campuses like Concordia's, changes in academic programs, in student lifestyle, in governance, in constituency relationships, and a lot more. I had experienced those changes and been in the midst of most of the struggles, some of which remained unresolved as I accepted the presidency of the college. I took it as my challenge in this address to declare how I understood both our challenges and our resources. I presented and appealed to traditional arguments and proofs including the liberal arts, the theological and biblical foundation of the school, and the strong tradition of community. The Gospel call to reconciliation was at the heart of my early leadership as I sought to address both a constituency and a college that remained somewhat unsettled by the dynamics of the 1960s.

LOOK TO THE ROCK
The 1975 Inaugural Address
Text: Isaiah 51:1-2

As the text for today, I turn to Isaiah 51:1-2, "Hearken to me, you who pursue deliverance, you who seek the Lord; look to the rock from which you were hewn, and to the quarry from which you were digged. Look to Abraham your father and to Sarah who bore you; for when he was but one I called him, and blessed him and made him many."

The writer of Isaiah addressed these words to a group of political exiles who were seeking deliverance and righteousness. He exhorted them to look to the rock of ages, that is, to Abraham, the father of the faithful. Abraham had been one, but had been loved by God and made many. Concordia is not in exile, but we seek God's blessing and direction, and so I invite you to consider with me the basic dimensions of the rock from which Concordia College was hewn.

College presidents come and go, and the significance of their going turns mainly on the transcendent qualities of the colleges they lead. The contemporary vocabulary of higher education trades on words such as "relevance," "accountability," and "secularization," and on the dilemmas posed by inflation, uncertain enrollments, government support and control. These words and issues may be different in three years and surely will be in ten. While we will all be accountable for our stewardship in dealing with these matters, I deem it important to reflect upon those resources and principles that have guided and shaped this college. We are not called to relive our past or to be a static and unchanging college—but in reflecting upon the rock from which we were hewn, we find reliable guideposts for dealing with the issues and opportunities before us.

The fundamental dimension of the rock from which Concordia was hewn is the Gospel of Christ—the Christ who called us to forgiveness and assured us of His Love, the Christ who called us to a ministry of reconciliation and assured us of His eternal presence.

The pastors and farmers who established this college may have had some heated arguments about whether the college should be located in Crookston, Grand Forks, or Fargo-Moorhead, and certainly the faculty disagreed about the content of the academic program. There was a good deal of political activity on both of these issues. But there were no arguments about the college's underlying purpose: "Concordia shall provide education and training for Christian service and leadership," they said. So, men and women called by the Gospel literally loved a college into being. In keeping with the Gospel, our pioneer founders were bold. They borrowed and raised money against good advice; they built buildings for more students than they enrolled; they beat the odds and survived economic depression; and they began talking about building an endowment in the early 1900s when such talk was more a measure of their faith than their capabilities. Yes, these were people made bold by the Gospel. By God's grace, they could dare, and they did; they could fail, and they did; but through it all, God gave the college an increase. A measure of both their pride and competitive spirit was best expressed by one of the founding fathers who said, "These people are preparing to open Concordia College in Moorhead. These people are going to do a work for Christ and His church for which even the sons of New England will yet rise up and call them blessed."

The Gospel that inspired and emboldened the founders of Concordia still calls and enables us. Because of the Gospel, Paul's words to the Corinthians are fresh today, "Such is the confidence we have through Christ toward God. Not that we are sufficient of ourselves to claim anything as coming from us; our sufficiency is from God, who has qualified us to be members of a new covenant; not in a written code but in the spirit; the written code kills, but the spirit gives life" (2 Corinthians 3:4-6). In our contemporary rhetoric, we speak of influencing the affairs of the world by sending into society thoughtful and informed men and women dedicated to the Christian life. It is a statement fully in keeping with the commitments of our founders, and it is a statement made possible by God's continuing work among us.

On the rock of the Gospel, we are enabled to undertake the risks and excitement of this ministry at Concordia. From my mentors, I have learned the meaning of faith in its institutional dimensions. It does not mean acting heedlessly, but it does mean acting in hope and confidence. The Gospel is sufficient for all seasons—seasons of drought and plenty, seasons of economic setback or public doubt, seasons of expansion or cutback, seasons of secularity or religious awakening. We know not what the next year or decade will hold, but we do know about Christ's faithfulness. It is on this rock that we sing the words of our college hymn, Soli Deo Gloria, to God alone the glory.

As we look to the rock, another of its dimensions is theology. In theology, we work out our understanding of the Gospel and its application to our human context. When the founders of Concordia said that Concordia would "provide education and training...in conformity with the faith, confessions and practices" of their synod, they were identifying the theological dimension of the rock from which Concordia was hewn.

There are some things that we Lutherans hold to be true about God, man, the world, and the relationship among them. Luther emphasized that God deals with us from the perspective of grace and that is a revolutionary concept in any age. It was Luther's view that man is both justified by grace and is also a sinner, so we need to take sin seriously. He emphasized that the world was not a place to escape but a realm of God's activity in which we are all called to address questions regarding the meaning and purpose of life, questions of human good, and issues related to faith and life. In short, it is a resource of central value to those engaged in the ministry of teaching and learning. It is a resource of special importance to the questions of this particular time.

For example, our technological prowess has created some disjunctions between what we know and what we do. Theologian Richard Salzmann says that we have lately tended to reduce reality to the pattern of our minds and thus ignore the laws of nature and supernatural issues. But God in Christ provides a basis for synthesis between Creator and creation, between knowledge and action, between neighbor and self. He makes new creatures of us and reconciles us to Himself and then enables us to be agents of reconciliation in the world.

Consider one of the dominant themes in recent social commentary—the search for dependable values and a legitimate style of life. The new president of the American Psychological Association recently chided his fellow psychologists for siding with self-gratification over self-restraint. Allen Pifer of the Carnegie Corporation expresses concern for colleges and universities in dealing with moral issues, and his is one voice in a chorus of leading educators speaking to this issue. Perhaps the sense of moral drift is best dramatized by the title of Karl Menninger's recent book, *Whatever Became of Sin?* Those familiar with Luther's *Bondage of the Will* are acquainted with most of the arguments that are being rediscovered these days. For Lutherans, there is a group of propositions that speak to the limits of secular knowledge and human will and the need for self-discipline and restraint in the sanctified life. Seen in the light of the Gospel, these propositions become means of fulfillment rather than self-denial, means of seeing our neighbor and the requirements of justice and mercy with new clarity and power. Lutheran colleges have something distinctive to contribute to the dialogue about the human good when such questions are in style, as they are becoming today, and when they are not, as has been the case in recent times.

Then there are the questions of Vocation that preoccupy so many of our young people today, questions that can be informed by what Luther had to say about the priesthood of all believers and the universal call to discipleship, a call that includes chambermaids and gardeners, surgeons and lawyers, businessmen and, yes, pastors too.

I believe our colleges are called to be Lutheran, to bring to bear on the great questions of life and meaning the resources of our doctrines and tradition. To say we have the answers to all questions is to deny the search for truth for which Christ himself stood. And to say that we have something special to offer from a theological perspective is not to compromise our academic commitments. We have something important to contribute to our brothers and sisters of all faiths. We can make our contribution in a manner that safeguards the freedom and integrity of the academic enterprise. Lutheran theology is a dimension of the rock on which we were built. I believe that, in taking seriously our theology, we may strike new fires in keeping with our historic mission. Let us claim this uniqueness, equip ourselves for it, and exercise it with joy and energy.

A third dimension of the rock on which Concordia was built is the commitment to quality liberal arts education. The commitment to good education was a matter of faith to the college's founders who must have been imbued by the spirit Luther reflected in saying, "If we wish to have excellent and apt persons for both civil and ecclesiastical government, we must spare no diligence, time, nor cost in teaching and educating our children, that they may serve God and the world...." This tradition of commitment to study in a religious setting goes back to Old Testament times; and Christ, in revealing Himself, made Himself knowable and so the study of His life and revelation has been a dimension of education since the early church. In view of these traditions, it is no wonder that the founders of Concordia had a deep commitment to quality education and it is appropriate for us to renew our commitment today. We are called to be a good college—called to excellence if you will, a word that lost its currency some years back through misuse. Several years ago, Dr. Alvin H. Rogness, then president of Luther Seminary, said he expected our colleges to be excellent academic institutions, "Excellence in and by itself is a part of our witness to the Lord," he said. So, it is today, we are called to develop our abilities to the maximum and to expect of our students the very best of which they are capable. The canons of academic excellence are the same at Concordia as at any secular institution, good scholarship and passion for the truth wherever it may be found.

In the early days of this college, there was a good deal of debate about the kind of educational program that the college should provide. Short courses in music, business, English, and the applied arts were the college's stock and trade until the early 1900s when a decision was made to develop a four-year baccalaureate level liberal arts program. It was nearly fifteen years from the date of that commitment to the awarding of the first baccalaureate degrees in 1917, but the issue was settled then, that Concordia should prepare students for Christian leadership and the liberal arts were the best means to that end.

Liberal arts education is based on the study of the most significant of man's traditions and the disciplines fundamental to understanding our world and ourselves. I appreciated Roger Goldwin's recent description of the value of liberal education: "We find we can develop very special skills that imitate the Creator himself, for we too can make new worlds, not out of nothing—but out of nothing more than a pencil, a straightedge, and a mind. Such skills... are called liberal because they free us from the restraint of our material existence and let us soar as free men and women in the realm of the mind." Through years of challenge from technology, unemployment, and vocationalism—we have remained in that tradition. Liberal arts education has been durable both because of the qualities it develops and its evolution. Innovation in content and method has transformed our program from time to time, giving it new vitality and currency. Our graduates have made distinguished records in the professions and in a range of careers including education, technology, agriculture, finance, and government.

As one looks to the present and future, the challenges confronting liberal arts education are rather immediate. We have agreed that diversity exists in higher education and that it is a good thing. After a decade of homogenization, it has also been agreed that uniqueness among individual institutions is a positive value. But in view of the challenges from a specialty-prone, job-minded and pragmatically-oriented culture, we need to give definition to the value of liberal arts education. As Steve R. Graubard remarked in assessing the future of higher education, "The liberal arts curriculum of yesterday would seem no longer to be adequate; there are few who detect very great vigor in what passes for 'general education' today. The issue of learning, its content and form, is recognized to be as important as any now confronting higher education." Graubard contends that what is at stake today is "the continued viability of the concept of a liberally educated person."

Indeed, what is it useful to teach and know? How shall we achieve the liberating skills and understandings essential to the late twentieth century?

Can we break down the walls of our disciplinary commitments? Can we resolve the confusion of voices on the issues of academic standards and goals?

I believe we should address these issues, and, being somewhat traditional in our notions about liberal arts education, our resources for this inquiry are close at hand. But I believe such an examination can and should take place at each liberal arts college, and there is some urgency about it for the challenges are immediate and our claims are more philosophical than those of other sectors of education. Our claims are also conceived of as being less provable in a society prone toward pragmatic judgment. Therefore, at a minimum, we must reconsider and reaffirm what it is we are about and then state our claims far and wide with eloquence and persistence.

Look to the rock from which you were hewn in all of its dimensions—the Gospel, theology, the program and finally, a nurturing community. The nurturing community that is Concordia is made up of the constituents who have surrounded this college with their prayers and acts, the faculty and staff called to the ministry of teaching and leadership, and the students through whom the mission of the college is fulfilled. In his inaugural address in 1925, Dr. J. N. Brown summed it up for us when he said, "There are no pages in the history of our Lutheran church in America so thrilling in interest, so filled with self-sacrifice, so far-reaching in permanent results as those pages recording educational activities of those far-sighted, freedom-loving, God-fearing Lutheran pioneers." The pages of Concordia's history bear out Dr. Brown's statement. Names like Guberding, Ness, Dosland, and Christanson abound in the chronicles of this college. Down through the decades, the roll of saints includes scores of people from across these Great Plains and woodlands who saw a need and responded. While the founding fathers may not have succeeded in building a large vested capital endowment for Concordia, their example has given us a living endowment of congregations and church people, alumni and parents. Small wonder that Dr. Joseph Knutson at his inaugural in 1951 could say with confidence, "I know that my God and His people will not fail to uphold Concordia, her teachers and students, with their prayers and gifts."

Another group of this community's citizens are those privileged to teach and work here. Grose, Bogstad, Rognlie, Wollan, Fjelstad, and Ylvisaker are among the men and women who gave definition to the word commitment. They and their colleagues shaped our traditions of scholarship and study and offered models for the intellectual and personal lifestyle of generations of Concordia students. In our documents, we say that the faculty and staff make more difference for good or ill than any other element in our college. That statement defines our challenge today as it has in the years gone by. Ours is a position of privilege, a position of almost unlimited possibilities for growth and ministry in Christ's church.

The other citizens of this nurturing community are the students. Their response to our teaching and leadership is what the college is all about. And again, the reputation that Concordia students have built is noteworthy. They have brought to the college great skill and good questions and have developed both to God's honor. With the help of those around them, they have gone on to distinguished careers both in this region and to the reaches of the earth.

The nurturing community that we call Concordia has always been more than the sum of its parts, and I think that is explained with the words Paul used in greeting the congregations at Philippi when he spoke of their "partnership in the Gospel from the first day until now" (Philippians 1:5). There has been a nurturing fellowship on the campus between the college, the constituency, and the church. The partnership has undergone change in composition and style. There were few among the early community who did not speak the mother tongue of Norway; whereas today, we come from a wider variety of creeds and cultures. In much of our history, the community style was more structured and formal than it is today.

Another reason for the tradition of nurture has been the strong sense of shared commitment that has been found among Concordia's members. The credit for the selection of the college's name is often given to Rev. J. O. Hougen. He said, "Concordia is the goodness of harmony...[the] opposite of discord... [it] literally means hearts working together, hearts working in unison." This should not lead one to the erroneous conclusion that there haven't been some battles here. Earlier I mentioned the faculty struggle over program content in our first decade, and I have been a participant in some great debates during the contemporary period. But the hearts have been working together, melded by the Gospel and the work of the Spirit among us; and disagreement and conflict have been possible here without fracturing the binding tie. The lesson is that we can continue to be a nurturing community by drawing on the resources of the Word and Sacraments. The music and worship traditions of Concordia are especially noteworthy, and few have passed through this campus without being influenced by them. With these resources, we are free to express the new idea or critical insight that is often the key to new levels of service in education. These resources also enable us to provide an environment in which hearts are affirmed and nurtured by the Gospel.

This community will have special opportunities in the next several years. For example, many voices from the academy have been predicting that our institutions will suffer from atrophy in the "steady state" and their view is based on the assumption that the only source of institutional renewal is new personnel. But I would argue that a stable community built on secure and affirming relationships possesses the conditions for being a self-renewing community. Admittedly, that won't occur without some attention and energy, but I believe it is possible and the signs at hand are most hopeful.

Another opportunity that lies before the nurturing community relates to emerging levels of awareness and aspiration on the part of women and minority group citizens. We have passed the first blush of public concern when conscience-stricken legislators passed laws and funding bills designed to deal with an accretion of limiting self-concepts and institutional injustice. The funding levels have declined, and we have all become aware that the wheels of social change move slowly. But our call to justice and equal opportunity comes from the Gospel and not the social chic of a passing decade. As we provide a nurturing community for these special citizens, they become stronger and our college grows richer.

Look to the rock from which you were hewn—in all of its dimensions: Gospel, theology, program, and nurturing community. Unlike the Israelites to whom our text was addressed, Concordia does not stand in political exile. But, like the Israelites, we seek direction for our future. We face the uncertainties of the future in the faith of our fathers. We affirm a future that holds new possibilities for reconciliation between and within disciplines and people and churches. We can make such an affirmation because the Gospel is fresh every morning and it gives us both subject matter and grace for the task before us.

Paul Ricoeur said, "Hope is the same thing as remembering." In remembering the rock from which Concordia was hewn, we find our hope. I pledge myself to the rock from which Concordia was hewn, to the God and Creator of all things by whose grace this college is an agent of reconciliation. I make this pledge in joy and confidence because God has promised to bless us with His love, His spirit, and His power. Amen.

Appendix B: The Vocation of a Liberal Arts College

Author's Note:

In 2003, I was back on campus as Concordia's interim president. Already in place for the coming academic year was a series of reflections on the role of a Lutheran liberal arts college in a changing world. I agreed to address this subject at the opening faculty workshop. It was a fresh opportunity to think about Concordia in terms of the postmodern conversation, the revived understanding of Vocation, and the rediscovery of the richness of the Lutheran tradition. I regard this address as the most comprehensive and cogent expression of my academic credo.

THE VOCATION OF A LUTHERAN LIBERAL ARTS COLLEGE
Concordia College Opening Faculty-Staff Workshop
August 22, 2003

I will take this opportunity to discuss the research I have been involved in recently with a focus on the Lutheran liberal arts tradition. In the spirit of that tradition, what I share now should be seen more as a series of hypotheses rather than a set of declarations in the sense that Lutheran colleges are very diverse in what and how they appropriate the elements of the tradition. There is not, in any sense, an official Lutheran theological perspective any more than there is a normative Lutheran liberal arts tradition.

The Lutheran commitment to learning dates from the Reformation itself. Luther exemplified St. Anselm's dictum that "faith seeks understanding." It was intellectual inquiry fed by religious anxiety that led Luther to his breakthrough reading of Romans on the nature of salvation. It was Luther's commitment to the laity, the priesthood of all believers, that led him to champion a universal education that would give people of both sexes and all ages direct access to knowledge. It was Luther's commitment to worldly truth that led him to exclaim, "How can you not know what can be known?"

It was his respect for human curiosity that led him to write the catechism with its recurrent question, "What does this mean?" following each creedal affirmation. It was commitment to the place of learning in church and world that led Luther and Melanchthon to spearhead a reformation of the curriculum at Wittenberg University. This is a significant history but what leads us to revisit the Vocation of a Lutheran liberal arts college in the first decade of a new century? Let me venture some answers to that question.

The first reason is because, beginning a decade ago, we realized that the Vocation of Lutheran liberal arts colleges (and other religious colleges) might be slipping away. As George Marsden related in his epic, *The Soul of the American University*, the hegemony of modernism marginalized humanistic and religious ways of knowing all across the academic landscape. It left religious colleges, at best, with what Douglas Sloan calls a two-realm theory of truth in which faith (values) and learning (facts) rarely intersected. In Mark Schwehns's analysis, the post Weberian preoccupation with the creation of knowledge edged out the discovery of truth and moral formation as desirable ends of learning. Academic excellence came to be defined by modernist, scientific criteria. Most of us were socialized in the modernist academy and its methods and values shaped our intelligence. Survey work led by Michael Beaty at Baylor University documents the impact of the two-realm theory of truth upon faculties at three highly recognized religious colleges and universities.

The recent history of religious colleges has been chronicled by several writers, mostly notably by James Burtchaell in his landmark work, *The Dying of the Light*. As Burtchaell and others note, the straying of colleges from their religious moorings was in some cases a deliberate action of the colleges. For example, in order to meet institutional funding needs many colleges sought to broaden their constituent base by generalizing their mission statements. In the face of change and incredible growth, many colleges sought to position themselves in a more ecumenical, secular, and less particularist mode. The influence of modernism and secularism was ameliorated on the campuses of many religious colleges for a considerable period of time through the ethos of the faculty who were part of the tradition, through relationships with sponsoring church bodies, and through religious rituals and traditions. But, over time, the rituals and traditions became less evident and important. Along with that, the ethos of the faculty was reshaped by professionalization, the shortage of candidates from related church bodies, the desire for diversity, and the leadership practices of the colleges.

A second reason we revisit the Vocation of a Lutheran liberal arts college is because of the powerful influence of material, individualistic, instrumental, and pluralistic values in our culture. Again, the historical accounts note the influence of a culture hungry for economic development, students motivated by narrow vocational goals, and a society preoccupied with glitz, consumption, and personal happiness. Many see a connection between these goals and the intellectual values that privilege the pragmatic, the material, and the individual. The cause of concern is not that material and personal issues are to be ignored, but rather that they are not contextualized within broader, transcendent values. Consequently, the two realms, faith and action, are unequal and largely disconnected.

A word about pluralism, the constructive value of pluralism is not the issue, but the relationship between pluralism and particularity is. The idea that we are a richer society today because of the plurality of voices and visions is borne out by our history. Bias and discriminatory practices have often jeopardized the richness and have led many to eschew any particularity, be it religious, ethnic, or gender. The challenge for a democratic society is to honor the particularities, the *pluribus*, that bring richness to our *unum* and the challenge for religious colleges is to sustain and enrich their particularity as they engage the pluralism. This requires courage, integrity, humility, and respect for others.

A third reason we revisit these issues relates to the critique of postmodernism. In the closing decades of the twentieth century, the foundations of modernism were shaken from both inside and outside the academy. As citizens sought a deeper sense of meaning and understanding (the spiritual dimension as some call it), the modern, objectivist-oriented academy was found wanting. As social/human crises continued unabated in a time of technological mastery, modernism's vulnerability became apparent. As the marginalized voices of women, the poor and persons of color were raised, the objectivist project began to shake.

While these external realities were being made manifest, the academy engaged in its own self-critique. The relationship between perspective and perception, between experience and knowing, between motivation and judgment, and between narrative and truth raised serious questions about the modernist project in general and other narratives, including Christian, in particular. A combination of new voices, fault lines in the social order, and the self-searching of the academy created a kind of an epistemic/ hermeneutical chaos. Critics complained of an incipient relativism that would lead to still more chaos. Some predicted the undermining of rationality itself and the descent into nihilism. But others saw the postmodern critique as an invitation to new voices in the academic process and new definitions of the academic project. We have an increasing body of literature from both young and seasoned scholars who are attempting to unpack the epistemological confusion and engage the desperate voices in common dialogue. This is a hopeful sign. (Particularly valuable are *Professing in the Postmodern Academy: Faculty and the Future of Church Related Colleges*, a collection of essays by younger scholars edited by Stephen Haynes, and *Religious Scholarship and Higher Education: Perspectives and Direction for the Future*, the work of established scholars edited by Andrea Sterk.)

The fourth reason we reconsider the Vocation of a Lutheran liberal arts college is because of the renaissance of religious intentionality in the culture and in the academy. Speaking of what he calls our smorgasbord culture, Miloslav Volf of the Yale Divinity School observes, "Communities of faith have not found effective ways to offer a compelling vision of an integral way of life that is worth living. Many people are seeking precisely that. They are unsatisfied with a lifestyle shaped only by the watchwords of contemporary culture: 'freedom' and 'prosperity.' This is signaled by the resurgent interest in spirituality as related to almost every dimension of life—from medicine to business, from arts to politics."

The last decade of the twentieth century has been a watershed for students and practitioners of religious higher education in America. Certain crises in the culture, the changing expectations and priorities of religious bodies that sponsor colleges, and the critical reexamination of intellectual paradigms already noted are among the key markers in this watershed. In addition, the Lilly Endowment has provided the essential resources and marshaled the competent talent that is prerequisite to a sustained and unfolding treatment of these developments.

But behind these developments lie the memory of a rich heritage, the restlessness of academics trying to come to terms with the discontinuities between experience and conviction, the growing spiritual self-consciousness of students and younger faculty, and the work of the divine spirit. The results are many and diverse: We see faculty renewal projects, the re-emergence of a robust scholarship in faith and learning, the reformulation of institutional missions, the reconsideration of religious identity, curriculum reform, the reshaping of campus life, the reemergence of religious symbols, and practices and new forms of relationship with the church. The products of this renaissance are already voluminous in both traditional and hypertexts. One recent sign of all of this is the Rutgers University website that now includes a feature on the reengagement with values and spirituality in higher education.

What then is the Vocation of a Lutheran liberal arts college? I believe that it finds its expression in three areas: purpose, substance, and pedagogy. Let me explore each in turn.

I. Purpose

The Vocation of a Lutheran college is expressed first of all in its purpose, and here the Lutheran idea of Vocation is formative. In Luther's view, God takes the initiative in the relationship between God and humans. We receive the righteousness of God through faith. We don't earn it or build our life toward that end. So, salvation is our starting point, not the goal of our lives. We receive this gift through faith and we respond to God's call through our vocation in service to the neighbor. The Lutheran concept of Vocation was and is unique and it begins with gift. In addition, it is distinctive in that it is inclusive of all occupations. Another feature of Luther's formulation is its comprehensiveness. For Luther, Vocation was occupation, but it was so much more than that—it was home and family and community and leisure and church - wherever one meets the neighbor. As Mark Edwards put it, "Luther spiritualized secular life, by taking the notion of spiritual calling and applying it to all honest walks of life."

Luther was concerned about the renewal of the church, but his larger concern was the renewal of society. Thus, he was concerned about the education and conduct of those called to be priests and monks, but he was just as concerned for those called to be shoemaker, farmer, judge, parent, and teacher; and so he called all of them priests! The calling to serve the neighbor leads us to issues of love and justice, it leads us to the community, and it leads us to concern for the common good. Again and again, Luther's centering ethic was expressed in the question "Does it serve the neighbor?"

In view of this, what then is the purpose of a Lutheran liberal arts college?

To call and prepare graduates to serve the neighbor. Luther made the case in his letter to the councilmen in 1524 as he wrote: "In order to maintain its temporal estate outwardly, the world must have good and capable men and women, men able to rule well over land and people, women able to manage the household and train children and servants alike. Now such men must come from our boys, and such women from our girls. Therefore, it is a matter of properly educating and training our boys and girls to that end."

Luther particularly underscored the necessity of good education for those who would be leaders, rulers, and authorities. So again, the Vocation of a Lutheran liberal arts college is to call and prepare students to serve their neighbor.

II. Substance

This leads to the second expression of our Vocation as a Lutheran liberal arts college and that is in the substance of the enterprise. Let me say a few things initially about the reformers commitment to what we refer to as the liberal arts. Martin Luther and Phillip Melanchthon were dismayed by the scholastic curriculum of their day, a curriculum that featured philosophy, a rote dialectic practice, and dogmatic formulations of belief and practice. In the 1524 letter previously referred to, Luther lamented about his own education in these words: "How I regret now that I did not read more poets and historians and that no one taught me them! Instead, I was obliged to read at great cost, toil, and detriment to myself the devil's dung, the philosophers and sophists, from which I have all I can do to purge myself."

In response to this, Luther and Melanchthon said, metaphorically, "Let in the 'light'." It should be noted that the reformers recognized the power and value of non-Christian contributions to culture. The great pagan poets and writers were to be taught in schools partly for their inherent value, partly as instrumental to the mastery of language and grammar for the study of scripture" (Richard Baepler, *The Lutheran Reader*). While Luther disliked Aristotle in general, he recognized the superior value of his moral ethics. For Luther and the other reformers at Wittenberg the mantra was "consider history, the languages and classics, develop critical perspective, study moral philosophy and, learn and practice a rhetoric that engages life." In the words of James Kittelson, for Luther and other humanists, "True knowledge was not universal and propositional in character, but concrete and specific to time and place. Its truths were not *scientia* or knowledge but *sapientia* or wisdom, which was to be found in the marketplace and in the conduct of daily life rather in the lecture hall or the monastery. Education thus had an end both temporally and finally. This end was the finished person that came out of the classroom and into society, the one who could apply general principles in a variety of specific situations" (James M. Kittleson, *Luther and Learning*). All of this is by way of saying that we have a legacy—a liberal arts legacy, a legacy of curriculum reform, a legacy that includes both the sacred and the secular.

But in addition to this liberal arts legacy, the substance of our collegiate enterprise is shaped by several theological themes and elements. In his book, *Quality with Soul*, Robert Benne writes that one of the distinctive resources of a healthy religious college is the Christian account of reality. This account is comprehensive, "It provides an umbrella of meaning under which all facets of life and learning are gathered and interpreted." It does not claim to have all of the data, but it offers a paradigm in which data and knowledge about the world can be "organized, interpreted, and critiqued." This Christian account arises from the Christian narrative and from the intellectual tradition that has emerged from it, and this intellectual tradition, says Benne, "...conveys a Christian view of the origin and destiny of the world, of nature and history, of human nature and its predicament, and of the human situation and of the Christian way of life." In other words, the Christian account provides a variety of substantive propositions that may shape the academic experience of a Lutheran college. While it would be presumptuous to even attempt to unpack all of this for our time and place, some illustrations may be helpful...six in all.

We begin with the Christian notion of *freedom* and its profound implications. Saved by grace from the burden of sin and the necessity of constructing our own salvation, we are free to serve God, free to explore all that God has done. This is a more profound notion of freedom than we find any place else in our culture. This leads most naturally to academic freedom, described in the recent draft of the college's statement of purpose as "the exercise of critical inquiry and the use of reason to discover the beauty, complexity and order in creation and contribute to the emergence of a just world." The practice of free inquiry, a right secured by the secular authorities in Saxony, enabled Luther to unlock the scriptures and emboldened him to set out his arguments for critical examination in the forum of public opinion. It is a legacy with both substantive and pedagogical significance. Indeed, our call to serve the neighbor requires that the truth be discovered and that the truth be told in a society that is always in need of reformation.

A second theme with implications for the substance of our work is Luther's *affirmation of the world.* Luther spoke of a God active in two kingdoms or two realms—the heavenly realm where grace rules and the earthly realm where reason and the law are indispensable. These two kingdoms are both arenas of God's activity and Christians are called to be active in both. What was distinctive about Luther's view was his affirmation of the world, the secular—his view that this is God's creation and the site of God's continuing activity, and so (as I noted earlier) Luther affirmed the study of so-called pagan authors and understood that they possessed knowledge that was essential in serving the neighbor.

A third substantive theme has to do with the *importance of the arts.* Music, in particular, played a key role in the Lutheran Reformation, more so than in the Calvinist Reformation with its rejection of graven images. Here was a creative explosion in the hymnody as well as a general cultivation of music. "Music not only banished earthly cares and became a vehicle for glorifying God, it seemed to mediate the presence of God in special ways" (Baepler, *The Lutheran Reader*).

A fourth theme is the *centrality of community* in Luther's writing and speaking. The Vocation of serving the neighbor brings us into community. Recognizing God's work in the earthly kingdom brings us to community. Confessing the third article of the historic confession of the church leads us to community. Therefore, it is not surprising that Lutherans have been distinctive among denominations in their engagement in the public sector. For example, in the United States, Lutherans account for only three percent of the population, but sponsor twenty-five percent of the nursing homes and the largest social and human service enterprise in the nation. In addition, Lutherans have pioneered the development of global assistance through Lutheran World Relief and the Lutheran Immigration Service has resettled more refugees that any agency except the U.S. government.

Moral deliberation of the sort Luther encouraged and exemplified begins with attending to the biblical narrative and the insights of the tradition and often ends by engaging the reflection and common sense of the community. In Luther's view no particular form of government or public policy was mandated by the Bible or tradition, so we need to use our reason to apply ourselves with wisdom. Luther modeled this paradigm, sometimes well and sometimes badly. Although he didn't deny his fallibility, neither did he use it as an excuse for inaction.

A fifth theme is what I describe as a *sense of contingency*. It is expressed in a number of ways, including the famous *simul eustis et pecator* formulation, the confession that we are simultaneously both sinner and righteous. We also see it in Luther's view on the limits of reason. Luther viewed reason as "the most important and the highest in rank among all things, and, in comparison with other things of this life, the best and something divine." But he was leery of Erasmus and others who thought they could rationalize divine grace and revelation, and he was sensitive to the ways in which persons who were simultaneously saint and sinner could corrupt reason.

The sense of contingency is also evident in Luther's preference for the paradoxical, the reality of the sometimes-irresolvable tension among alternative ways of understanding and negotiating reality. This sense of contingency leads to a sense of intellectual humility. It may also enable Lutheran intellectuals to be less bothered by the epistemic and hermeneutical chaos of postmodernism—but that is the subject for another day. Finally, it perhaps accounts for the "ethical realism" characteristic of Lutherans, the idea that we are called to work for change without the expectation of heaven on earth. This apparently sensible insight has led others to suggest that our "realism" may lead to quietism.

The theology of the cross perhaps best exemplifies the Lutheran sense of contingency. In view of the human suffering, we have experienced in the past century and already in this new one, this theme is worthy of our attention. We are called to think *coram deo*, that is, in relationship to God. And we find God in suffering places, places where we encounter most dramatically the limits of human wisdom and action. In weakness, we find God's strength; in human folly, we find God's wisdom; in the cross, we find God's victory. To seek God in such crosses is a profound quest, one that opens us to both spiritual depths and heights, to our own human limitations and our human possibilities as messengers of God.

A decade ago, Nicholas Woltersdorf, a guest on this campus on more than one occasion, lost his son in a mountaineering accident. He experienced a long night of grief. As he emerged from this experience of the cross, he wrote: "To believe in Christ's rising and death's dying is also to live with the power and the challenge to rise up now from all our dark graves of suffering love. If sympathy for the world's wounds is not enlarged by our anguish, if love for those around us is not expanded, if gratitude for what is good does not flame up, if insight is not deepened, if aching for a new day is not intensified, if hope is weakened and faith diminished, if from the experience of death comes nothing good, then death has won. Then death, be proud."

A sixth substantive resource emerging from the Lutheran tradition is *the incarnation*. Luther's idea was that the finite, that is, human beings and other created things, are capable of witnessing to the infinite, which is the divine. As the bread and the wine convey God's gift and presence, as prayer and word give us access to God's spirit, so also does human work in the community make a difference. That work may be making good shoes or good beer, or it may be aiding the poor and disenfranchised, or it may be engaging in the hard and often ambiguous work of moral deliberation but we are God's creatures who in spite of the dirt on our shoes and in our souls are called and enabled to convey God's truth and mercy in whatever station we may find ourselves.

III. Pedagogy

We have not exhausted the Lutheran themes that may bring substance to a Lutheran liberal arts college, but, hopefully, we have exemplified the possibilities. Let me now turn to the third of the ways in which the Vocation of a Lutheran liberal arts college may manifest itself and that is in our pedagogy.

First, from a pedagogical point of view, we are reminded of Luther's high praise for, and confidence in *human reason* as a means of understanding God's revelation and gaining wisdom and skill to live out our vocation in the world. His reservations about the limits of human reason notwithstanding, Luther and his colleagues had high expectations for the intellectual rigor of their work and the work of their students.

The Lutheran preference for *dialectic* constitutes a second contribution to pedagogy. It is framed by the themes of contingency, the limits of reason, and by our human nature. But it is also shaped by our callings in the world, the need to bring the insights of our faith to bear on the burden of our callings. Returning again to Robert Benne, he argues for a dialectic that will reveal the alternative worldviews that shape our academic disciplines. For example, let the worldview assumptions of classical economics be in conversation with those of Christian ethics, let the disciplinary assumptions of literary criticism be in conversation with those of natural science. If we are to transcend the two-realm theory that dominates the academy, then conversation between the disciplines and the Christian intellectual account, or between faith and learning, is both a promising and necessary activity. From a Lutheran point of view, the objective is not to Christianize or somehow "convert" the disciplines because we regard them as having integrity in their own right. Rather, the goal is to engage the disciplines in the service of holistic understanding, a holism that recognizes the sacred and secular as two realms of a single reality, that is, God's creation.

A third pedagogical resource is our notion of *paradox*. As noted before, this has strong roots in the substance of the Lutheran theological tradition. But it has pedagogical implications as well. It may provide a modality for understanding complexity and ambiguity. Richard Hughes raises a warning flag worthy of consideration. He points out that while paradox is a unique gift, it is also a weakness. In nurturing both sides of a paradox, it is easy to sacrifice one side for the other. In Hughes words, "When paradox dissolves in this way, the risks can be absolutism on the one hand and relativism on the other." This tendency is especially apparent in considering the Lutheran formulation of two realms. If we accentuate the realm of God, we may absolutize our religious vision as the Scholastics did. On the other hand, if we accentuate the realm of the world, we run the risk of relativism. So, our challenge is to maintain the tension. I believe he advises us wisely in this matter.

In conclusion, for many good reasons Lutheran liberal arts colleges are revisiting their sense and understanding of Vocation. The implications go well beyond those noted today, but perhaps this will suffice as a beginning. As academics in a Lutheran setting, we have a goodly treasure.

Let me close with the testimony of one who speaks about our tradition from outside of it, Richard T. Hughes. Here is what he says about us: "The Lutheran tradition possesses some of the most potent theological sources for sustaining the life of the mind that one could imagine. It encourages a dialogue between the Christian faith and the world of ideas, fosters intellectual humility, engenders a healthy suspicion of absolutes, and helps create a conversation in which all of the conversation partners are taken seriously."

It seems to me Hughes says it right, and he sets a standard worthy of our highest aspirations.

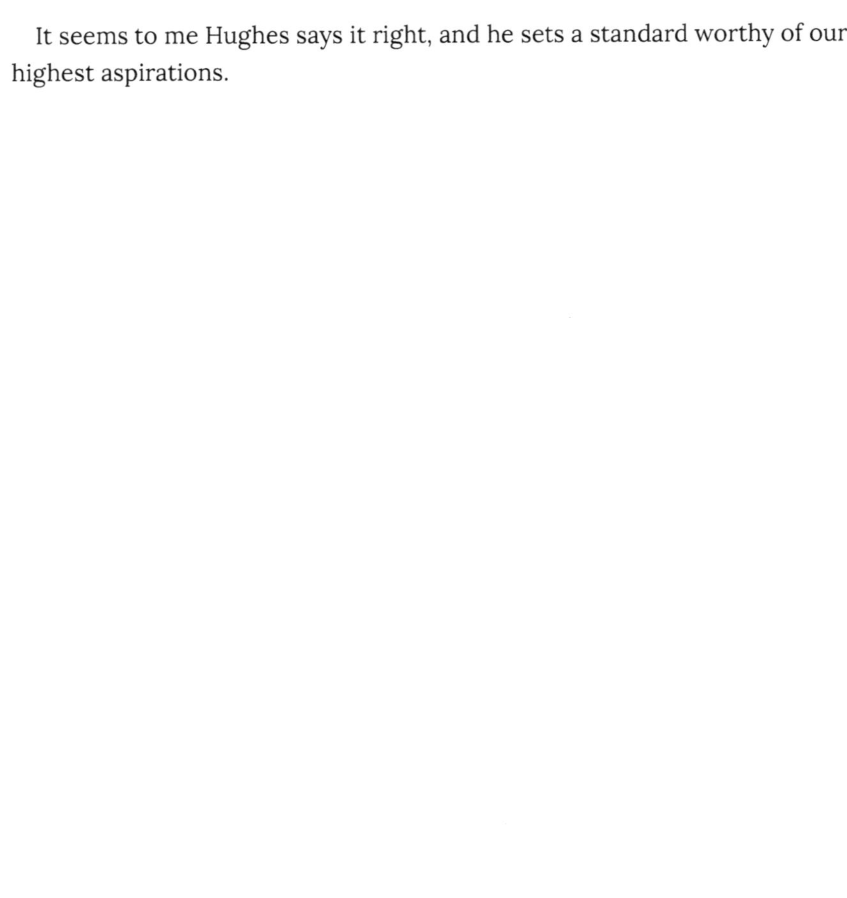

Appendix C: Reflections on Leadership

REFLECTIONS ON LEADERSHIP
Lorentzsen Center for Faith and Work
February 12, 2016

INTRODUCTION

While I have previously spoken about various aspects of leadership, I have not previously prepared anything like a comprehensive set of reflections on my own leadership. When I accepted the invitation to be with you today, I wasn't sure what this would look like. But I am glad for the invitation because it has turned out to be such an interesting assignment.

My approach today is to identify principles that have emerged from practice. I will identify those principles in three categories; that is, faith principles, leadership principles, and organizational principles. These three are, of course, inseparable so I hope that you will see interconnections as we move along.

This program is under the auspices of the Lorentzsen Center for Faith and Work. The central assumption of the Center is that our faith influences everything. I concur in that assumption and that's why faith principles come first today.

FAITH PRINCIPLES

1.

The Creation Principle: This is where it begins for me. I believe "that God has created me and all that exists," and further—in the words of Martin Luther in his explanation of the first article of the creed—I believe "God has given and still preserves to me my body and soul, my eyes and ears, and all my members, my reason and all the powers of my soul."

This statement is the foundation of my faith and my view of the world. I also believe that we have a proclivity to mess up God's world through guile and cunning, neglect and incompetence, and self-centeredness. Sentiment at times clouds my judgment. I have lacked the courage of my convictions. I have been satisfied with convenience when I should have gone outside of my comfort zone. In the words of Paul the apostle, "The evil that I would not, to that I am sometimes inclined, and the good that I should do, that I am inclined to postpone." All of this is what Luther called it "original sin." It is the reality that leads me to the second of my faith principles,

2.

Redemption: In his explanation to the second article, Luther wrote, "I believe that Jesus Christ...is my Lord who has redeemed me, a lost and condemned creature, bought me and freed me from all sins, from death, and from the power of the devil." We could easily call this the grace principle—it is the source of soul cleansing, of peace making, of life changing. This grace is inexhaustible, we are never out of reach of God's mercy. This mercy is often mediated by my family, my friends, my co-workers, and even strangers. They are people who often show me the way to a fuller life through their example, their good counsel, and their forgiveness.

3.

Gratitude: This leads to the next faith principle, gratitude, gratitude for God's creation and for God's mercy. After writing about the many gifts of God's creative activity, Luther wrote, "For all of this I am duty bound to thank, praise, serve and obey him." It's about gratitude, it's a push from within my soul. It's about the joy of participating in God's work.

I have been using Luther's language here, but I submit that the language of St. Thomas or St. Benedict or John Calvin regarding the work of God may be different, the core beliefs of these denominational traditions are very similar. It's about the joy of participating in God's work.

4.

Principle four has to do with *Vocation*. Some people use the word "calling." I believe that I am called to care for the creation and to care for my neighbors. As one grateful for God's abundance, I am open to God's call. The Gospels express that call in many ways: "feed my sheep," "cure the sick, raise the dead, cleanse the lepers, cast out demons." Or one could turn to the blessings of the beatitudes for additional specificity about our callings as peacemakers, as comforters, as givers of mercy, as those persecuted for righteous acts, and the list goes on.

Vocation gets a lot of attention these days in both secular and sacred settings. The best book I have read on leadership in the past year is David Brook's *The Road to Character*. He writes, "No good life is possible unless it is organized around a vocation. A vocation is not found by looking within and finding your passion. It is found by looking without and asking what life is asking of us."

Brooks offers an extended critique of the self-actualized approach to vocation that emphasizes success and status and winning. He refers to the self-actualizing person as Adam I. In contrast, Adam II "works to love intimately, to sacrifice self to service of others, to live in obedience to some transcendent truth…." "While Adam I wants to conquer the world, Adam II wants to obey a calling, to serve the world." In the words of Frederick Buechner, Adam II asks, "At what points do my talents and deep gladness meet the world's deep need?"

5.

This is an ennobling vision of life and calling. But I must bring some reality to all of this nobility. That leads me to the fifth principle, *Contingency*. Life is complicated, I am complicated. My calling is complicated. My Vocation gets messy for, as noted earlier, I am in bondage.

And there is that wonderful Lutheran discovery, paradox. I can't get it all done, so in choosing the one thing I neglect the other. And in selecting one strategy that will be of benefit to my neighbor, I may disadvantage another neighbor; think of downsizing or taking advantage of technology. Customers may be better served but employees may not be. Must I choose between keeping my business profitable and serving my neighbor when, in reality, I can't do the one without the other?

In the midst of my Vocation there is a cross, inconvenient but inevitable. The cross is central to the Christian story and is exemplified in the suffering and death of Christ and foretold for us too when Jesus said "take up your cross and follow me."

- A cross appears when the budget doesn't balance and there are human consequences.
- A cross appears when I must confront an employee who is my friend because of his or her ineffectiveness.
- A cross appears when there is dissension in my work place and no obvious compromise.
- A cross appears when for reasons of confidentiality I cannot explain my actions to a doubting and critical public.

In my early years of leadership, I had difficulty resolving the paradox between my feelings and my calling. I would be personally anxious about a decision, fearful of the conflict and criticism that might ensue in response to a decision that I was called upon to make as dean or president. But I came to understand that this matter was not about me and my feelings, my desire for approval, or an escape from a certain kind of personal grief—it was about the college, about its well-being. Without a healthy, stable, effective college the mission could not be accomplished. I struggled in coming to terms with that paradox.

I have often told emerging leaders how important it is to claim the office to which they are called; that is, if you are the dean, the community needs to have you discharge the duties of that office in spite of your feelings. If you think leadership is going to be easy or without conflict, redirect your calling. Or as Harry Truman put it, "If you can't stand the heat, get out of the kitchen." Whether you are the assistant dean, the comptroller, or the president, the same principle applies.

6.

Yes, it can get messy. How are we to deal with such messiness, with so many contingencies? This leads me to the sixth faith principle:

Transcendence. I believe that God is at work in the world. We are not lone rangers, castaways on an island of loneliness and despair. I can access God through prayer and confession, through God's word and the lives of the saints. And through deliberation, not just any deliberation, but moral deliberation. These practices became staples in my daily life as a leader.

Luther's counsel to those caught in paradox was to engage in all of these practices. In addition, he suggested that it was prudent to seek the counsel of friends in faith, people who share your commitments, who think with comprehensive wisdom, who work with diligence out of a passion for the neighbor. And such deliberation will often involve seeking the counsel of people who hold different views than your own, or who view the world from a different perspective than you.

7.

And, finally, to principle seven, *Accountability.* I have been called to be a neighbor—no, more than that, to love and heal and seek justice for my neighbor. This implies an ethic of excellence. If I claim my calling, I must also claim its obligations: to teach well, to heal effectively, to forge a secure weld, to provide efficient service, to keep people safe, to provide a reliable, high-quality product—and the list goes on. After all, my God and my neighbor are calling on me to do my best and, if that's not good enough, to find someone who can do it better. Holy prayers and beautiful melodies will not excuse my lack of proper stewardship in behalf of my neighbor for piety is not an excuse for mediocrity.

I believe that God will forgive my shortcomings, but God will not spare me the temporal consequences of my failings—failings to my neighbor which could lead to failing in my employment. I do not wish to close this discussion of faith principles in such a somber note because, remember we are loved, we are redeemed, we can be renewed in our spiritual lives and in our Vocations, as many have been. We know them. Maybe we are in that number.

LEADERSHIP PRINCIPLES

1.

The first of these principles is *discerning our gifts*, naming and claiming them. I know this goes against the grain of our militant modesty so, if you must, keep your lists to yourself but at least make that list. No, seriously, we have all been gifted and naming and claiming those gifts is very important if we are to serve our neighbors well. My skills for organizing, analyzing, and communicating had a lot to do with the way my Vocation continues to play out. There are in place several skills inventories that are helpful in this discernment process. We also do well to be self-reflective about what we're good at, what our neighbors tell us, and the sage advice of our mentors and elders.

I believe it's also good to know what your deficits are and how to manage them. The popular theory today is that you lead and serve from your strengths, and I think that's great advice. I also believe it's good to know where you are not as strong. In response to that, you may want to figure out how you will minimize those deficits, how you will work around them.

David Brooks, whom I mentioned previously, wrote about a number of well-known figures in our history. His examination of their lives included consideration of some of their personal and leadership deficits:

- Eisenhower had a difficult temper that he learned to control;
- Dorothy Day dealt with her self-indulgent life style through a life of religious discipline;
- George Marshall did not excel academically, but he did excel at neatness, organization, and self-control; and
- Frances Perkins, longtime cabinet secretary of labor, overcame her personal reticence through her commitment to a greater cause, and the list goes on.

It was my experience that my relationship skills were not a great strength, I didn't read people as well as others. I often neglected to show appreciation for people who worked hard. I often lacked patience. My political skills diminished over time. I sought to improve these skills, and I came to depend on others to fill in the gaps; I was always on the lookout for people who could bring to our team gifts that were not already abundant. Warren Buffet's sage advice applies here: "It's better to hang out with people better than you. Pick out associates whose behavior is better than yours and you will drift in that direction." Worked for me!

2.

Principle two: No matter where you serve it is essential to cultivate key habits and values. Habits like reflection, listening, persistence, discipline and values like respect, transparency, honesty, and compassion.

3.

With an awareness of one's gifts and the practice of such habits, one is positioned for the *discerning of one's calling.* It begins by seeking clarity on that earlier question: What is life asking of us, what is needed now, and where and how can I best serve my neighbor.

- We may be motivated by a push—when we're told our gifts don't fit with what the organization needs now,
- or by a pull, a sort of persistent sense that you belong in a certain job at a certain place at a certain time,
- by a tap on the shoulder when people whom you know and respected tell you where you are needed and why,
- or by the gracious serendipity of the Holy Spirit in which you simply find yourself where you are needed.

Early in my life, I experienced a long period of discernment. Some told me that, because of my experience in youth ministry (we called it Luther League in those days) and my academic and communication skills, I should be a pastor. On the other hand, I had grown up on a successful farm and could see possibilities there. A faculty mentor asked, "Have you ever thought about teaching?" I waffled on all of this until, during a year of theological study, I discovered that my Vocation, that is, my calling to serve the neighbor, could be lived out in a number of places and what I needed to do was pay attention to my gifts, to the counsel of my wise mentors, and to the things that brought me joy. So, I found my way to teaching and eventually leadership roles in the academic world. It is a Vocation that continues to unfold in my life in new ways and stations.

4.

Let me talk next about *partnerships*. Some call it community or collaboration. I simply cannot envision leadership as a one person show. The needs of my neighbors require gifts beyond my own so I need partners. This is not to say that I lay off my responsibilities on others; rather, it is to say that I need the gifts of others to meet the needs of neighbors.

Jim Collins, author of the bestselling *Good to Great*, offers sage advice about having the right people on the leadership bus and sitting in the right places. Once you do that you unleash the power of collaboration. One way you do that is by leveraging the variety of gifts possessed by the people on your bus. Halfway through my presidency the members of our leadership team all took the Myers-Briggs inventory, and we spent an afternoon discussing the findings and the implications. We became a much more effective team thereafter because we began to self-consciously leverage our strengths. And that worked because of the power of a common culture and a common cause. We were loyal to each other because we shared essential values and commitments.

5.

The last leadership principle is *renewal*. In today's world there are myriad sources of stress. The great recession compounded those stresses for many people and leader burnout is the all too frequent consequence. It is instructive to recall that Jesus would take occasional leave from his ministry to escape the crowds and even his coworkers. We are told that he would find a quiet place, a place for prayer and reflection.

6.

There is, almost inevitably, stress in our vocations, and that is why more attention is being devoted to maintaining healthy lifestyles and cultivating practices of spiritual, emotional, and intellectual renewal. I could not imagine doing my work without the quiet times for meditation and prayer, without the stimulation of colleagues from other schools, without the resources of a joyful and supportive family, without the intellectual stimulation of an annual theological conference, without the infusion of new insights from the things I read and the concerts I attend; or without the respite and renewal I find at our lake cabin.

ORGANIZATIONAL PRINCIPLES

1.

It begins with the formation of an organizational culture. And that begins with a clear mission and an explicit set of values to shape the environment and the conduct of the enterprise. There are several tools that go with this such as vision statements, goals, and strategies. I believe that healthy, effective organizations use all of these tools in shaping culture.

Concordia is blessed with this strong, vibrant mission: "To influence the affairs of the world by sending into society thoughtful and informed men and women dedicated to the Christian life." This mission generates our core values and is our most valuable asset. As president, I believed that my first and foremost responsibility was to uphold, nurture, and extend that mission.

2.

The second principle is the *hedgehog principle*, which I have also drawn from the work of Jim Collins. He says an organization needs to be clear about what it does best...that's it's hedgehog. This is a way of simplifying a complex organization by identifying what makes the organization succeed. It may take some time to sort that out, it may not be obvious to an onlooker or someone new to the enterprise. For example, Walgreen's figured out that its hedgehog was building drive in pharmacies at convenient locations. And

Starbuck's hedgehog was providing a simple, high-quality menu at, again, convenient locations.

Concordia's hedgehog is combining the liberal arts and the practical arts or, if you will, the liberal arts and career preparation. The synergy created by that juxtaposition is magical and our graduates recognize and celebrate it. It works and the college is always upgrading it, fine tuning it, and moving in new directions. It's about knowing what makes you successful.

3.

This leads me to the *generative principle*—that is, the encouragement and creation of new ways to enhance the mission of the enterprise. Again, Jim Collins points out that great organizations foster a productive relationship between continuity (your hedgehog) and change. They are always picking the brains of others. Max Bazerman, author of *The Power of Noticing*, warns about ignoring inconvenient evidence, about complacency when things are going well. I believe that effective organizations prioritize creativity by providing time, space, and encouragement for creative, out of the box people.

Let me cite a few examples.

- The Concordia Language Villages is the product of very creative people, Jerry Haukebo, Dell Bjerkness and Christine Schulze—and college leaders had the good sense to support and encourage them.
- Or look at the health care administration program, the brain child of Ted Heimarck.
- Think of the contributions of the late Paul J. Christiansen and the contemporary Rene Clausen to the choral life our church and nation;
- Or Hiram Drache's contributions to our understanding of the history of this region;
- Or Charis and the Communiversity, the progeny of Jim Hofrenning;
- Or the student leadership initiatives of Morris Lanning;
- Or the May Seminars, another of Dell Bjerkness's ideas;
- Or the Offutt School of Business, the result of a generative process led by the beloved Pam Jolicoeur;
- Or the National Book Awards affiliation, formed out of the initiative of Scott Olsen and Tracey Moorhead, and the list could go on.

You get the idea—successful organizations privilege and practice the generative principle.

And before I leave this topic, I share with you that what I enjoy most about leadership is the generative; about anticipation, planning, innovation, and problem solving. I find these activities energizing and joyful. (The long-range planning initiatives of the sixties through the nineties, we called it the Blueprint process, engaged the whole community and produced scores of ideas for strengthening and extending our mission. Our cabinet made an annual retreat, an event that always made time for exploring new possibilities. The several capital campaigns were exciting opportunities to share the story, engage our constituents, and move the college forward. Fun Stuff!)

4.

Ah, but back to reality and the *assessment principle*. Strong organizations know what and who are working effectively. They will not survive, much less succeed, without rigorous attention to performance. Are we meeting our goals? Is the strategic plan on course? Is our financial plan working? Are people playing well with one another? How is our market changing and are we responding effectively? And the list goes on.

In higher education, as we have shifted our focus from teaching to learning, we have experienced the challenge of figuring out how to assess our effectiveness, especially when learning goals are affective in nature. And as organizations we identify the critical indicators of performance and track them, almost continually working them to be as certain as possible that we are measuring the right things in an effective way.

5.

The *character principle* is another dimension of the assessment principle but I set it out separately because everything else rests on it. Character is about our mission and our values. Are we living them out? Do our actions match our words?

Jim Collins has a book on this subject. Its title is *How the Mighty Fall*. He identifies the derailers; arrogance, neglect, the undisciplined pursuit of more, confusing big with great, denial, and desperation. Any one or any combination of these may lead to organizational confusion or dysfunction or failure.

I think of many colleges, once clear and comfortable with their religious identity, that camouflaged and then diminished that identity for the sake of enrollment, or status, or financial support. It's the result of a failure in institutional character. In contrast, Concordia's faithfulness to its mission and the neighborhood it serves is exceptional, an example of enduring character.

Jim Collins observes that many successful organizations experience tough times, and great organizations will be strengthened because of them. It begins with character, that is, mission and values, and then our capacity for organizational change.

6.

Which leads me, finally, to the *renewal principle*. I take Collins' observations as an argument for, among other things, continuing attention to organizational mission and values. It's not enough to revisit them every decade or so and then print them in the handbook. They need to be cultivated and sorted, illustrated and re-examined almost continuously if they are to retain their relevance and impact in the organization.

Leaders, more than anyone else, are responsible for ongoing organizational renewal. It's not a sideline leadership function; rather, it's at the core of what leaders are called to be and do. I believe that has been and continues to be a distinguishing mark of this College. This place tends to its mission and values scrupulously. It is what accounts for the loyalty of our constituents, and the unity of the community even in challenging times. It is a great gift, mediated by the work of God's own spirit.

CLOSE

As many of you know, one of my favorite metaphors is restlessness, inspired by the biblical story of Jacob wrestling with an angel. I believe restlessness is a gift and it is what makes life interesting and productive; it is what keeps good organizations alive and effective. So, I close with a quotation from one of my favorite theologians, the late Joseph Sittler. He wrote: "Our whole life is an effort to approach, to appreciate, to some degree to participate in, the absoluteness of God himself. But we can never do it; that's why our whole life is restlessness. This restlessness may make us want to throw in the towel—or pull up our socks. You can play it either way.... One of the goals of the Christian message is to join together the people of the way, the way of an eternally given restlessness, and to win from that restlessness the participation in God, which is all that our mortality can deliver." But, I submit, that is quite a lot.

ABOUT
PAUL J. DOVRE

Paul Dovre was raised on a farm near Porter, Minnesota, and completed his high school education in Canby, Minnesota. Dovre earned his B.A. degree from Concordia College after serving in the United States Army. Dovre attended Northwestern University, earning his M.A. and Ph.D. degrees. He came to Concordia in 1963, first serving on the faculty and then as vice president for Academic Affairs. Paul J. Dovre became the eighth president of Concordia in 1975 and retired in 1999, but returned to the college twice to serve as interim president and in other capacities of leadership and support over the years.

Paul Dovre has remained active in the Fargo-Moorhead community and has earned multiple recognitions for his contributions and leadership, including the 2024 Legacy Leader Award from the Fargo Moorhead West Fargo Chamber of Commerce. The Dovres continue to reside in Moorhead, Minnesota, where they are active members of Trinity Lutheran Church and enjoy spending time at their lake home on Bad Medicine Lake.